DO YOU ASK THESE QUESTIONS?

- Why are we so separate?

- What has happened to us that increases our separateness and makes us cling to it all the harder?

- What are we doing to avoid union with another person and with life?

- How can we come out of our self-made isolation and learn to love?

- How can we make a permanent bond with another human being so our soul can put its energies into getting on with our life's work instead of hiding?

- How can we surrender to all things in life so that we can experience the deepest kind of love that is truly all of life?

- How can we find the love that heals and restores the dwarfed and emaciated emotional part of us that has hidden so long in its separateness?

JESS
NATIONALLY FA
AND LEO
HELPS YOU
ANSW

D0452023

Fawcett Books
by Jess Lair, Ph.D.

"AIN'T I A WONDER . . . AND AIN'T YOU
   A WONDER TOO!"   23688 $1.95
"I AIN'T MUCH, BABY—BUT I'M ALL I'VE GOT"   23585 $1.95
"I AIN'T WELL—BUT I SURE AM BETTER"   24193 $1.95

This offer expires 10/1/81

SEX:
IF I DIDN'T
LAUGH, I'D CRY

Jess Lair, Ph.D.

FAWCETT CREST · NEW YORK

SEX: IF I DIDN'T LAUGH, I'D CRY

THIS BOOK CONTAINS THE COMPLETE TEXT OF THE
ORIGINAL HARDCOVER EDITION

Published by Fawcett Crest Books, a unit of CBS Publications, the Consumer Publishing Division of CBS Inc., by arrangement with Doubleday and Company, Inc.

ISBN: 0-449-24336-2

Printed in the United States of America

First Fawcett Crest Printing: October 1980

10   9   8   7   6   5   4   3   2   1

To Jackie, after 31 years together, the person I more than ever would most want to be stranded on a desert island with.

Contents

My Opening Note to You

There's a ton of talk today about sex. But there is a silence about the real important part of sex, our failures and our feelings, that's just as bad as the silence about sex of the prudish Victorians we laugh at so. Here is sex, a force in our lives that is next in importance only to air and food for most of us, yet usually there is no one with whom we will honestly share our feelings and experiences.

This silence about our deep feelings and attitudes about sex has meant that a lot of our crucial attitudes are unexamined. Many people who listened to me tell about my feelings and attitudes found that deep down they believed in some things they weren't aware of and so weren't acting on. A long time ago it was said that an unexamined life isn't worth living. As you hear me talk in this book about the attitudes and ideas I have come to, it can help you examine, sort out and clarify your own ideas.

When I said my last book, *"Ain't I a Wonder . . .",* to the nurses in Columbus, Ohio, in 1976, I mentioned I was planning to write the next book on sex. Jackie spoke up and said I couldn't write a book on sex because I didn't know anything about it. She said a true thing. But, the next day, I told the nurses that while I didn't know much about sex, I did know enough about it to be worth four or five dollars to some people. So that tells something about the kind of sex expert I am, a four-or five-dollar sex expert.

When I started teaching in college, I saw that quite a few of my students would have sex with each other when what they really needed was closeness and wholeness. But there wasn't one in a hundred who could admit to their honest feelings about themselves and the other person. It seemed like everyone was doing the wrong thing to the wrong person for the wrong reasons. I just shook my head at all the madness, and thought if I didn't laugh, I'd cry. When I talked to my students about sex and feelings, they would always get very quiet and still, because they were so absorbed in my puny little efforts to open up to them. Later I found adult groups just as hungry. So I decided if I ever learned enough about sex I would write a book about it.

In June of 1977, I felt I was ready to start. I put on a two-day seminar in Minneapolis. It gave me a chance to better organize my thoughts, feelings and experiences. In February 1978 I presented two one-day seminars in Seattle and said most of the first half of this book the first day and the second half the second day.

What I said was then offered as a set of cassette tapes.* The tapes, the responses of the people who were in Seattle for the two days and those who later purchased the tapes helped me arrive at the final form for this book. It is written almost directly from the tapes, so in a way, you will be a part of that group for those two days. I think being a part of a group of people is very appropriate for a subject like sex, where our desire to be left alone is most challenged. A sexual relationship is about the only thing there is we can't do alone.

At the end of each session, our group in Seattle would all hold hands. I told them, each time, the point of holding hands is that we are all in this mess together, and only together are we going to get out.

Jess

---

* If you are interested in hearing what was said in Seattle, a set of eight tapes is available for forty dollars from Jesse Lair Tapes, P. O. Box 249, Bozeman, MT 59715.

CHAPTER 1

If Sex Is So Good, How Come It Can Hurt So Bad?

Neither you nor I can ever know the true power and beauty of sex, because never yet has a man without an ego gotten in bed with a woman without an ego. Sex is opening our hearts to one another and then opening our bodies. When we open our bodies to each other in sex and won't open our hearts, sex becomes a terrible pain. But when we've opened our hearts to each other in the deepest way, then sex is a beautiful confirmation of the closeness that has already happened between us. These ideas best sum up what I've learned from ten years of intense study, thought and observation of sexual behavior.

I'm not going to tell you anything you don't already know. All this book will do is underscore certain feelings you've had about sex but were unsure of because so many voices today seem to be saying things opposite to what you have experienced. What I say will help you have more confidence in some of your ideas so you can act on them more often and more freely as you take more responsibility for what is happening in your life.

When I worked out the ideas in *"I Ain't Much, Baby—But I'm All I've Got"*, in the spring of 1969, I was speaking to a group of nurses on how to communicate. They thought I was going to be telling them about how to write short sentences. Instead, I found myself telling them that the most important part of their communication with others was having a good heart towards that other person. The way to get a good heart towards that other person was to get a

9

good heart towards themselves. So I told them about my ideas and experiences on getting a good heart towards myself.

Late in the second day of talking to them, I was horrified to find myself talking to them about sex. One part of me was shocked because sex didn't seem to have anything to do with communication. But another part of me knew it did. If our attitudes towards sex are distorted so we're preoccupied with sex or push sex away, then we will have trouble communicating with women, or men, or both. It means we'll have trouble with at least half the human race or all of it, including our feelings towards ourselves.

The material in that book that I came up with in talking to the nurses opened my eyes to the world of sex and started me examining my own needs, attitudes and behavior on sex.

As I started looking at myself and the people around me, mostly students at the time, I was really shocked at what I saw. Here was sex, potentially one of the most powerful of the forces in each of our lives, being distorted by almost everyone to some degree. The wrong people seemed to be doing the wrong things to the wrong people for the wrong reasons. In sex I couldn't find hardly anyone whose life showed a deep and honest happiness with the results of their use of sex.

I saw it was like the closing scene of the movie *Bridge on the River Kwai*. The captured British general who had been forced to build the bridge for the Japanese ended up trying to stop his own commandos from blowing up the bridge. A British major was watching and groaned, "It's madness, madness." I felt the same way, and from that feeling the title for this book came to me.

So I had a title but I didn't have anything to say after I'd said the title except a feeling that sex wasn't working out well for people, that I couldn't support with any evidence or understanding. Now, ten years later, I can see and understand sexual behavior so much more clearly and I have an understanding of why sex works positively in many people's lives and negatively in so many other people's lives.

The most crucial mistake I see that we make is when we separate sex from the rest of our lives. The sex books I have accumulated concentrate almost exclusively on sex. People who read my books often tell me the first chapter they turn to is the chapter on sex. They don't understand that the earlier chapters of those books have more to do with improving their sex lives as well as their whole lives. What people so often don't see is that sex isn't something we do, it's what we are. We don't need sex, we need wholeness. We aren't searching for a sexual partner, we're searching for the other half of us, who can complete us in the deepest union possible with another human being. Only our union with our higher power can be deeper than sex, but we really can't compare the two, because they are such different things.

So sex has a lot to do with our higher power, God as we understand him. But you'd never guess that as you read and listen to the people clamoring to put forward their ideas on sex. Many today in the current fashion see sex in a very limited way as an entertainment, a distraction, with no understanding of its deeper significance and its relationship to the rest of their lives and their higher power, some force outside themselves. Others go so far over on the God side that they are equally out of balance and they write of a hearts-and-flowers sex where everything is perfect and no one should make any mistakes.

In between these two opposing viewpoints lie the great majority, who are confused and troubled at how little they can understand and use the enormous power of sex. They wonder why they have so many strange feelings and why they have so little control over the ways they express those feelings.

It's taken me all these years of study to come up with understandings of sex that can work to untangle and solve problems for me and produce good fruits in my life.

In the past few years, I have seen a number of explanations of sex and love and marriage that make sense to me and are essentially the same. The clearest of these experiences and the one that speaks most clearly to me is from the late Eva Pierrakos, a woman who lived in New York City.

She sees that we are each separate souls who are desperately guarding our separateness despite its cost to our souls, which have to see their oneness with everybody and everything and come into union with other people and our higher power, God as we understand him or her. Love and sex are the crucial forces that break down our separateness and give us our first taste of what a loving and perhaps physical union can be.

She divides love and sex up into these parts: the romantic force, the sex force and the love force. The romantic force is first seen as puppy love and each of us usually meets it a few times after that. It's the attraction that pulls two separate souls together. The romantic force has to be so powerful to overcome our desperate struggle to hang on to our separateness. Under its overwhelming spell, which is so strong kings have given up their kingdoms for it, the two souls put down their separateness from each other for a while and come together.

The sex force is then at their disposal to express their new oneness, to experience the wholeness of union with each other and with all the rest of life and to build a real love between them that will bond them together for the day when the romantic force starts to lose some of its power. So the love force, then, is the force that holds the two together after the romantic force has brought them together.

This breakdown of hers is helpful to me because it so clearly outlines the major areas of problems I see. First I see that our sense of our separateness is so strong and hard to break down that millions of single people who want a marriage or permanent relationship don't dare risk it because they have been hurt so often. Millions of people in marriages are in the same trouble. The marriage partners are using an arm's-length marriage to meet some of their social and family needs, yet each is determined to stay very separate.

The romantic force is misused by those people who seek romantic love and then, when it dies out, go on looking for the next romance. One of the old movie stars was recently quoted as saying that a romance was the only possible reason for her being with a man. When that romance was over, her marriage or relationship was over. The hundreds of millions of copies of romantic novels we read are partly an attempt by us to re-experience romantic love in a safe way, at second hand.

There are times when a man and a woman, reading romantic novels at the same time in the same room, could have a real romance with each other if they weren't so afraid of their separateness being broken down.

The sex force is misused by the pornographic people, who try to separate sex from the romantic and love feelings. They want sex without intimacy. This can be one of the worst addictions and leads to a need for more and more sex and more and more extreme forms of sexual stimulation to produce the necessary escape. Just like the wino who needs to drink more wine to get drunk, so the sex addict seeks a bigger and bigger sex thrill to get relief from his or her pain.

Sex addicts seek to rationalize and justify their self-destructive behavior, so they build convincing and very legitimate-sounding arguments for what they are doing. Because of everyone else's fascination and preoccupation with sex, the sex addicts find a large and ready audience.

The third force, the love force, is hardest to misuse and least misused. But even such a great and beautiful force can be twisted and distorted into seeking love without any of the messiness and hurt of romance and sex. There is a place for celibate loving in all of our lives at some time and in some of our lives all of the time. Pope John XXIII's beautiful life, which moved the whole world, is a good example. There can even be marriage partners who come to choose celibacy as a mutual choice. I've studied the Shakers and I make reproductions of their beautiful furniture. Their communities practiced celibacy and their lives were moving examples to the people around them of their love for their God.

But there are many people in marriages who are trying to get as far away from sex as they can, because they think they like love but they don't want to bounce around in bed with their partner because it's so undignified. Actually, they're afraid of their separateness being broken down by an unfeeling oaf or a mean old nag like the one they're married to.

When the three forces aren't misused, we can have the kind of deep, truly permanent relationship I see so many people, unmarried or married, hungering for. That is where two separate souls experience romantic love together. Then the sex force is added in to the relationship when it is appropriate, according to the higher power of their understanding. The two take advantage of all their closeness and all their giving up of their separateness to build a deep and true love between them that will keep them in union with each other and all of life. This love force will be so strong that, as the romantic force loses some of its power and as the sex force loses some of its fascination, the love force holds the two people together and keeps them living out in the open, not hiding from each other, for the rest of their lives. The biggest thing that happens from living in union with life, rather than separate, is that each of the two can go deeper and deeper into themselves and be more and more the beautiful souls they were meant to be but can't be when they are using up all their energies desperately clinging to their separateness and pushing the world away.

So these are the ideas and issues this book will deal with. Why are we so separate? What has happened to us that increases our separateness and makes us cling to it harder? What are we doing to avoid union with another and life? How can we come out of our self-created isolation and learn to love? How can we make a permanent bond with another human being so our soul can put its energies into getting on with our life's work instead of hiding? And, how can we so surrender to all things in life so that we can experience the deepest kind of love that is truly all of life and that heals and restores the dwarfed and emaciated emotional part of us that has hidden so long in its separateness?

The biggest obstacle I had in my search was that I was full of ideas that weren't so; they wouldn't work in my life. I had to be nearly killed with a heart attack, open-heart surgery, and a death verdict of cancer (that turned out to be benign) before I was willing to put down my old ideas and humbly go seeking my truth.

The best thing you can do for yourself as you read this book is temporarily put aside your belief systems and consider the ideas I offer in light of your personal experience and observation rather than what you believe. If you're at all like most people I talk to, you're like the seamen of Columbus' time. You believe the world is flat and if you aren't careful, you'll fall off the edge. In your fear you are constantly hugging the coastline. You are constantly being shipwrecked on the coastal reefs because of your fear of the open sea.

As my friend Wally Minto of Alpha Awareness says, "It doesn't matter if you believe or disbelieve what I say. Test some of it out and see if it works in your life." I'm going through this in my own life right now in some other areas that you'll probably be hearing about in later books. I'm seeing some ideas I don't believe in, in fact I'm even violently opposed to them, but they produce results I like in my life. I'm putting aside my old notions in favor of what works for me. It's hard for me, just as Columbus' trip was hard for him.

Some of you will feel I'm talking about right and wrong. So much of your feeling that way is because sex is so full of right and wrong for you. You can't see that your concepts are very destructive to you and they are really opposite what you claim to believe in.

The ideas I'm offering you didn't come from right or wrong. I couldn't make my right and wrong ideas work in my life. They nearly killed me, the way I was using them. So I threw all that away and went seeking what would work in my life. These ideas are what has worked for me. What works in my life is my psychology. I'm a psychologist; I'm not a theologian. But I've found that the closer I get to what works in my life, the more the theologians say to me, "That's good theology, Jess." Well, that's fine. But I'll keep on looking for what works to produce the results I want in life.

What are those results? What I'm looking for is a way of life where each day is filled with *life* all day long instead of dying. I'm looking for a life where I'm in harmony with the people around me: my wife, my children, my friends, and my community. I'm looking for ways to live my life that give me more life instead of less life, more laughter and more honest tears, more feelings of all kinds and less of me sitting on my feelings, lying about them and not being able to express them. And I'm looking for a clearer sense of my being, so I can be more the creative, outgoing personality I was meant to be.

So in this book I will often sound very dogmatic. That's not because I want you to go the same way I'm going. It's because I've tried a lot of dead-end roads and seen they were dead-end roads for me. But I've also seen they were dead-end roads for most everybody who went down them who wanted the kind of results most people wanted.

You can be a cook without a measuring system, but I've never seen a good carpenter without a rule. So I'll sound real positive when I'm talking about the necessity of a rule for the kind of woodworking I'm seeking.

Some of you might not want these same general results for you. That's fine. You're a beautiful person the way you are. I want you to stay the way you are so you can keep getting the results you're getting. I don't want you to be different. I don't want any one of you to change. None of you need to.

There were two purposes for me saying these ideas to the people who were in the sex seminars in Minneapolis and Seattle and writing them down for you in this book: The first purpose was so I could learn. The second was to offer to any of you who wanted them some new ideas you could try out in your life if you want different results than what you're now getting.

As I say, when you feel me being positive, that's not against you, that's just that I feel strongly that some certain idea is very helpful or very harmful in achieving the results I need. I feel a deep compassion for my students, the people who come to me. Many have been so hurt they seem powerless to break out of their old ways or make contact with some power that can help them.

Let me express my compassion for you and my best wishes for you as strongly as I can. Then let me offer you this idea: I've told you that these ideas of mine are useful only if you want results like the ones I have described and will describe. But the results I'm seeking are very personal results. You will have to think for yourself about what results you want, because you're a separate person.

If you remember all that and still find yourself getting mad at something I say, you can use that to help you. I'm saying what I'm saying because I'm me. If you get mad at that, that's you getting mad. It's easy to say it's because of me, but is it? Is it partly because I'm stepping on one of your old ideas and it's your pain that's making you feel the way you do? You see, if I look wrong or stupid to you, that's nothing to get mad at. That's something for which I need to have your compassion, your sympathy and your prayers. So think about keeping your mind open and ready for new approaches to test as you go along with me on my search for myself that may throw a little more light on your search for yourself. It shouldn't surprise us when my search throws light on your search, because you and I are one, we truly are. All the spokes lead to the center of the wheel.

Oddly enough, in sex it's our terrible need, or what we see as our terrible need, that creates most all of the problems. Just as a starved man is, at first, intemperate with his use of food, so do we show all the signs of the sex-crazed individual. This idea clears up so many questions I used to have.

There are two common ways we show our terrible sexual need. We act out our sexual need and seek a lot of sex promiscuously. Or, we deny our sexual need is really there. So two very different ways of reacting towards sex I can see now are really the same. I'll never forget how puzzled I was when a nice matronly woman with all the outer appearances of respectability asked me in class one day, "What if, going deep into my self in acceptance, I find that I'm a sex maniac?" I thought she meant the kind of sex maniac who molests little children and reassured her that I'd never seen that happen in acceptance, only in lack of acceptance, just as the people who accept their alcoholism don't drink *today*.

I see now she had a different fear. She was very correctly seeing the sex-starved and sex-crazed part of herself and she was afraid of the sexual side of herself, which demanded satisfaction. She was sitting on that side of herself and not letting it show. The young guy or gal in class sitting on either side of her could easily have been doing the opposite and trying to satisfy their sexual demands, but they were finding the more sex they had, the more they wanted and the less it helped.

So, yes, Virginia, there is a sex maniac in each of us, for reasons I'll discuss later, but he has no real power over us. It's just our fear that gives that maniac so much seeming power. Once we look carefully at that part of ourself as it truly is, without fear, it loses a big part of the hold it has over us. We need to stop identifying with that part of our personality and its demands on us and see that our personality is a lot bigger and more complete than just being a sex maniac.

As long as that part of our personality has a hold on us, we're very immature and sex for us is pretty much like what the high school kids do in the backseat of a car. After we get free of that one small part of our personality that seeks to dominate us, then sex can be magical sex, which is what happens between two fairly mature people during one to four hours spent together in bed after they've had hours previously of the ordinary intercourse of talking and loving each other in their lives during the day.

When we are deep in seeking to scratch our sexual itch, figuring if we scratch long enough and hard enough it will go away, we're usually in deep trouble. We find we just can't get the results in our lives we want. We thought if we had enough sex, like enough money, we would be happy. But we found more sex wasn't what we needed, though we may still loudly proclaim it is.

To defend our actions as we search for all the sex we're sure will finally solve our problem, or as we deny our needs for sex and push it away, we build up a set of attitudes that justify our behavior. Once we've done that, we all of a sudden have two problems, a sex problem and a sick-attitude problem. When you take the bottle away from the alocholic, he's just as crazy as he was when he was drinking. All the sick attitudes he had that started him drinking and that he developed to defend his drinking are still there, causing him all kinds of troubles. Now that the bottle is gone, he also has a new problem. He hasn't got the bottle to blame his craziness on or to take away the pain of his craziness.

Same with both the sex addict and the sex rejector. Their attitudes got sicker and sicker as they were forced to justify their increasingly harmful behavior. When a person says, "Sex is no good, I don't need it," or when they say, "I can have sex with anyone, no problem," they don't hurt me or others. They only hurt themselves.

It's not the sex they have or don't have that's the problem. Some person who doesn't have sex because they think it is ugly and disgusting has a problem with their attitudes. Pope John didn't have sex because he chose not to though I'm sure he had a better sense of its true power and beauty than most people who do have sex.

The person who has a lot of sex with anyone argues that anything goes. A rock star, in *People* magazine, estimated that the first woman he really loved was the 2001st woman he'd been with. He says he has a new attitude now and she's the only woman for him. I hope he can do what he says, but I don't see that most people can change their attitudes that easily.

Many people feel that in sex anything goes. I think very little goes. I say this not from the standpoint of the results I want but from the standpoint of the results I see most people around me wanting. Better than three fourths of single people want a permanent marriage. Most married people want that too. To achieve a permanent marriage I think there are some general principles that apply to everyone despite all the defenses the sex addicts and the sex rejectors throw up.

In a study on abortions, we see a horrible example of what can happen to our attitudes when we try to justify our behavior. There are a lot of abortions now. About a fourth of all babies conceived are aborted. You can say abortion is good from your standpoint. Maybe. But look at the study by Paul Cameron.*

Shortly after Gary Gilmore was executed, researchers asked more than three hundred residents of Pasadena, California, whether they were totally against the death penalty, favored it for heinous crimes, or thought it should be used more frequently. They also asked, "Would you serve as executioner if our society had the death penalty?"

In this conservative community of Pasadena, 75 per cent favored capital punishment. Twice as many women as men were opposed to the death penalty. Only one fourth as many women as men would serve as executioners.

Among women who had had an abortion it was a very different story than among women in general. Only 6 per cent were against the death penalty, as compared to 26 per cent of the women who hadn't had an abortion; 22 per cent of those who had had an

---

* *Psychology Today,* November 1976, p. 44.

abortion were willing to serve as executioners, compared with 8 per cent of the non-aborters.

In interpreting the results, Cameron felt that the women who valued life less were more likely to have abortions or they changed their attitudes to justify the abortion. He said, "It's a vicious cycle. As you take human life you are pressured to justify your action by holding life less dear. You are then led logically to press for social policy that holds human life less dear. . . . As in so many social issues, some of the best of intentions lead to unforeseen and unwanted results."

Is Cameron's study accurate? I don't know. But the basic point he makes I've seen operate in alcoholics and others so often that I suspect his study is very accurate.

I know the gals who have had their abortions are feeling, "Hey, you're making me feel guilty." I'm not making anyone feel guilty about abortion. I'm just talking about the attitudes we develop out of necessity to defend our actions and how harmful those attitudes are to us. There's almost no way we could find the guys who had a part in the necessity for those abortions, but I'd bet their attitudes would show the same changes. So the issue here is not the having of abortion or not, it's the question of what it tells about our basic attitudes towards taking life and how it can change our attitudes.

In the current mood of our society, it seems strange to ask if there is an ideal in the area of sex. I believe there is an ideal for each of us, and that ideal is very close to the common ideal we all have.

What chaos music, art and literature would be in if we didn't have a higher ideal! Why does an artist destroy many of his paintings? He sees that they are not part of his higher ideal for himself. But, today, so many of us are in such a violent reaction against any consideration of an ideal in sexual behavior that we've rejected the very idea was workable for us. I think much of this is because so many of us are so driven sexually that we feel we have no choice but to throw away the ideal for us because we see in our behavior we couldn't come close to any idea.

Now, remember, I'm not talking about the right-and-wrong idea taught by some of the religious and much of society. If painters and musicians followed those ideas of society and religion, there would be no new art or music. I'm talking about the same higher ideal a painter or composer uses to guide him to a new truth for him rather than let him wallow in chaos.

What is this great power that is in sex? It is so strong a man will give up everything he has and run away with a woman he finds can give him what he always wanted. Men and women have left their homes, their families, their spouses and their positions to be with a person who made them feel complete—and then have been reasonably happy they did what they did.

The only other thing men and women have given up so much for is the power of an idea they were dedi-cated to. It might be an idea for a personal vocation, a business, a political movement or, most commonly, a religious belief. To me, it seems the common thread running through all the deepest pursuits of men and women is a search for wholeness. I think it is really an urge towards a union with God at the deepest level. This union can occur just as much in the dedi-cated rock climber who has completely given himself to the climbing and his companions as it can occur in the minister. Both can be men of God, because what counts is the spiritual dimension of their lives, not the outward religiousness or lack of it.

C. S. Lewis talks about "mere Christianity." Most men with a professed religion I've seen who came into Alcoholics Anonymous or other twelve-step programs found to their horror that all they had was "mere religion" and that it took a bunch of former drunks to teach them how to find a personal and truly loving God.

It's easy enough to say, as some do, that we have lost this natural language of the spirit that we had at one time in the past. But the more anthropology I read the more I see that no age was all that spiritual. I see that in each age and each culture men and women in that culture were each moving towards God in their own way at their own pace. But whatever the past may have been, we have only today to live in. I see any present lack of spirituality as no problem, because the minute I was humble enough and hungry enough to really seek, the spiritual teaching I needed was all around me. All I had to do was reach out my hand and take it.

But I had to be nearly killed before I could be humble enough to reach out in the least little way. The more I was wounded by my pain the more I was open to the spiritual lessons life had for me.

The problem I see today is that sex is completely out of context. It was also out of context in the old days, when sex was such a no-no. As our present generation of young people grew up, they couldn't see that sex meant that much to their parents or anyone else in our generation, the fifty-plus age group. It was just a touch more than a handshake. So the young folks shook off all the old sex taboos and used sex with hundreds and even thousands of partners.

What this book is is an attempt to put sex in a different perspective. Where does it fit? And where doesn't it fit? Those concepts are very foreign to much of the current discussion about sex, which says there are no rules for anyone, each make their own rules. It's true that each person must find their own way on their own spiritual path. But it doesn't follow from that that this is a world without lawfulness.

There is a deep and fundamental order each of us must appreciate. We can't offend those laws any more than we can offend the laws of gravity. If we jump off a building we pay the price. If we use sex indiscriminately and offend the basic lawfulness in sex, we pay the price.

Today I see two generations paying the price for using sex carelessly: the younger generation who weren't afraid enough of sex and generally used it quite loosely are paying the price in their inability to live together with one of the opposite sex in harmony; and the older generation, now mine, so frequently divorcing after twenty-five or thirty-five years of marriage because they were too much afraid of sex and didn't really face it. So we have millions of lonely people, young and old, hungering for permanent partners but afraid to get hurt again in another union they fear won't work.

What's more, even within the marriages that are still unbroken, sex has trouble making its proper contribution. A survey of good marriages found the general attitude of the partners was "Sex is all right for us but it sure could be better."

What I've seen, as I've taught people of all ages, is that there are two deep hungers in them. When I touch one of those two hungers, I can always count on a deep hush and a deep attentiveness to fall over my audience. These two areas are sex and our individual spiritual quests. As I said earlier, I think both are part of our deep and fundamental search for wholeness and our movement towards the God of our understanding.

You and I need love to live, just as much as we need food and water and air to live. We can meet our needs for love only in relationships. But, because I am afraid of myself and I'm afraid of you, you and I are both alone, rather than loving one another.

You are the most precious thing in the world to me. You have what I need to take away my pain, my discontent, my aching heart. But because I'm afraid to love you, I am alone and you are alone. When I say that, because I am afraid, you and I are both alone. It's not that I am unduly blaming myself. I'm simply talking about the only part of the process I know anything about, which is my part. In most of our loving, in one way or another, the closer we get to each other the more sex rears its ugly head. In the world of loving, sex is the great glue—but sex is also the great dynamite. Sex is beautiful and gross and ugly. Sex is so hard to cope with just because it is so powerful. But sex has to be so powerful to break down the walls that you and I put up around ourselves so two very separated people can be united.

The big problem in talking about sex is that there's lots of talk about opinions and theories and ideas and fantasies but very little honest talk about personal feelings and difficulties. Much writing on sex makes it too pretty, makes it seem simple, makes it seem too technical; and cleans it up too much. There's a lot of talk about actions and theories but almost nothing about feelings.

There's a beautiful legend from ancient Greece that originally man-woman was one creature, with two heads, four arms and four legs. This man-woman creature was so happy and so joyful that the gods became jealous and angry. What do you think the gods did? They split the two apart. Ever since then, the man part and the woman part have been trying to find each other so they could come back together again.

We hook up with lots of people who aren't the true other half of ourselves and hurt ourselves and hurt the others. We're all crying in various degrees because the little boy or little girl in us is hurt and we can't help them because we don't know where they hurt. In most of us, the little child was hurt early and often. We all look like we are well and smart, but that's an illusion. It's only outward appearances. Inside, we're all, to some degree or other, crippled, dwarfed and deformed. Despite these terrible handicaps, we and our partner have to climb a mountain together, because what's at the top of the mountain is what we need to feed, build and heal our bodies. We need to learn to handle the screaming, insistent, prodding sex part of ourselves to get it quieted down enough to work in harmony with the rest of the parts of ourselves so we can be a smoothly functioning whole. We are like a symphony orchestra where sex has such a hold on us that sex is the drums and they are drumming so loudly the noise drowns out the rest of the music.

The paradox is that all we have to work with to find our way out of our difficulties are the crippled instruments we have. It would also seem nicer if we weren't so often in the position of denying the very thing we need or refusing to take it when it is offered us.

Sadly, we can persist for a long time in our delusions about sex and our twisted attitudes and feelings when our bodies seem young and strong. They can seemingly absorb any evil we throw at them. By the time the damage has accumulated in its effect so much that we're forced to see it, we've done even more damage to our already damaged instruments—the very instruments we need to save ourselves.

We'll spend the rest of the book filling in the picture of how sex can play a better part in all our lives. I'm going to talk about the obstacles we face as we try to meet our need for sex coming out of our terrible childhood deprivation. I'm going to talk about how our self-centeredness and our fear of intimacy make us shy away from sex. Then I'm going to talk about the escapes we use to avoid intimacy and sex simultaneously.

I'll talk about learning celibate love, because we've got to love somebody where we aren't going to have sex with them before we can really learn to love somebody where we are going to have sex with them.

I'm going to talk about learning to love sexually where we start out doing a poor job and we end up, hopefully, a lot better.

I'm going to talk about what I think is the most crucial dimension of sexual love, which is surrender and moving towards the total surrender, which none of us will ever achieve. I'm going to talk about bonding and how the more surrender there is, the more bonding and the closer and tighter the bonding is. Along with that, I'll talk about the thing that I had always wondered about in sex, this tremendous intensity we see at times in sex. I wondered, should sex always have that intensity for us, throughout life? A lot of people are chasing that sexual intensity. They chase sexual intensity with one person, then they go and chase it with another person. What I've come to see now is that sexual intensity can't persist. There's no way you can climb Mount Everest the twenty-seventh time with the same excitement that you climbed it the first time. But that intensity doesn't have to persist, because if you can achieve a tremendous amount of surrender and have this tremendous intensity, you get the bonding. Out of the bonding comes a tremendous closeness and attachment and fastening together of two people which helps them through so much, through the rough time. And then there's a feeling between them that pervades the whole rest of their lives.

At times, some of that intensity comes back into the sexual relationship and goes back out for a while. But the knowledge that it will probably come again and again in varying degrees in the lifetime of the relationship is a very important thing. But, most crucially, the bonding the intensity has helped create is there. So that helped explain the place of intensity in the sexual relationship. We'll talk more about that later.

Remember, we're all in this mess together, and it's only together that we're going to get out.

CHAPTER 2

Our First Big Obstacle to Sex—
Our Terrible Deprivation

As near as I can see, there are two big obstacles to meeting our needs for love and sex. In every civilization I've ever looked at and studied, the people in it had to contend with their separateness, their loneliness, and come into harmony with each other and some power outside themselves. In the legends of the American Indians it's common to find stories of their getting out of touch with their god and becoming more separate from each other. In the book of the Hopi, their legend tells that their people were wiped out by water, then by fire, with only a few survivors each time.

We want to romanticize and idealize primitive society. The South Sea Islands have been portrayed as a paradise, especially a sexual paradise. But even there we see the case of the man who would all of a sudden run amok. He had been a good man, good husband, good father and a caring member of his community. All of a sudden he would grab a spear and start killing people in his village.

The Crow Indians believe all their people go to the big camp in the sky except for people who commit suicide or kill a member of their own tribe. These people's spirits are doomed to endlessly roam the earth as ghosts. When you come into a tepee or a house, you have to leave by the same door or window or hole you came in. Otherwise you will leave a hole for the ghosts to enter.

These are just a few examples of man's separateness even from members of his own tribe and his god.

That's why I believe every society has had to cope with the problems of separateness and coming into relationships with his or her fellow men and fellow women. But in addition to that problem, I believe we have another problem that is so sad that it makes me want to cry about it. It is so sad that some of you are going to cry about it. It's our first big obstacle to meeting our need for love and sex—our terrible deprivation of emotional love and body contact in our infancy, which has then been carried on by us throughout our life.

What is deprivation? It's a technical psychological term that means that you don't provide something an animal or human needs. When you take a rat and don't feed him you are depriving him of food. He is not deprived of air, because you are not depriving him of air. Typically he is not deprived of water, because if he was deprived of water very long, he would die. Or we can deprive him from being able to see other rats, of smelling or hearing other rats. The deprivation can also be a partial deprivation, in which the rat is given a very small part of the food he needs, rather than being completely cut off from all food.

So deprivation is a technical psychological term talking about a process in which somebody doesn't get something they need. The longer they don't get something they need the greater the deprivation. So we are going to talk about your and my deprivation.

A good example is a concentration-camp inmate who isn't given enough food. That happened to many during World War II. As you go longer and longer with inadequate food, the deprivation becomes more and more severe and the thought of food becomes so strong and becomes such an obsession it overwhelms you. It's like I said earlier about the drums in the symphony. Drums are a beautiful thing in a symphony. We need them in all the appropriate spots, like in Wagner where the gods are storming. So they are a fantastic thing in the symphony. But if the drums go crazy and beat all the time and beat too loudly, we can't hear the rest of the instruments. Well, that's exactly the effect a severe deprivation has on us. We become so obsessed with some one thing that we have been terribly deprived of, that it rules and controls our whole lives. It twists all the rest of our lives out of shape, just as the drums going crazy in the symphony orchestra twist the music out of shape. It doesn't matter what beautiful music the violins are playing, and the tuba and the delicate little flute, the drums are making so much noise you can't hear any of the rest of the symphony.

Most of us come to an awareness of the symphony of our own life at the point where the drums have already gone crazy. As we come to a consciousness of ourselves increasingly through early adolescence, teens and early twenties, all we hear typically is the insistent noise of the drums. We don't understand what a symphony is. We have no comprehension that, buried beneath the terrible racket that the drums of our deprivation are making, are the sounds of delicate little oboes and flutes and violins and intricate harmonies between the horns and the woodwind instruments and string instruments. There is even the sound of the little bells of the tambourine, such a delicate little sound it makes. But we don't hear any of these sounds. All we hear is the roar of the drums.

So it will help us to take a look, and we don't need to look too far back, oddly enough, to see what extreme deprivation of emotional love and body contact can do. In the 1910s and 1920s the majority of infants put into orphanages and hospitals died. This shocking death rate was reported to a meeting of the American Pediatric Society in 1915 by Dr. Henry Chapin. In ten infant asylums he surveyed in the United States, every infant but one under two years of age died.

At the same meeting, Dr. R. Hamil reported that he

had the honor to be connected with an institution in Philadelphia in which the mortality of all infants under one year of age was 100 per cent.

Dr. T. S. Southworth of New York City gave an instance from an institution where the infant mortality was so high it was customary to enter the condition of every infant on the admission card as hopeless. That covered all subsequent happenings. This was only sixty years ago. Why did the babies all die? They died from lack of body contact, lack of being touched. They were fed, but they died anyway. Why didn't somebody touch them? Partly it was because the method of child rearing put forth by doctors of that time, which said you don't touch babies, drowned out the common wisdom of mothers for millions of years. The doctors taught that you let them lie in their beds. You fed them at rigid times, and you put them out of doors alone and gave them lots of fresh air.

Now it seems impossible that such an idiot notion could be propounded, but this is a testimony to us university thinkers that we could come up with something like that. That was the prevailing medical idea on how you cared for children. Besides, the orphanages were understaffed and there weren't enough people to care for the babies. So extreme deprivation of body contact and of love in infancy kills babies—almost 100 per cent.

Back in those days, we had another experiment that was offered us by the conditions of that time. Two kinds of homes were studied. One was called a foundling home and one a nursery. In this particular foundling home in the mid-1920s, the children had enough care so that most of them lived—they had enough body contact. But in the nursery the mothers had been confined to the hospital and so the baby also got the mother's care and got the special kind of body contact the mother can give a baby.

So we had these two conditions: The foundling home,

where the kids got touched some, with eight to twelve babies in the care of each nurse, and we had the nursery, where the mothers were there to touch them in addition. In the foundling home 37 per cent of the children died in the first two years. But even for those who lived, there was a big problem: The developmental quotient, or D.Q., was used as a measure of their complete development. D.Q. is a combination of I.Q., social development, perception, body movements and social relations. In the foundling home the developmental quotient at birth for the group averaged 124. This dropped to 45 by the end of two years. In the nursery, where the babies had the mothers' touch in addition to the nurses', the group averaged a 101 D.Q. at birth and it increased to 105.

So the infants in the foundling home who didn't die were still severely deformed emotionally and developmentally. They were simply imitations, in a sense, of human beings. They *looked* all right, because they were nourished physically, but inside they were a mess. The children in the nursery got so much more of the mothers' care that their developmental quotient increased over the two years.

A study up in Canada during World War II found that infants suffered drastically from any kind of separation from the father or mother, whether from enlistment in the armed services, divorce, illness or what have you. Any kind of separation, even a father who traveled on the road a lot, left a mark and hurt the child. So separation of any kind hurts the child. How can you say to a baby who is a year or two old, "Your dad's gone because he has to go out on the road to earn some money; he can't get a job in town"? How is that different for the baby than where the father just leaves and goes on the bum and deserts the baby? You can't tell a year or two-year-old child in a way they can understand, why their father or mother left them.

In my own case, when I was about a year and a half

my mother was severely burned in a fire. All her hair was burned off and she was burned all over her face and down one arm. She nearly died. In fact it was a miracle that they saved her life. We lived in southern Minnesota at the time, so they rushed her to Mayo Clinic, at Rochester. It was in the early days of skin grafts, but they were able to save her life. She was away about two years off and on, and she came out of there a very grotesque-appearing woman, with livid, red scars. She was so disfigured at first, when the scars were fresh, that when she walked down Main Street in our little town people would stop and stare at her.

Of course there were grave consequences for my younger brother, who was born during this time, and for me, as I was a year and a half old when it happened and over three when she came home for good. In addition, there were all the problems in her own life and her life with my father as a consequence of her burns. This is just an example of separation in my own life. During that time, I was raised by my grandparents.

Recently I was meditating on those early years of my life, using the ability of meditation to carry me back through the subconscious mind where my conscious mind couldn't take me. I found myself in an upstairs bedroom at my grandfather's house crying for someone to come. I cried on and on, and no one came. All of a sudden I felt that the reason no one was coming was that there was something wrong with me. I saw that the nebulous "others" I had tried to impress with my good behavior in school, college activities and business may very well have had its origin in that experience. I can't be certain of that. But my basic personality defects are just like those in other infants who were separated from their mothers.

A guy was interested by the fact that in photographs and paintings of mothers, they held their babies in their left arm. He wondered why that was. Then he realized that if a baby is held in the left arm its head is up against the mother's heart. He checked to see if this was because the woman was right-handed and would feed the baby with the right hand. He found left-handed women also held their babies with their left arm, with the head against the heart. In the study, 83 per cent of right-handed women and 88 per cent of left-handed women held their babies on their left arm. It had nothing to do with handedness.

You might think the mothers were simply doing the socially acceptable thing. But no, there was an aspect to his research that shows something much deeper. The horrible thing he found was that if the baby and the mother were separated for a period of twenty-four hours or more at the baby's birth, as in the case of premature birth, the arm used to hold the baby was reversed, with over 80 per cent of the mothers holding the baby away from the heart. Whether they were right- or left-handed, only 20 per cent of the mothers held the baby with the head against the heart when there was the separation at childbirth. The only exceptions were when mothers were able to hold one of their other children during this time a premature baby was away from them. Those mothers showed the same preferences as when there was no separation.

The doctor doing the research recorded the sound of a heartbeat and put it in one nursery, and in the other nursery there wasn't the recording. Those babies who heard the heartbeat did better. They gained more weight while they were in the hospital.

What goes on between the mother and the baby is very complicated. But we can see from the research that two things stand out. The obvious need is touching and loving. But there is another need on the part of both the mother and the baby, and that is for the bonding that goes on in the first few moments of birth. There is much more going on there at birth between the baby and the mother and father than our feeble intellect can imagine.

After all these years, the American Medical Association finally adopted a statement supporting mother-infant bonding and asking hospitals to review their policies on delivery and, if necessary, develop and formulate new guidelines respecting all aspects of professional support for the birth and nurturing process.

The medical profession is finally recognizing something that's been obvious from the research for a long time. But the delivery process has been run for the convenience of the hospital, the nurses and the doctors, and it is the way it is because it meets their emotional needs. I don't believe very many hospitals will change their ways very much. It would make too many doctors and nurses cry.

My wife has written a book called "I Exist, I Need, I'm Entitled" which will be published in 1980. She tells how she was watching a film of a normal delivery where the baby is spanked and then one where Dr. LeBoyer delivered the baby gently and gives it to the mother so they can both stroke it and play with it. The film made her cry both times she saw it, because she wanted to be that baby so badly.

The problem with the AMA statment on bonding is that they don't recognize the emotional factors that produced the mechanical treatment of the baby by the doctors who control the process.

You can't just tell doctors to start delivering babies like LeBoyer and to stroke them and be loving and gentle. Most doctors, if they could have done that, would have long ago. It takes a person like LeBoyer, who is well developed emotionally and spiritually, to do what he's doing. Will the AMA create new classes for their doctors to return to so they can learn the emotional and spiritual development needed? When you put the question that way, you can see that it would be an impossible task to re-educate the emotions. A person who seems not to be deeply affectionate in their behavior can't be easily changed.

Another sad part of the AMA statement recognizing bonding is that they acknowledge it is partly an attempt to head off home deliveries: "The House action is a vital step, Dr. McQuarrie added, in combatting the surge of home deliveries in recent years, which some studies indicate lead to fetal risk six times that in hospital deliveries."

There are two problems with that statement. One problem is that home deliveries are just getting started again, because the midwife system pretty well died out. So there are midwives who are poorly prepared. But well-trained midwives can produce birthing risks as low as or even lower than the hospitals.

The Farm is a large commune in Summerton, Tennessee. They have delivered their own babies and those for people nearby since 1970. They were quite inexperienced at first. But their perinatal mortality for babies delivered on the Farm for 694 babies was 11.5 per 1000.* This is a very acceptable level compared to good hospitals. Even when the twenty-eight high-risk pregnancies that were taken to the hospital are added in, the perinatal death rate from all causes is still only 19.4 per 1000, which is still lower than some hospitals achieve.

But there is another advantage for the mother and the baby to birthing by the Farm midwives. In their system the mother and baby and the bonding of the two is the primary concern. There is a lot more to being born than just coming out alive! We can see enough as we look at studies where children weren't loved and see what happened to their emotional development to be able to guess at some of the conse-

* Ina Mae Gaskin, *Spiritual Midwifery*, Revised Edition (Summerton, Tenn.: The Book Publishing Company, 1978).

quences of lack of bonding and lack of mother love. We saw that when the mother and baby were separated and couldn't bond, she held the baby away from her heart, with at least some negative effect.

In a very comprehensive article on this problem, Ashley Montagu shows the physical and emotional consequences of a lack of mother and father love in the first six years of life; some of the earlier studies I mentioned are from his article.*

Montagu cites a 1948 study by Fried and Mayer, of dependent and neglected children at the Cleveland Jewish Orphans Home. They found the severest disturbances in growth and development to be in the emotionally impoverished, derelict children. The child who has been inadequately loved, neglected, or abandoned by its parents exhibits socio-emotional disturbances that are reflected in his growth and development. Drs. Fried and Mayer conclude that "socio-emotional adjustment plays not merely an important but actually a crucial role among all the factors that determine individual health and physical well-being. . . . It has become clear that socio-emotional disturbance tends to affect physical growth adversely, and that growth failure so caused is much more frequent than is generally recognized."

Montagu in his article goes on to cite a large body of research that shows the three major consequences of a lack of loving for the babies who don't die. Those consequences are a lack of physical growth, a weakness in the physiological system that makes all the psychosomatic illness so much more common and the emergence of an "affectionateless" character.

This "affectionateless" character is well described in the work of Dr. John Bowlby, the English psychiatrist who headed a study for the United Nations World

* Ashley Montagu, "A Scientist Looks at Love," *Phi Delta Kappan*, May 1970, pp. 463–67.

Health Organization reported on as *Maternal Care and Mental Health.**

In a study of forty-four juvenile thieves, Dr. Bowlby found that a large proportion exhibited an inability to establish affectionate relationships with other persons and displayed "the affectionateless character." Fourteen of the forty-four delinquents were of this type, and of the fourteen there were twelve who had suffered a prolonged separation from the mother at an early age. These affectionateless characters were significantly more delinquent than the other thieves, constituting over half the more criminal and chronic offenders.

Two other books that cite similar data are *Children Who Hate,* by Drs. Redl and Wineman, and *Children in Trouble,* by Dr. Frank Cohen. Ashley Montagu says in his article on love, "At the International Children's Center in Paris, Dr. John Bowlby and Jenny Rudinesco have seen that children who have not been adequately loved grow up to be persons who find it extremely difficult to understand the meaning of love. Such children are awkward in their human relationships, and they tend to be thoughtless and inconsiderate. They have little emotional depth, hence they enter into many sorts of human relationships in a shallow way, drifting from one marriage to another with bland, emotionless ease. They are affectionateless characters who suffer from a hunger for affection. Awkward and ineffectual in their attempts to secure it, they often suffer rejection, becoming still more embittered. They find themselves in the paradoxical situation of hating people because they want to love them. They have attempted to love them but have been repulsed and so end up hating them."

One of my basic points in this book is that a majority of us both in the older generation and in the younger, suffer from a lack of love. The lack of love we

---

* John Bowlby, *Mental Care and Mental Health* (New York: Columbia University Press, 1951)

suffered wasn't enough to kill us or to make criminals of us, but I see that so many of us are "affectionateless characters," who are awfully poor at getting love. So in addition to the problem of separateness that all souls face, I see that so many of us have a second terrible handicap, our impoverishment of love at an early age so we don't know how to get the thing we lack so much.

We know we need love, but our need looks so big that we feel helpless to meet it and don't know where to start. When we look at this childhood stuff, in a way it appears like we are almost doomed. But I think if we keep on looking more deeply into the problem of our deprivation we can find some ways out of our dilemma.

Our skin is the largest organ, by far, in the body, far larger than the liver or the lungs. Our skin, for most of us, if you spread it out would be about the size of a single blanket. Here's this huge organ and we know it needs good stimulation. We know, from the babies' case, that if it doesn't get stimulation from being held, it dies, or the rest of the body dies because that big organ isn't gettting the stimulation it needs.

We can understand that we need food. We can understand that we need water. But it's hard to understand that we need body contact. However, the evidence, to me, is overwhelming. It's absolutely clear that we do. And when you look into these studies like I've looked into them, it's very simple to see that there is no way that any of us could have possibly been raised right, from the standpoint of our upbringing meeting all our needs for body contact.

I am completely convinced that there isn't a single person who wasn't deprived to a substantial degree of body contact during the formative part of their childhood period, during their first, second and third year of infancy and childhood. I think it was a severe deprivation in most all of our cases and in some of our cases it was nearly catastrophic. It nearly killed us. A little more deprivation and we would have died like some of the babies did back in the study in the 1920s.

Many of us are just like the infants in that foundling home. Our development and our social abilities were so retarded and suppressed by our lack of body contact that we are hollow shells of what might have been, had our situation been reversed. But it wasn't. One of the funny things is how unable and how unwilling we are to recognize our inner handicaps.

When I was saying this book to the seminar in Seattle the first of the two days, a man named Harold was in the audience in a wheelchair. Here was good old Harold in his wheelchair, so it looked to the rest of us like Harold had a handicap. But Harold's physical handicap wasn't the real serious handicap in the room. It is you and me who've got the severe handicap. Good old Harold can solve his handicap with a wheelchair and a willing helper. But the kind of handicap that you and I have inside us, that really handicaps us. There aren't any wheelchairs made for that. There aren't any pills or medicines. There isn't anything to do for our problem except one thing, and that is so hard for us to handle that we push away the very thing we need. What we do in our lives would be just like Harold sitting home saying, "I don't want my wheelchair," and destroying it when it's his passport to freedom. Okay, why do we do that? I see that there's a good answer for us in this little experiment.

Take some monkeys and put them in separate cages when they are born. They'll be able to see other monkeys but they won't be able to touch or get any touching from the other monkeys. Their mothers won't be holding them and preening them. And they won't be playing with each other. What kind of monkeys do you think we'll have? Research clearly shows us that we'll have a very violent and very hostile monkey who won't touch or let himself be touched. So the monkey got to the point, because of lack of touching, where he wouldn't receive the thing he needed. He couldn't receive it, and that, to me, is the dilemma we're facing here.

It isn't the hostile, aggressive part of us that concerns me as much as the fact that we run away from both the physical touching we need and the symbolic touching as well. In any kind of closeness, there is symbolic touching at least. When we run away from this, it interferes with and makes difficult all our human relationships. There was symbolic touching from all of us who were in that seminar room together in Seattle, because I was talking about my feelings and they were listening. Anytime there is emotional closeness, there is symbolic touching. I don't know whether two monkeys can get as much out of sitting across the room and looking into each other's eyes as humans can. I hope so. Because there can be more touching in that exchange than much physical touching we received.

Jackie Smith, my friend and my student from Bozeman, was in Seattle sitting in the front row. I looked at her and she looked at me in a very special, nice way. That was almost as if she were touching me physically. There was some of the same kind of warmth and feeling, because there was an openness of her face and eyes to me and, hopefully, of mine to her.

That's why our deprivation and its effects are so traumatizing. It wouldn't be so bad if we just pushed away sexual contact, because we can live without that. Some of our happy priests and other happy celibates show us that you can live without sex. So that's not the problem, really, as much as the fact that we push away all other kinds of not just physical touching but symbolic touching in intimacy with our brothers and sisters, which is everyone. See how crazy it is that we push away what we need to save our lives. We push away what we are deprived of. We push away what we need. We push away what can heal us and save us. That is the nub of the problem. The fact that we do this tells me about our deprivation.

We can infer or guess at the extent or depth of our deprivation by how we act. If you starved a bunch of rats, some of them for five days, some for ten days and some for fifteen days, and you couldn't see how skinny the different groups of rats were, you could tell something of their deprivation by how greedily and how long they ate afterwards.

In the same way, you could sort out the monkeys raised in the cages. Leave them in sight of the monkey colony so they can see all the social relationships going on but not in their individual cages. You do that to three sets of monkeys, giving them a little time away from touching, a moderate time away from touching and a long time away from touching. You'll be able to sort the monkeys out by how violently they fight off touching. The ones that don't fight off touching so violently from their fellow monkeys weren't deprived long. The ones who fight off touching moderately violently were in the middle group and the ones who fight off touching most violently were in the most deprived group. You see what that opens up to us? You see what it tells us about ourselves? A person says, "Well, I'm not a toucher," as if that is just another thing about them; you know, like "I've got pimples." That tells me about their deprivation. It isn't an original part of their nature. As humans, we weren't made that way or we wouldn't have survived for millions of years. It just *seems* to people that that's their nature, because they've always been that way. In a small sense, a child of five can say I'm not a reader because I can't read. But if he opens his mind, he can see that he can learn what he doesn't have.

Some of these studies I'm telling you about were like thunderbolts to me, because they explained things

I'd always wondered about. Why? Why is it that way? I didn't learn about touching until I was forty-two years old, ten years ago. I started touching people, made a lot of dumb mistakes, got knocked down a few times, but found there were some people I couldn't even touch with a stick, but I'm learning. The difficulty I had and am still having learning to overcome my fear of touching and meeting my needs for touching tells me about me. It also offers an explanation for violence in our society.

A lot of people want to argue that violence in our society is because we show our kids all the violent television pictures and give them all these violent ideas. I don't believe that. This was a violent society before television even happened. I come from one of the most violent of states, which is Montana. People say, "Oh, you live in that lovely pastoral paradise out there." We've got some of the maddest, most angry people in the world. If you look at the states with the highest rates of violent death per capita, it's Alaska, Nevada, Wyoming, Idaho and Montana. Any idiot can see the pattern. What's the pattern? Simple. Two things are involved there. When you are isolated from your fellow human beings, you are going to be more violent, just like the monkeys. Secondly, there is something different about the kind of people who leave the cities and come to this area so they can get a long way away from those other people; they aren't really very sociable. That's why I get so excited when they characterize us as the "Howdy" state. You've heard me say that. It's "Howdy" the first year, yes, but twenty years later it's still "Howdy" there. And the guy has never stopped long enough to find out any more about you than what your name is and what you do. He'll help you out, but he hates to have to be in a position where he needs your help. Most of all, he isn't interested in how you feel. In fact, he doesn't want to know. And the worst thing you can do is say anything more than "Howdy" back.

Sure there are lots of friendly people in Montana, but it isn't the friendly state it looks to be on the surface. Otherwise, we wouldn't be among the leaders in the nation in our per capita rates of violent deaths, alcoholism and divorce. People, including children, who have violence already in them, seek violence in all forms, including TV.

Speaking for myself, I understand the monkey who is lashing out at his fellows instead of accepting what he needs. I understand violence. When violence comes out of me, it is a reflection of the anger in me coming in part from my severe deprivation. This is an extremely violent society. Because of the increasing difficulty we're having in our country with holding marriages together, we are, I think, going to have ever-increasing violence in our society that will make the violence we have today look tame. That's because it's hard enough for a husband and wife living in a society without any close support from other adults like they would have in a tribal society to give their children a fraction of the loving they need to be less violent. It's even harder for a mother or father living alone to meet the needs of the infants and young children. And we're going to keep on having more divorce and more violence and hostility until the whole bunch of us in our society find some way to arrest the increase in broken homes and poorly functioning homes. I don't know what's going to stop the trend. I'm just now learning a lot of things about being a father and a husband twenty-five to thirty years after my wife and kids needed me the most.

I'm not surprised at violence and hostility any more. I can predict it in given situations, because I think I know where it's coming from and television isn't the cause people see it as. To me, it's just another symptom of our violent leanings, that we need to see them acted out. Now, television may tip some kid over to say, "I'm going to shoot six neighbors today the same way I saw it last night on 'Kojak.' " But that kid didn't change from a nice, peace-loving little kid to a violent person all of a sudden just because he saw "Kojak."

Then, of course, there's two kinds of violence. There is the going-down-to-the-bar-and-getting-beat-up kind of violence. But there's another kind of violence which I find more scary, really. That's the kind of violence I've seen in those so-called calm, quiet people. They're against a lot of things, but they're against them in a real quiet voice. But there's so much anger leaking out of those people.

One place I see a lot of this expression of violence is in the anti-smokers' movement. I haven't smoked since I was seventeen years old. So I'm a reformed smoker. But I really have a deep sympathy for smokers for all the hell they are catching from some of the violent nonsmokers. They tell me some of the worst of the anti-smokers are smokers who have quit and are mad at the people who are still doing what they want to do.

That covered-up violence is so bad because it is so deceptive and it keeps leaking out. When you're around quiet violence, you aren't aware of it at first, but you're getting all these arrows in your stomach. You look like a pincushion. You keep wondering why you feel so bad. But the person you're with says, "I'm not doing anything to you." Yet they're cutting holes in your stomach, leaving gaps so big they can see all the way through you. But they insist they're not doing anything to you. "I'm a nice, quiet, peaceful person. I love other people."

So, again, both forms of violence are bad, but disguised hostility is the worst. A lot of times it comes across as pretended love. One of the saddest things, of course, is when that violence is in mothers and fathers who are raising children, and that's you and me.

Rollo May, in *The Meaning of Anxiety*, points out that what produces anxiety most isn't rejection but rejection that's denied by the parent. He found that unwed mothers who had been openly hated and rejected by their parents didn't have much anxiety. The ones with anxiety were the unwed mothers who had been raised in homes where their parents rejected them but pretended to love them. So pretended love is far harder to handle than hate.

A while back, I went out to feed my horses. They had busted down a corral pole and gotten in my hay. They tore my hay bales up and made piles of manure on my three-dollar-a-bale hay. I was angry. So I yelled at them to get out of there. I've got a colt named Doctor Jim who's three and a half years old. He's got a personality like mine: he's feisty and aggressive. After I went over to the tack room to get a hammer and nails so I could nail things up, I left the door open. The colt went in the tack room and sniffed around. I yelled at him and he got out. I did some more work and he went right back in again. I got through with my work and yelled at him to get out. He backed out and scooted by me. Just as he went by, he kicked up his heels at me like he was going to kick me. I grabbed my training whip out of the tack room and gave him a crack across the butt.

The whole thing was stupid. He wasn't really being bad. And even if he was, the only time you can ever punish an animal is within a second after they misbehave or they can't figure out what their punishment is for, because by then the colt was just standing looking at me. It was pure stupidity on my part, just anger. So I understand violence.

I told my group in Seattle that if we wanted to have a contest to see who was the most angry, hostile person in that group, that I would win. It was just like one time I was speaking to an AA convention and I said I was a supreme egotist. I practically had to fight everyone in the hall for the title.

So what does my violence tell me about me? I can see now that it tells me about the degree of my deprivation. I don't know what it was that happened in the first few years of my life. I can just guess at some of the things by the results I see in myself.

Now we get into another problem. My mother is a nice woman. She was as fine a mother as she could be, and today she is a fine, very kind lady. Okay, how come she and my dad didn't do their job right? A lot of reasons. First of all, I defy any one of us to study over the research on child raising and then take a baby into our homes and raise him right. We've got too much anger and hurt of our own, just like me with that colt. In my head I know a lot about horse training, so that was one of the dumbest things I ever did. But that didn't keep me from doing it and it isn't going to keep me from doing it again sometime. I don't do it very often, but I don't need to do it often to do plenty of harm to my colt.

He's the only one of my six horses who comes running up to me every time he sees me. I love having him do that. But if I keep on treating him inconsistently, how long before he starts to run from me, like the rest do?

I can have all this knowledge in my head and see that it doesn't help much. And it's a very small matter, handling my colt, compared to the importance of how I am with my own children.

With my mother, also, all I need to do is look at her mother and how she was with my mother and her brothers and sisters. My grandmother was a ring-tailed terror, that lady was. I just remember her up to the time I was eight or nine years old, but she was really mean. I'll never forget the time we stayed with them one winter. She had been so mean and growly to

my brother and me each morning at breakfast that
my dad finally took me out in the barn and told me,
"It's all right, Jess, we're not going to have to be here
much longer. You're just going to have to put up with
her the best way you can." He showed a great compassion with me.

How come Grandma was such a ring-tailed terror?
Well, I know the story of my great-grandmother. She
came over here from Norway as a widow on a boat,
and God knows how she got the money to carry herself and five kids, four girls and a boy. I don't know
whether she was really a widow or just such a nag her
man couldn't stand to live with her or what. But
anyway, here was this mother all alone. Imagine what
a frantic and difficult task she had to completely move
herself and five children away from her homeland and
family. I don't know why she left there, or why her
brothers or parents didn't say to her, "Hey, you can't
go to a strange country." But she tore herself away
from all her roots and came here and then gave one of
her sons to a family that didn't have a son and gave
one of her daughters to another family. It was a
kindness, in a way, because they could do more for the
children than she could. The other children, she raised
as well as she could. One of those girls was my grandmother, who married young and was moved by her
husband down to a part of Montana where the former
Indian reservation lands had just been opened up to
settlers.

So I come from a long tradition of deprivation. And
I know some of the stories on my father's side of some
of the difficulties that were in the families of his
mother and father. His father, my grandfather, was a
very sad and terribly depressed man. I loved him a
great deal, because he raised me in those early, formative years. But I would have loved him anyway,
because we had many characteristics in common. One
of his problems was that it was so hard for him to

show a feeling. He was really kind of a tyrant in his family. Though he was a deacon in the church and had a big library of theological books, he wouldn't give my grandmother a nickel. He even bought her pots and pans, her clothes, everything. Every once in a while, he would decide to go to town. My grandmother was a social person, she just loved people. My grandfather would come in the house and say, "Well, Net, I'm going to go to town in ten minutes." If she wanted to come, she'd by God better get her clothes changed and her new girdle on or she would be left behind.

When I spoke in my books about some of these things my grandfather did, it made some of my aunts mad. But one of them said she did have to agree, Dad did have that stingy side to him. But some of my aunts were holding him up on this pedestal, which is what we do as a way to hide what really happened. We want to dwell on what we thought was good. We excuse that as a kindness and as a good thing to do, but it isn't. It's necessary to see our handicaps. We don't have to blame anyone for them, but it helps to see the truth.

There's a third reason why all of us had some degree of childhood deprivation. We may have had the best two parents in the town. They may have loved us with every fiber of their being. We may have been the most loved and the best loved children we've ever seen. But there is something we can't see, because it runs throughout our society so much we're unaware of it.

When we study some so-called primitive societies, we see that the mother and father aren't alone in loving and raising the child. They can get three things that are almost impossible to get in our society, expecially to the degree that these three things are in a tribal society!

First, the mother and father aren't tied up too much

with work, so they both are more available to give love to the child and to get love from their fellow tribesmen and tribeswomen.

Second, the mother and father have lots of help in loving the child. There are all kinds of other people to love and accept the child as he or she is.

Third, the mother and father aren't so alone in the society. They have lots of kinfolk and friends to give them the love they can pass on to the child.

You can't give away what you don't have. The more love you get, the more you can give, especially when there's time to give that love at the precious moment. A life like that is a perfect honeymoon and a long one.

So, for all these reasons, each of us had at least a little childhood deprivation and some of us had a lot.

As my old friend says, "If we're working on a problem, it helps to know what the problem is." I think if you and I are going to work on a problem, it helps to know what the problem is.

I think our problem is a severe childhood deprivation of body contact. And we were doubly unfortunate in a way. I've seen people who are suffering so much, it almost seems to them that it would have been better if they had been killed by their deprivation. Because if they were dead, they would have some peace. But we weren't killed by it. Some of us seem to have just enough body and just enough life in us to go through the motions. Yet we look at others' physical bodies when they are young and think, "Ain't they pretty!"

It's just like this friend of mine. He'd been married twice and was shooting for a good number three. I told him, "Bailey, you idiot, what's wrong with you is that you are looking at the outside of a woman instead of the inside of her. You'd better find a woman who has got a good heart for you." He'd been a student of mine, so I could talk to him this way. And Bailey said, "Yeah, yeah, I know." We were riding up the ski lift about five minutes later and he was looking over at this gal coming down the slopes. "Wow, Jess, look at that!" I said, "Bailey, you can't tell anything about her heart from here." But that's the way we are so much.

Another way of conceiving of it is if we could picture that these physical bodies of ours are just costumes we wear. We can look at it just like we're a bunch of actors wearing costumes, doing Shakespearian plays. We've all got these outlandish costumes on, very different from anything we've ever seen. We know that in everyday life the actors under those costumes look totally different.

Imagine that this emotionally dwarfed, emaciated, handicapped, deprived little soul that is inside us comes to the costume-rental place and rents a King Lear costume—or a King Arthur or a Guinevere. There's no relationship between the costume and the thing that's inside. But this is what we're judging people by. Some guy looks at a gal's face and body on the beach and says, "Wow!" What's he looking at? He's looking at her body, her costume that she just checked out at the theatrical rental agency. He isn't looking at her soul, but it's her soul that he needs to love and live with the rest of his life.

Another way of putting it is it's just like a bunch of us were going to go mountain climbing and we're going to pick partners. So here are these twisted, dwarfed, deformed emotional bodies and we all go in and buy mountain-climbing suits. We're in northern India on the way to the Himalayas to climb Mount Everest. We buy our mountain suits and we're all wearing these neat new suits. You know how good clothes can hide a lot.

So I've got my nifty mountain-climbing clothes on and someone says, "Whoopie, I'll take you as my partner to climb Mount Everest. What can't they see? They can't see that, underneath, I've only got half a hand and half a leg and the two don't work together worth a damn. Yet we're going to be roped together climbing Everest. If you take the bunch of us, it's a hard job coming up with a whole person between us. So we're climbing up Everest and it goes pretty good along the flat. But the minute there gets to be a little pitch, things start going to hell immediately. The steeper it gets, the more the crippled, deformed, deprived thing inside the suit reveals its weakness. Our partners looks at us in our groovy mountain-climbing costume and think, "My God, the defects that pretty suit is covering up." And we look at our partners and their groovy little lederhosen and think, "There's more holes than hosen."

So this is the vision that I saw. I always used to be troubled by the paradox of my college students. They looked so pretty. The gals looked so pretty and the guys looked nice and neat. Yet, most of them couldn't do what they needed to do when their personal situations got tough. The minute they started having a love relationship, that was when things started to go to hell, right there. In easy things, they did great; it was just like walking on the flat. But the minute they tried to have any kind of a relationship worth a nickel with someone, boom! they were in trouble. The jealousy, envy, possessiveness and self-centeredness all came out.

I finally saw that the problem wasn't with our bodies, the costumes we wear. It's that dwarfed, emaciated, deprived little soul inside that is so deformed by what happened in infancy. That is the problem. I saw that vision and I saw it so clearly. Then I saw the tremendous need to have compassion for myself and to have compassion for you. I don't do very well at having compassion for you and me, but I saw the need to. I don't have much more compassion for you than I do my colt. But I see the need to.

Okay, what are the consequences in our life of this

deprivation? Simple. Now I can understand this constant preoccupation with sex in our society. As an advertising man, all I have to do is show a big pair of breasts to you guys and I get all of your attention. Wow! And to you gals, all I have to do is show some good-looking guy with a nice dark complexion and I can sell you a ton of cigarettes. How come? We're all so damn' deprived, we're push-overs.

This is why all the sexual temptations of life have such control over us. You get businessmen away from home and buy them dancing girls and you own them. You and I are like slaves. We can be bought and sold like slaves. They talk about the old South, where the plantation owners bought and sold slaves; you and I are in that same kind of slavery. In a sense, it's worse, because when a black person was stood up on that auction block he knew he didn't want to be sold and he knew if there was some way he could get out of it he would, including killing himself.

But you and I don't have that much freedom. We're bought and sold just like cattle. And the currency is the rottenest currency there is in the world: a cheap, rotten imitation of what is one of the most beautiful things in the world, which is sex.

Prostitution is a good example. You look carefully at that and it's one of the most awful things in the world. I didn't realize until I saw this television show on prostitution that, by and large, you are not supposed to kiss prostitutes. How weird can you get? You can't hug them or kiss them, but you can have intercourse with them. That, to me, is the craziest thing. In the show this guy was going to bed with a prostitute. Meanwhile she was arguing with some other prostitute about something. The guy was getting undressed and the prostitute was getting undressed, but she continued her argument with the other gal. He finally said, "Hey, what about me?" She said, "I'll get to you." So the other gal left and the guy goes to embrace the

prostitute and she pushes him away: "No kissy-kissy."
That is worth a lot of money?

I still do the advertising for my friend George Jacques
in the hybrid seed-corn business. About eight hundred
of us from the Jacques Seed Company were out in San
Diego for a convention. The girls in San Diego heard
about us being there, of course. They slipped calling
cards under our doors for their massage parlors, instant service in your room. They are used to most
business groups, where only the guys go. And that's
again another interesting thing. In our company, we
always bring the wives and, half the time, the children. But in the business world, we're very rare because we travel with out families. So here's these
calling cards slipped under the door, and the wives
are seeing them and they're saying, "What the blankety-
blank goes on here?" But I'm an old advertising man.
I know people don't waste money on advertising that
doesn't work. Those ladies didn't go to all the expense
of printing those cards up and slipping them under all
those doors if their percentage return wasn't adequate.
How sad that a husband would put on the line so
many things he stood for and spend big money for
some dumb thing like that.

It's just as if I needed a new valve in my heart and
instead of getting the good valve I needed, I went down
to the junk shop and bought an old rusty valve as a
cheap substitute and shoved it in my heart instead.

Pornography is another example. Hugh Hefner came
out with *Playboy* magazine and almost instantly he
was a millionaire, a multimillionaire, because he found
a way to dress up pornography and make it more
socially acceptable by getting learned people and ministers to write articles alongside his pornography. Then
the other guy comes out and shows other parts, so
Hefner has to do more and they've got this little war
going on in the newsstands. In the meantime, the

guys are chuckling in glee and the money rolls in. That's crazy.

Not being a gal, I can only guess at how gals react to the same deprivation. I think, as near as I can tell, and you gals are going to have to decide these things for yourselves, the way many gals handle this terrible need is, rather than reach for some twisted and distorted form of sex as guys do so much, gals tend to over-romanticize sex and they kind of want it all cleaned up with all kinds of white curtains and frilly little rosebuds on it and kind of push it away if it won't quite meet those tests. The sale of the Harlequin romances, which are absolutely "clean" is a good example of this. Sure there are some very big-selling romances for women that are very sexually explicit. But they won't come close to matching the sales of Harlequin books.

You can't generalize too much about any group of people, but I see some women going toward seeking this overly romanticized version of love. "He came riding up on his white horse and swept her into his arms and they rode away into the sunset." I grant that has happened once in a million years, but other times it doesn't really make much sense. To me, overromanticizing sex isn't quite as tawdry, it isn't quite as awful, as so much of what we men do, but it's equally effective as a way of pushing away the real thing that's needed.

There is also a growing percentage of girls and women who show their deprivation just like most men by constantly seeking sex in any form. But even in the most promiscuous women, there seems to be a difference between them and men. They seem to want to be held and be close, but have to give sex to get that momentary closeness. I don't see hardly any women who want the kind of anonymous sex men find with prostitutes, where the emphasis is on the genital contact without any loving and holding.

There seems to be a lot of truth to the statement that men give love to get sex and women give sex to get love.

To me, these things are simply ways by which we show the extent ot our deprivation in infancy and childhood and should be interesting to us as we see ourselves using these things in our own life. To what extent am I pushing away the body contact and physical love I need? What are the particular devices by which I push away what I need? How does my resistance to something that there is overwhelming evidence that I need tell me about the extent of my deprivation and what I really need?

The letter to Abby, instead of saying, "Sex has never meant anything to me and I can take it or leave it," should really say, "Probably because I was so severely deprived as a child, I have such a repugnance and fear of sex that I have held it at arm's length all my life, and what can I do about it?"

In James Bond books, in *The Carpetbaggers*, in *Semi-Tough*, the way they treat sexual intercourse is one of the most awful things I've seen. Sure, I know they're a put-on. But not completely. And because that viewpoint is so widespread and sells so well, it tells me so much about all of us. I don't say these books are so awful as any moral judgment. I'm speaking about them from the results of that kind of sex. If you like nice, shallow relationships with lots of physical sex with anyone who is handy, fine. Then you're getting the results you want. If you also want the other consequences of shallow emotional relationships in your life, like catching the first sickness that comes along and dying as quick as you can, that's fine too. Because I've seen that escaping into sex has these later consequences. People often disagree with me on these later results, but I've seen enough evidence to convince me. I've seen a lot of people die in this town at an early age, and I'm able to be plenty accurate about who has a way of life that will sustain them and who doesn't. But, as I say, this isn't a moral judgment. It's a psychological prediction based on my study of what people need in their lives. Most people I know don't want a short life, and they don't really want a life filled with shallow relationships where there is no real love for them from the people around them.

It's easy for me to carry my point about the sex portrayed in books too far. I enjoy James Bond and I got a kick out of *Semi-Tough*. But I had better be sure I appreciate that the sex in those books is a spoof and not try to act on those ideas.

Philip Roth was horrified at all the fuss *Portnoy's Complaint* stirred up. Here he had gone along writing novels that were moderately well read, searching for the combination of his theme and his skill that would produce the dream of all writers, the great American novel. Then he wrote the story of Portnoy's love affair with his organ and everybody was interested, and eight dollars and ninety-five cents interested. He sold tons of books. But he told how his reputation was hurt as a serious writer because critics attacked him for portraying a Jew lusting after gentiles, and besides, most people were sure the book was purely autobiographical. Again, what does the success of *Portnoy's Complaint* tell us about us? To me, it shows us our intense, yet hidden-from-ourselves, preoccupation with our genitals. I think it shows us that too much a part of too many of us is firmly focused downward trying to scratch an itch that gets worse the more we scratch it.

If all this sexual writing I mentioned was just some harmless fantasy that didn't tell anything about us, it would be different. But it isn't. It's too close to the truth. You see this when you see things like Playboy Forum. In Playboy Forum they have letters from guys telling about all the wild, wild things they do with women, and it turns your stomach. There are stories in there like the one where the guy came home and he finds the baby-sitter lying on the bed masturbating and she's having such a wild time and he joins her and then they have wild intercourse and then his wife comes home and she's carried away by this fantastic thing that's going on, so she jumps in and participates and they have this wild, wild orgy. Even if something like this could happen, think of what feelings there would be afterwards. How is that fourteen-year-old-girl going to feel? How is the wife going to feel? And how will the husband feel? The claim is they don't have any feelings later but good ones. How can that be? But, ridiculous as the whole situation is, what is really ridiculous is that guys have taken stories like that to their wives and said, "Why can't you be like this?" And that hasn't happened just once, but more than once, and there are a couple million guys reading stuff like that.

To me, that's one of the most awful things, because what a terrible way to treat two delicate sexual instruments, a man's and a woman's, which are like fine computers where we need special air conditioning and dust filtering and stuff for those instruments. Then we put them in the hands of idiots like you and me, who take them out in any damn' kind of weather and they get rained on, snowed on and dirty and dusty. Then after about twenty years of mistreatment, we get into a situation where we want the damn' things to work and we wonder how come they won't work! Isn't that a surprise?

What happens, we're just like a bunch of little kids in a tremendous, terrible level of immaturity, frozen at the genital level. To have any kind of sensation, we have to have a bomb go off. We can't appreciate some subtle little thing like a guy just touching a woman's elbow. That's a beautiful thing. There's a fantastic feeling. No, we have to have a bomb go off before we can tell anything happened. When we are that immature, frozen at the genital level, the only way we can get any kind of feeling is jump right into the bomb of sex—boom! And we detour all the rest, all the other stuff. What we do is we lose all the good stuff and the end doesn't mean anything anyway.

All we need to do is look at our lives, our faces and our bodies and we can guess from what we see what we've done to our instruments and we can guess at what happened.

I think there is probably some difference in men's and women's sexual natures. But, like I said earlier, I think deprivation has done nothing but enhance that difference. I think women do need more subtlety than men, but I think the deprivation has accentuated those differences, made them bigger. Guys don't seem to be able to be platonic lovers, but a lot of that, I think, is because of the deprivation, where they'll jump in the sack with practically anything that's got two legs. It's like the world of sex as I used to describe it to my college students from the man's point of view. It's a very immature man's point of view but a very common one.

The world of sex for the guys on campus is each woman has a mattress on her back and there are all these little shacks around campus. Anytime any guy sees some gal he likes, he just points to her and they run and jump in the little shack together and she lays down real quick without a word said but of her eagerness for him, and it's slam, bam, thank you, ma'am. Then he says, "Well, I'll see you around, you know." And he goes on about his business.

The world of sex as a woman sees it is, instead of little shacks, there are huge houses with white columns and a bunch of rooms. If she sees a guy she fancies, they go into the first room and play music and talk endlessly, hour after hour. Then, if there's some kind of feeling between them at all, they go to the next room, where the lights are lower and there's food and wine and softer music and darker lights and they talk some more. If there's a special thing between them, they go into the third room, where there's a couch and even less light and they talk endlessly and occasionally might even touch each other some. If that works out great, they would touch each other in deeper ways. There is a door out of that room which is partway open. In the adjoining room there is a bed, but the covers aren't pulled down, because if the covers were pulled down, that shows it was premeditated, see? And with the guy who passes muster in the third room, she floats into the bedroom and into bed and magically all the clothes disappear, because taking off clothes is cold-blooded and unromantic. So they hold each other tenderly for a long time and there's all kinds of soft talk, but gradually their feelings mount and they are both carried away despite themselves and they come together in a sexual way.

Okay! How do you match up those two worlds? There's no way. They just won't fit together. But, again, a lot of this is our immaturity, and the way our terrible deprivation magnified that immaturity, that makes those worlds seem so far apart.

When I told that story to the sex seminar I gave in Minneapolis in June of 1977, one of the guys argued, "I don't want to be characterized as a slam, bam type." And, of course, there is a loving and tender side of every guy under the right conditions. In a recent book, *Beyond the Male Myth*, by Pietropinto and Simenauer, it is said 98 per cent of the guys surveyed were concerned that their partner be satisfied sexually, which is almost the direct opposite of what Sherry Hite found in her survey. She found that women were tender, loving things and men were beasts who didn't care about their satisfaction, so women weren't having orgasms. But there are a couple of simple ways to solve that problem. The woman can handle it herself if she's desperate enough. A much better way is to just ask the husband. And why didn't she? It's like the story that's supposed to be true of the woman who wanted her husband to blow in her eyes during sex because her father did that to her as a young girl and it really excited her. She finally divorced the guy because he didn't blow in her eyes, but had never told him what she wanted.

As for *Beyond the Male Myth*, where the study shows 98 per cent of the men are interested in satisfying their women, the answer to me is that it is equally off target, because I've never in my experience seen anything like that. If half the girls felt their husbands were interested in satisfying them, that would be high. So the guy may think he's interested in satisfying his wife, but the other person of that relationship doesn't think that he's very interested in satisfying her. There are terrible misunderstandings here.

Those misunderstandings, of course, go back to how come there are women on earth. Originally there were just guys down here on earth. There was a lot of poker playing and elk hunting and just having a good time. But eventually it kind of got boring just telling lies. So the men held a council, because they realized they needed some excitement. They agreed to call God up and tell him, God, send us down some excitement. So God sent down women for excitement, and there was a great time making love and playing together. Beautiful, fantastic. But after a while the fighting, yelling and screaming broke out. Then the headaches started. So the guys had a council. They called up God and said, "Hey, God, this is too much excitement. Would you please take these things back?" So he took back the women.

The guys went back to their elk hunting, poker playing, whiskey drinking and lying. They kept on and it got kind of boring, but they said, "No way." And they went back to their activities and it got more boring and they said, "No way." And they went back and it got even more boring, so they finally said, "We give up." They had a council· and the upshot of the council was that they would call up God and say, "Okay, God, send them back. We can't live with them, but we can't live without them either." So that's how come there are women on earth. Now, some of the ladies, I'm sure, would like to have me turn the story around. I would be glad to. They can tell the story any way they want to. I don't understand women so well that I would want to try to tell the story for them.

The point of the story of how come there are women (or men) on earth is the oppositeness of men and women. That oppositeness is a source of great pain. But it's also a source of great power. In the first chapter, I told of the concept of a relationship where two separate souls make an agreement with each other to spend their life stripping away their own separateness and each going deeper into themselves. That relationship can be between two people of the same sex; when it doesn't involve sex we call it friendship, when it does involve sex we call it homosexuality.

But, either way, the relationship is not as deep as one with the opposite sex, because of that very oppositeness. A homosexual relationship will often even try to get some oppositeness in it by the two partners taking male and female roles.

I see a lot of running from sexual oppositeness today. Women are trying to act like men, men are trying to act like women. Everything is all mixed up. By opposite, I don't mean the woman is a slave and the man a master. I mean it in each person asking themselves what it means to have a man's body or a woman's body and try to be what they are, not what they aren't. I see that our oppositeness is such a big problem to us partly because our deprivation has made it harder to handle. We are so frantically pulled towards the other sex by our need, yet we are so awkward in meeting our needs that our inappropriate behavior causes us so much pain.

How do we keep our children from going through the same problems we've had? There's a simple answer. All we've got to do is love their father or their mother. As one of my young students said, "The greatest thing a father can do for his daughter is love her mother."

What's the answer, then, to our deprivation? We've got to recognize our problems and see our behavior as it is and accept where we're at, rather than lie to ourselves and justify and rationalize our behavior. A good example is when people say, "having sex, for me is just like taking a drink of water. It's that natural." I know they are big liars.

How many of you have any trouble with your water-drinking techniques? How many of you are disturbed about the way you use water, to excess or not enough? How many of you don't have a wide variety of approaches to water, as I do, ranging from "I'll just take a sip casually" to, when I'm up in the mountains and I've been riding all day and I come to a mountain stream, I'll get off and I'll slosh it on my face and I'll practically roll in that stream it feels so delicious.

I have available to me the whole gamut of water-drinking techniques, with a complete lack of self-consciousness, with a complete confidence that I have a mastery of water drinking. I am fully as good a water drinker as anyone who ever lived in the world. I am no better and no worse. And I know everyone feels equally confident of their water-drinking technique. Water is so abundant we have no problem meeting our needs in that area.

But sex is not like a drink of water. It's dynamite. It's very different for us, because we've all been deprived of body contact to some degree and so it's hard for us to learn to get a little closer to sex being like a drink of water.

The most crucial study I have seen offers us some hope and a way out of our dilemma. The common psychological notion is that what was done to us in the first five years of our life sets our life pattern and we've had it.

The answer is, that is false. There is a study by Prescott which is one of the most important studies I've ever seen. He's the one who did the monkey study I mentioned earlier. That study led him to see the vital importance of body contact and its relation to violence, particularly. But we must remember the monkey wasn't only violent; he pushed away touch. So that's got sexual implications, as well as a lot of others.

Prescott took a look at a whole bunch of cultures, especially at their child-raising practices. If their child-raising practices were very loving and affectionate, it meant the children got a lot of body contact, like those born to Eskimo mothers who constantly carried their babies on their backs against their bare skin. For the African mothers there was a lot of holding of the babies, as I told in the Zulu story in "*I Ain't Much, Baby—But I'm All I've Got.*"

Prescott found that most of those societies with good child-raising practices weren't violent. They didn't go to war hardly ever, and when they did, they were kind to their captives. But Prescott found that some of the societies with these good child-raising practices *were* violent. The Plains Indians had very loving child-rearing practices, yet the young men turned out violent. By violent, he meant they went to war a lot, and when they captured people, they were cruel to their captives and tortured and punished them.

So he said, "Hey, is there some other difference in a culture that would help explain the fact that societies with good child raising aren't all non-violent?" He looked for some other variable. The variable he chose was a liberal attitude by the society towards premarital intercourse. That's another thing that will give you a lot of body contact, premarital intercourse, with all the petting and other touching that goes on.

Now, don't get this wrong; in our society, we have a lot of premarital intercourse, but we don't have a liberal attitude towards it. Many of our young people and some of our older people pretend to have a liberal attitude, but we don't. In our culture today we have young people who think they have worked out a new morality for themselves. They have, in their conscious minds, figured out they can have all the sex they want. The problem they don't recognize is that their subconscious and unconscious minds, which came out of our culture, have far more control over them than they realize. I don't see many guys who prefer as wives women who have had sex with two hundred guys because these women will be more experienced lovers. We can't ignore our unconscious that easily. We can't jump out of our culture. This isn't Tahiti in the 1800s. This is America in the 1900s; whether 1900 or 1980, it is much more alike than it is different, no matter what pretty stories we dream up for ourselves.

I knew one young couple where they had both been married to other people and divorced quickly. Supposedly they had good liberal attitudes towards premarital sex. When they started going with each other they had intercourse and she got pregnant before they got married. That bothered them so much it contributed to their divorce from each other. They were doing something they thought was all right, but deep inside themselves they found their attitudes and society's attitudes were deeply against what they were doing. So we don't have as liberal an attitude, a lot of times, as we think we do.

Societies that do have a liberal attitude produce situations like in Denmark in the 1870s, where one third of all girls married in Denmark were pregnant when they married. That's very possibly an evidence of a liberal attitude towards premarital intercourse.

So Prescott added this new idea into his study. When he looked at sixty societies where there were both loving child rearing and a liberal attitude towards premarital intercourse, there was no violence in the societies.

But here is the amazing aspect of his study: Prescott found that societies that had harsher child rearing and a liberal attitude towards premarital intercourse were just as non-violent as the ones that had the loving child rearing and a harsh attitude towards premarital intercourse. So it didn't matter much when you got your loving, you could get it early or late; either way, the society was fairly non-violent. See what a radical thought that is! It directly contradicts the common notion that what happened to you by the time you were five rules you for the rest of your life.

To me, that says that if loving in the age sixteen-to-twenty-five bracket does as much for you as the loving you get from age one to five, then that means that even forty-, fifty- and sixty-year-old people can get the loving we need in our lives. Think of that! I just found out about that study fairly recently; yet it had sat around in my files for a couple of years and I hadn't realized the implications of it until I studied it for this book. It says we can change our childhood deprivation by changing the way we live our life today. We aren't doomed because of our childhood. All we need to do is to get over our terrible, terrible resistance to getting what we need.

See what I'm saying? Our goose isn't cooked just because Ma was so mean that her milk would have curdled and just because she wanted to knock us on the head and sell the milk, and just because Pa hated her and she hated Pa and he didn't want us around, either, even though they both pretended to love us. Those things don't need to doom us forever. And just because we were such mean little kids that we wouldn't sit still for the affection later on and we didn't get it then because we were pushing away what was needed, that still doesn't mean that our goose is cooked. So this was the most hopeful research finding I had seen in this whole field of physical-contact deprivation and its results.

So, all we need to do is go out and dance and love up a storm and get all kinds of contact. Here's this organ, as big as a blanket, and any place it can get touched in a good way is going to get at some of the deprivation. It's going to change.

What kind of love am I talking about? Not just physical love. When a child is raised in a loving way, he gets body contact and loving looks and feels the love. Now that we are older, we can better feel love. So the love I'm talking about can run the whole range from a truly loving relationship with a God of our understanding, all the way to fumbling attempts by two people who may not be married to each other but who manage to give each other a feeling of being loved, where they both have a healing.

I have seen that, for most of us, we seem to need to learn to love on the physical level before we can experience much of God's love. Or maybe it's just that the first way of experiencing God's love is through his creatures. But I know so many of my students and friends have come by the love they needed by ways in which the great judges of our society didn't approve.

But here I have to listen to the words of my old friend who said, "Jess, you ain't the judge. Who appointed you judge of the universe? You can't judge anyone, not even yourself. When you condemn yourself, you condemn an innocent man."

When I face dilemmas, contradictions and paradoxes like those found in how we meet our needs for love, I'm really confronted with the great mystery of God. I find I can't always follow the rules other people have so carefully figured out. I can't even follow my own rules. I believe that when I get God all figured out, then I am God.

The only guide on how to meet my needs for love is to look for what works for good in my life. If the God of my understanding only produces long-term good in my life, then that good truly is from God. If it doesn't produce long-term good, then it isn't from God. I have made plenty of mistakes, but I find that as long as I'm asking for the help and guidance of my higher power, what look like mistakes don't hurt me or others nearly as bad as when I don't do anything because I'm paralyzed with my fear of making mistakes.

A while back, we buried a friend of mine. His wife seemed like a real nag to me, but he was a life-loving guy. Some time later, I was speaking to a group and mentioned my love for my friend. A woman came up after my speech and said she really loved my friend too. She said he was in the habit of stopping by in the afternoon for a cup of coffee. The gleam in her eye suggested to me that he may have had much more than a cup of coffee at her house.

Another friend of mine started getting some loving from the other husband in her bridge foursome. It went on for some years while she was learning to love her husband better and to love the people right around her better. Eventually she stopped loving the other guy physically but kept on playing bridge with him.

So I see there are two ways we can go as we set out to get the love into our lives that can heal us: We can live the law and follow all the rules and suffer the consequences. Or we can turn our wills and our lives over to the care of God as we understand him and try to live the law of loving one another as God loved us. Then we face endless questions and see ourselves making what we think are mistakes. But these people trying to live the law of love are the ones I'll throw my lot in with, because in their fumbling attempts to

let love into their life, they show an awareness of
their own imperfect humanity that I can identify with.
Human weakness and frailty, I have no trouble identifying with.

Oddly enough and sadly enough, one of the biggest
ways that we refuse and can't let love into our life is
we're so overwhelmed with our sense of inadequacy
that we're all sitting here saying, "Yeah, but nobody
could love me. I'm inadequate. Poor little old me." So
we're going to deal with that next.

CHAPTER 3

Our Second Big Obstacle to Sex—
Our Self-centeredness and
Our Fear of Intimacy

How do we solve the problems created by our deprivation? It was fairly simple for the inmates of the concentration camps who had been food-deprived. They gradually learned to eat without all the wild feelings they first had, even though for many of them their deprivation left a lifetime mark on their use of food.

But the monkey experiment shows us touching and closeness must be a far deeper need, because, when deprived of it, the monkeys later wouldn't allow themselves to be touched. We may have an advantage over the monkey in that we can think a little better and have a more elaborate language. We also, though, have an extra problem that the monkey doesn't seem to have. A monkey can only be a monkey. We humans can be a human, or a monkey or a jackass—often all three in the same day. The problem is our ego, our self-centeredness. We are all born alone and separate. Our ego, or self-centeredness, strives to keep us separate and alone, self-sufficient, meeting all our own needs. But human contact, talking, closeness, touching and intercourse are needs we can't meet by ourselves. To meet those needs, we have to put down our desire to be separate and self-sufficient. But what a struggle it is to overcome our ego and come out of ourselves!

In its early stages, science is a demonstration of common sense. Psychology as a science is still in its infancy. The scientist Sigmund Freud gave many the impression that if their childhood was bad their personality was fixed. The scientist I mentioned in the previous chapter, Prescott, shows us that we can take in love and closeness in our late teens and early twenties just as effectively as in our childhood. To me, Prescott demonstrates what is common sense.

We've all seen adults where love came into their lives and changed them. The love could be a deep physical love from another person, it could be a mental love, a devotion to some high ideal, or it could be a spiritual love—an infusion of love from God. In all cases, real deep love came into adults' lives and changed them. They were different people because of it.

All of those people who were changed by love thought they were lovers before really deep love came along and hit them. Then they saw the love they had known before was just a pale imitation of real love. Here's where we really need to keep our minds open. I can't think of a person I've ever heard admit they were a poor lover. It's always the people around them who are poor lovers. They are good lovers who are constantly being hurt by love.

I think we need to remember back to the studies in the previous chapter where we saw that infants who didn't get enough love in infancy were awkward and ineffectual in their attempts to love. As Montagu said, they ended up hating people partly because they had tried to love them and couldn't. That strikes a responsive chord in me because I now find it easy to see what a poor lover I was and how awkward and ineffectual I was. My heart attack and my search for what I believed in made me see that if I didn't learn to love, I'd die on my feet and then die in my body. So I saw there were two powerful forces that drove me through the difficulties of learning to love: my need for love to become more what I was meant to be and the knowledge that if I didn't find love it would kill me. I don't pretend to be a great lover now. But I am getting a little better than I used to be. I see my improvement as a lover in the increased love that's in my life now, and I see the effects of that love in my improved health.

I see from my experience and others' that we can take advantage of the hope Prescott's studies give us, that it's never too late to get more love in our lives and get all the benefits of it. It's like stopping smoking. You can stop smoking at a fairly advanced age and get almost all the benefits of a person who stopped smoking twenty years earlier.

For anyone who has any lingering doubts about whether they need to start loving or whether they should stay isolated, there's some powerful evidence to think about in Lynch's book *Broken Hearts: The Medical Consequences of Loneliness*. Lynch compared the health of people who were married to those who were single for any reason. He found single people had way more illness and died quicker than married people. In one kind of cancer, the death rate was nearly ten times as high for singles as marrieds.

We know that in half the marriages the partners would just as soon start over, so think what Lynch's study would show if it was a comparison between singles and the best half of marriages.

From another study we see that even a so-called bad marriage has a lot to offer, because the rate of serious sickness and death increases so much after the death of a spouse, seemingly without much regard to how good a marriage it was. So it looks like any kind of a relationship is vastly better than none.

I can hear the single people screaming at me that I'm being too hard on them. I'm not being hard on them; the research is. If you're single and screaming at me in your heart, learn from it. It's a pretty good sign you've got a problem, because if you were single for some very good reason you'd see that what I'm saying doesn't apply to you. A happy celibate lives to a good old age. That's partly because he or she has lots of beautiful relationships in their life. Sister Theresa of Calcutta isn't going to die of a broken heart because of her loneliness. But someone who is single because they are awkward and ineffectual in their attempts to love is very likely to die of a broken heart. So we need to get on with the business of living and loving and getting into relationships with the people who can save our lives; save them emotionally first, and physically also.

I see no choice. I have to reach out to get everything I hold dear to me. But as I start trying to reach out, I find I have the twin foes to reaching out: my awkwardness and ineffectualness that comes from my deprivation, and my self-centeredness that comes from my ego.

It is very important for us to see what life would be like if we hadn't been deprived of love in our infancy. It helps us see that, good as life would be, we would still have the problem of our ego to overcome. So we see that not all our problems of reaching out come from our childhood deprivation. Our big fat ego is in there holding us separate too.

In my first book, *"I Ain't Much, Baby . . ."* I told how I had heard Reverend Ellertson tell about how happy the Zulus were. He told how the mother carried the baby at her breast or on her back all day long with the baby's bare skin against the mother's bare skin. The mother carried the baby as long as she could physically carry him before the baby was finally put down. But all the other children and adults loved the young child and held it and played with it. So the young person didn't grow up with all the questions I had, like: "Who am I?" "What am I?" They knew who they were.

That story was very appealing to me, just as I'm sure the experience of seeing the Zulus' lives was appealing to Reverend Ellertson. But that's the point. He and I saw and heard what we wanted to see. I was just like my wife, Jackie, crying when she watched the film of LeBoyer stroking the newborn baby. She wanted that for her. She needed that. So did Reverend

Ellertson and I want and need a Zulu upbringing.

The longer I thought about the Zulu story, the more trouble I had with it. It meant that primitive man living in his tribal culture had no problems. That didn't make sense.

Most of our Western culture and tradition comes from a bunch of nomadic Semites who wandered in the deserts three thousand to five thousand years ago. Their history in the Old Testament doesn't tell of a paradise on earth. They had all the problems we have today. Now, I agree they probably had many of the advantages of the Zulus and it would look that way to a minister or anthropologist of today who was able to jump time and go back and visit them. He would be struck by the laughing, happy children.

The South Sea Islanders are people that we have really romanticized. We think they had a paradise, especially before we brought them civilization. But our romanticization of them tells us a lot about our need and maybe not much about their culture. The first bare-breast picture didn't run in *Playboy*, it ran in *National Geographic*, back about 1907. We've had a steady stream of bare breasts in that magazine through three generations of boys, some of whom later became anthropologists. Supposedly a scientist isn't influenced by his humanity. He or she is nice and objective. Not so. Our deprivation is built into us like patch pockets on a suit. It's so deep in us we aren't aware of it.

All you have to do is take a closer look at the South Sea Island paradise. As I said earlier, our word running "amok" came from Polynesia, for the man who would all of a sudden go crazy and kill his fellow villagers. Recently, a sixteen-year-old girl ran amok out in California and shot thirty times with an automatic rifle at a school, killing two people.

A tribe in South America had a ceremony where, in the middle of the night once a year, women who hadn't been able to have babies went to a large hut. The men came in in the dark and had intercourse with as many different women as possible. It was taboo to talk or do anything that would give away your identity. The rite supposedly solved the problem of the occasionally sterile husband. But there is more than a sneaking chance that some ladies went into that hut who had children. And maybe some men had a sex orgy more on their minds than the inability of some distressed wife of a dear friend to get pregnant. That scene is something like today's swinging sex clubs, where anything goes and no names are disclosed.

Michener's book *Hawaii* tells of the sexual beauties of paradise, but he also tells of the terrible fear the natives lived in because of their superstition. If you stepped on the king's shadow, you were killed. The gods were capricious, and it was hard to know if you had really done right by them. So you lived your days and nights in periodic terror that you had offended a god in some way and would be killed for it. Sounds like home.

So it isn't paradise—or the lack of it for ourselves—that is the problem. I'm convinced it's the human condition. The story of the Cheyenne Indians pretty well cleared up the paradise myth for me. Their legend was that the one way in which all the people were created equal was their loneliness. Loneliness means being separated from others, separated from a sense of the harmony of the universe and separated from God. The Cheyennes saw the crucial part of each person's life as their spiritual quest, their journey to harmony with their fellow man and their God.

The first Cheyenne legend I read told of how individual villagers would sneak down to the stream and see their reflection in the stream and talk to it, telling the reflection how they felt. It made them feel good, but they didn't want to admit their need to others, so they kept what they had done secret. Then two little children, a boy and a girl, went down to the stream together and saw their reflections in the stream and openly told how they felt. It made them feel so good they rushed back to the village to tell the others. When they told their story to the villagers, they became very angry at the children for what they had done. The children asked, "Don't you do this?" The adults denied it. They tried to kill the two children, but Coyote, a god of the Cheyenne, came and saved the children. Doesn't that sound just like home too?

The Cheyenne society raised their children with great love. By our standards there was little or no emotional impoverishment in childhood, but as adults they were just as afraid of opening their hearts to each other as any two doctors or university professors I've ever met. They'll speak in the intellect all day long, but just try to get one to say how he feels about himself as a human being.

What does all this have to do with sex? Everything. If the biggest part of real intimacy is opening our hearts to each other, look at the two big obstacles we face: our childhood impoverishment, and being born so separate we feel the desperate need to protect that separateness even if it kills us. And it will. We can see that as we watch people around us die on their feet at an early age.

As I mentioned in Chapter One, romantic love is a great force that can help the soul come out of its separateness. But most of us are in relationships where we long ago used up or destroyed romantic love without getting the amount of openness between our two souls that we could have achieved. Some of us have misused romantic love so many times that it won't work for us in any more relationships. Most of us are so awkward and ineffectual in our loving relationships that we aren't able to communicate our love and our closeness to someone else except through sex. But using sex as an all-purpose communicator is like having a one-word language: it doesn't serve us very well.

What we needed as babies was more loving, which to a baby primarily means more touching. We aren't babies any more, so we can give and receive love through other means than physical touching. But I find that physical touching is tremendously valuable to us as a gauge of how able we are to reach out and love. We need the touching for itself. But we are so good at lying to ourselves about our ability to love that only touching can keep us honest. Touching is visible. We can see if we're doing it or not, and we can see the effects of the touching. Friends meeting on the street in Europe touch each other one hundred times an hour. When you or I meet a friend on the street, we touch each other only three times an hour. Is that all we feel for our friends? Is that how we want to go through life, all locked up and inhibited? We weren't meant to be all locked up and inhibited. We were meant to be creative, outgoing personalities who aren't all tied up in their deprivation and their ego but who can joyously go out into the world and take, who can partake of this splendid feast that God has prepared for us. There's nothing we need to do to earn it. We are sons of the King. All we need to do is take.

There is only one caution I need to give, and in a way it may seem very sad but it isn't. Stella Brewer, a young woman from Africa, wrote a beautiful book, *The Chimps of Mt. Asserik.* In it she tells how some chimps who had been raised in captivity since babies became too big and active for their enclosures. Rather than put them in iron cages, she determined to take them out in the jungle and teach them to live there. Over a period of two or three years, she succeeded. But not as completely as she had hoped. Her chimps could live in the jungle, but they couldn't fit in with wild chimps. They didn't know the language of gestures and cries. So now Stella's chimps have their own little group of semi-wild chimps and enjoy the jungle that way.

Stella and I were being interviewed on Bev Baker's radio show in Seattle. As Stella told of her wild chimps not being able to fit in, she saw the tears in my eyes. She said, "Jess, are you crying?" I told her I was because I saw that I was like her chimps. I had found a good, loving society for myself, but I didn't have the natural language that would let me fit in a wide variety of social situations. In many social situations I'm still very awkward and ineffectual, and I often find myself fitting in only by sitting and watching.

Stella was concerned at my tears, but I told her it wasn't all sadness; part was relief and joy because it helped me accept that I'll very possibly never be able to be socially at ease in a wide range of environments but I'm so thankful for what I already have and the improvements to come. It was a very moving experience and a very valuable one for me, because I saw that as I have been learning to make contact with the world in the past seventeen years since my heart attack, I've really been like one of Stella's chimps. I've tried to reach out as well as I could in as many ways as I could, and the people around me have been my teachers, showing me the appropriateness and inappropriateness of my responses.

So let's look at touching, one of our most valuable tools in reaching out and one of the best ways we can see how our twin foes, our deprivation and our ego, hold us back as we try to reach out to meet our needs by touching the world around us.

What seems to me to be the toughest test for us is not intercourse but touching. It's like the prostitute story I told earlier. You can have intercourse with her but not hug and kiss her. There's something about intercourse that is very temporary. When it's over, it's over. But touching, when attention is paid to it, is a deep and loving way of making contact with the world outside ourself, most specifically with another human being. So touching isn't usually taken as lightly as intercourse. I think that's partly why women so often bemoan the lack of preliminaries in intercourse. The intercourse doesn't require too good a heart towards the other person, but touching is different. You can't fake touching someone lovingly, and you don't even want to try touching them if the heart is bad towards the other. The answer for both parties in intercourse is often, let's have sex and get it over with.

So, touching the loved one, or anyone else, is hard. Yet it's a good place to start, because like the monkey who can't touch and meet his needs, we need to see just where we're at in being able to meet our own needs. Then we have to set out to meet them every way we can.

Now, I understand that physical touching is just a part of meeting our adult needs for human contact. Symbolic touching, emotional openness and closeness to the other is probably the way we'll meet our needs most of the time. But touching helps us here, too, because we can kid ourselves we're really being close but if we find we can't reach out and physically touch the other person in some way, we probably aren't as close as we thought we were.

I can hear voices shouting, "Not me, I'm not a toucher!" No question about that. But the more I've studied touching, the more I feel that what you tell me about yourself is not some special part of you, but your deprivation. When you and I can't touch where it is appropriate, I think we're just like the monkey as he pushes away what he needs.

With all this background, we're ready to make a frontal assault on touching and the problems of it. I gave the group in Seattle a demonstration of touching. The best way to communicate what I said would be to treat you as if you were there and let you hear what I said to them:

I said, "I'd like to give you a couple of little demonstrations on touching. Where's the guy I was talking

to at the break—Hal, was it? Yes, there you are, Hal,
come here. Sure, all of you thought I was going to pick
out some pretty girl, didn't you? You see, the thing is
that if I show you about touching and I pick some cute
gal like Jackie Smith, you say, 'Come on, that doesn't
count. That's simple.'

"But with Hal here, who's an old beat-up guy like
me, what I'm saying and doing makes more sense."

I want to show you the first few steps in touching
that most people overlook; they don't even know about
them. Some people say, "I'm a toucher," and they
touch most everybody whether it's right for the other
person or not. They may think they are meeting their
needs, but it's insensitive to the feelings of the other
person. Other people say, "I'm not a toucher," and
they don't touch anyone in a feeling way even when it
is very appropriate and sometimes even when it's
desperately needed. That frustrates the need for touch,
and it's also very insensitive to the feelings of others.

On touching, a lot of people don't know where to
start. I found why I had trouble with the girls in high
school, but I found out twenty years too late. Once in
a while some gal would say, "Boy, you're sure fast."
Do you know what "fast" is? First it's an expression of
the Forties for a guy who was, well, fast. What I
finally found, not too long ago, is that you are called
fast not for what you are doing but the sequence in
which you are doing it. If you get things in the proper
sequence, you aren't ever fast. But when you skip a
step or get a step out of place, then you're fast. Now, I
wish I could have known that when I was a high
school kid, because I'm sure I could have figured out
what the steps were and what the order was if I could
have just known that that was what was important.
I'm sure I would have been very willing to start at
step one to get to step twenty-eight. But in my ignorance and selfishness, I was in a rush and kept want-

ing to skip steps. So it's very important to understand the steps, or that there even *are* steps.

The first two steps in touching someone are before you touch them. Most people don't realize this. That's why they get in so much trouble touching and are so heavy-handed. When you touch people inappropriately and at inappropriate times, the touching not only doesn't meet your needs, it frustrates you. If you have this kind of problem, you need to pay special attention to the first two steps of touching, which come before the touch. The first step before you touch is to be really aware of the other person, and the situation you are in with them, to see if touching is appropriate. When you're a banker and you're telling some stranger that you're not going to lend them money, that may not be the right time to touch them. But you can be the same banker who, minutes later because of circumstances, has to tell that man that his wife was just killed in an accident, and it might be very inappropriate not to touch him, even though turning down his loan was your only previous contact. So the first step in touching is an awareness of you and the other person and the situation. Many people's faces are the biggest clues; they just seem to shout: "Don't touch me." There's no specific suggestion on what to look for in a face that says don't touch me. Maybe it's a tightness in the face, a feeling of fear on the face, a coldness in the eyes and mouth. I think if you look closely at the other person's face and body and read what's there, you'll get a pretty clear message. So pay close attention.

The second step comes when it seems to you that it is appropriate for you to touch the other person. Just start to reach out to touch the other person and pay close attention to their face. As your hand comes towards them, you can tell by their expression if you can even touch them at all. They will show their unwillingness to be touched by you in that situation

with at least a flicker of pulling away and they will go
as far as drawing back away from you so you can't
touch them. As you move your hand out and you see
you shouldn't touch the person, stop and draw your
hand back.

It isn't until step three that you actually touch the
person. The most neutral place we can touch the other
person is on the outside of the elbow or the point of
the shoulder. For our part, the most neutral way we
can touch is with the tip of a finger, and the more
lightly we touch, the more neutral.

So I reached out and touched Hal. As I told the
group, "As soon as I touch Hal, I find out some important information. If he starts wincing, that's a bad
sign, isn't it? He hasn't winced, so I reach out more
and touch him with my hand on his elbow or on his
shoulder. Okay? Instantly now, I have a whole bunch
of new information. Not just from his face, but from
my fingers touching his body. Hal's body hasn't moved
away. He hasn't moved into my touch, but he hasn't
moved away, either. So even without looking at him,
without picking up that information, just from feeling
what his body tells me alone, I can tell a lot more
about touching him, you see. Even without looking at
Hal, I can get all the information I need, just from my
hand.

"Now, it's foolish to disregard information that's
available to you. So if I were doing this in real life, I
would be looking at his face, too. But I just wanted to
show you that I can feel for myself how my touching is
going by feeling how his body is responding to my
hand, negative or positive or neutral. And Hal's response is pretty much neutral. He's just standing there.
Now all of a sudden it's negative, probably because
I'm embarrassing him. So, okay, I can tell just how to
touch Hal. In this case I'm pushing my touching of
Hal much further than I would ordinarily, because he
isn't sending me signals that he wants me to touch

him. I don't touch people just because I want to touch them. They have to tell me by their signals that they also want me to touch them. You see how that goes? So this is the kindergarten of touching. Thank you, Hal."

"How about that lady. Can you come up here, Shirley? Step two, graduate from guys to girls. I picked Shirley out for a very special reason, because her face has been sitting there in back of the room just lighting up at all of what I'm saying.

"I see you like some of the things I've been saying, Shirley. That's nice."

"Right."

"I picked Shirley for another reason. With no insult to her, she's a little closer to my age than Jackie Smith is. There's an unfortunate situation in this country and it isn't fair to the ladies. The guys tend to go for the younger girls, but the ladies don't seem to go so much for the younger guys. That produces a kind of inequity that women by and large feel a little resentful of. So I wanted to demonstrate touching with a lovely lady so you wouldn't feel, because the woman is only twenty, Jess is just some dirty old guy."

"You're not a dirty old guy."

". . . and that's why Shirley is letting Jess touch her."

"Now, Shirley has indicated to me by her actions, her face, her tone of voice and the way she's standing here that I can touch her and that she would welcome it and it's not a problem to her. So I can put my hand down around her waist and stroke her back a little. My hand is telling me how Shirley is reacting."

At lunch just before this, someone was telling me, "Well, I can touch somebody if I know them." And the answer is sure, that's where we start, by touching someone we know. But the problem is that's so limited, and our fear shows up by not letting us touch someone we don't know very well. Earlier, I mentioned the study where, in Europe, when friends met they touched each other one hundred times per hour of contact. Here we average three touches per hour of contact between friends. So if we start by touching someone we know, then touch them thirty times as much, we'll get as much touching as Europeans. See how limited we are? We need to learn to touch our friends more and to be able to touch all kinds of other people. I touched the lady in the camera store yesterday who showed me how to load my camera so nicely. I had never seen her before. By all of us not touching each other, we've been making a meal out of just spinach and lima beans. What we could have when we can touch a lot is like eating a full meal, a real banquet.

So we need to broaden out our touching. It is dangerous, very dangerous. But it's even more dangerous not to. Because if you don't make contact with the world outside you in some way, you die, or you'll starve to death inside and be just a hollow shell. That makes you a setup for some of these kinds of distorted sexual stuff that I've been telling you about. So I like to hold a woman; it's lovely. It's lovely just as it is. Now, sure, the problem is sex always rears its ugly head but, fine, let it. Oddly enough, the more you satisfy your feelings and needs for touching, the better able you are to handle all these things, you see.

"What do you think, Shirley?"

"It's nice to hold you."

"Well, thank you. You're a very lovely woman, beautiful."

"I feel I know you from your books."

"That's nice; I've got all kinds of friends I haven't even met yet. That's nice.

"Thank you, Shirley."

I started touching about nine years ago and I'm learning. I've had some terrible problems. There's one story in my third book, "*I Ain't Well . . .*" It tells about touching this gal. She had been a student of mine and we got along great. Then we were having a bad time between us for some reason. But, one day, she gave me a big greeting and I thought things were all right between us. I reached out and touched her arm in some way, and she just glared at me. It gave me a terrible feeling. It was no fun. It was an ugly experience. It happened in the hall over at the student union building. It really hit me. So that's terrible.

But what's more terrible is not doing it. If I decided I'm not going to take a chance like that again, I take the biggest chance in the world. In a sense, I do the most deadly thing in the world. I literally condemn myself to death. It's like pointing a gun at my head and killing myself. So you start dying inside and pretty soon the body dies. You've seen these people who are walking around waiting to die. They are people who have given up. They have seen that what is true for them is: "I push away everything I need. No fairy prince is going to crash through my barrier, so I'm going to die inside here." Now, I don't like that way as an alternative to the dangers of touching. To me, that way of holding back isn't just risky, it's certain death. I've found I can reach out and touch people, men and women. That's kind of risky, but like I say, it ain't certain death.

"Jackie, do you want to come up here? I saved you until last. Okay?" Some of you saw me touching Jackie Smith on the way in here. What you don't understand is the whole situation. Someone was saying to her at the lunch table where I was sitting with Jackie and eating, "My gosh, I wish I could do that," because Jackie had her hand on my back and was stroking it. And I said, "Well, you misjudge. You don't understand." Jackie was at my school this summer. There were about sixty people there, about thirty-five gals and twenty-five guys. But of all those people at the school, Jackie was the one I felt closest to. Now, it isn't because she's young and pretty. At the sex seminar that I did in Minneapolis, in June, the gal I had a tremendous feeling for was about fifty and gray-haired. She and I really hit it off. There was a tremendous mutuality there. So what Jackie and I can do in the area of touching gives you a very distorted idea of what is usually possible. It's only under the rare circumstance of a deep mutuality that such closeness is possible.

Jackie took all the trouble of coming from Seattle to Montana to come to school to me for a week, which says already she's responded to something very special in me. And of all the sixty people who did come, Jackie and I found that we had the most mutuality. I don't know why it is that she and I fit together. I don't know why it was in June that I fit together with that gray-haired lady. It's just mutuality.

But, typically, you look at the way Jackie Smith and I can be so easy and close with each other and you look at it as a downer for yourself. You say, "Well, I wish I could do that. Why can't I do that?" You use it to put yourself down without understanding and appreciating all of the special conditions that have gone into our situation. There aren't any women here I can touch or who can touch me as I am touching Jackie and as she is touching me, because any other woman here and I probably wouldn't have the same fit as Jackie and I have. There might be some people here I could get to be this close to, but we haven't had the chance to work together closely like Jackie and I did for that week in Bozeman. We had a chance to really find what mutuality was there. There might be some one of you here, and it could be a guy, where we have this great mutuality between us and consequently we could be very close, as Jackie and I are. But, again, that's my point. As we meet the world openly, we will find all kinds of different relationships and we will find some that are very special for us.

What do you do about where you are now? Simple! You don't compare yourself, you don't criticize yourself, you don't condemn yourself. You simply go out and find the people you have this mutuality with. You go out and love the easy ones. Out of a whole bunch of easy ones, and this is the case with Jackie, you'll find one that's super easy. So when Jackie is touching me, that really feels great. With all due respect to Hal and Shirley, I don't fit with them to the degree that I fit with Jackie. In Shirley's case, because she and I were pretty much strangers even though she'd read my books, she wasn't free enough and it wasn't appropriate for her to rub my back and stroke me in other ways. So the touching Jackie can do with me is a far deeper kind of touching.

I don't run into situations like this very often. I had thought I had told Jackie that I was coming out here to speak. I've been writing to many different students in my classes. Jackie had written me three or four months ago and I thought I had told her I was going to be out here. But it turned out I hadn't. She just happened to hear about it. It was lucky for me she did. So she just showed up here. I didn't even know she was going to be here.

But these are the kind of things that happen in life when you start looking for them and are open to them: great experiences. Along with them are all the good experiences like it was lovely for me to be able to hold Shirley and it was lovely for me to hold Hal.

One of the most beautiful holding experiences I ever had was holding a guy who was in a scream-therapy demonstration in Princeton a couple of years ago that my friend Walther Lechler was conducting. As he was screaming, he lived out his feelings and probably went way back and was screaming and sobbing almost like a little child. It was one of the greatest honors of my life and the tenderest feeling to be holding that man and to share such a crucial experience. He was about six foot five and weighed about 280 pounds. He was so big I could hardly hold onto him as he was standing there. I had to clench one hand around my wrist because my arms gave out, holding the guy. But it was an overwhelmingly sensuous, wonderful kind of feeling.

Okay, as Jess Lair goes about satisfying his deprivations in life, these are the kinds of experiences that I can have because nine years ago I read a book on touching which said it was good to touch people. The book was Gunther's *Sense Relaxation: Below Your Mind.* It was there that I read the study I mentioned earlier about how Europeans touch thirty times as much as Americans. I said to myself at the time, "Hey, that's right." Us Norwegians, you know, we wouldn't know an emotion if we met one on the street. I didn't know what a feeling was. So I'm a very poor, poor student and a very poor beginner. But I started out, though, because I was a desperate person and I realized I'm going to die and I didn't have an unlimited hunk of time. So I started out using the time I had as well as I could, doing what I could with the time and resources and the crude, twisted, damaged instrument that I had. I did the very best I could. Nine years later now, I can often touch people. I don't do it in inappropriate ways hardly at all, because I've learned how to do it by being willing to make mistakes. I've learned through the mistakes how to tell who I can touch and who wants to be touched, because I'm getting what I need.

Now, Jackie Smith here would argue that she's getting what she needs as I hold her. But that's not why I'm doing it. I'm not touching Jackie because, of the people here who need to be touched, she's the one who needs it the most. I'm only doing it because I recognize my need and I'm meeting my needs. I'm the only one who can meet my needs. Again, where we get in so much trouble in life is we say to the other person,

"Hey, you other person. Meet my needs. Guess what my needs are. Meet my needs. Push down my barriers that I have put up. Crash through them and come in here and meet these needs of mine."

Well, life doesn't work that way. I'm not in the business of loving porcupines. If a person wants to be a porcupine and say, "Hey, love me even though I push you away," I'm not going to do that. I will reach out my hand in love and friendliness and try to awaken some poor soul. But if they tell me, "No, don't touch me," I respect that no, and I give them the results of their behavior. I walk away. A lot of times people will say, "Oh, but I didn't want you to walk away. I wanted you to stay and persist."

And I say, "No, it's not going to be that way, honey. You're going to have the fruits of your own pushing me away, which is loneliness. So you can have as much loneliness as you want until you're ready to give up loneliness. Because I don't belong in your life unless you invite me in."

This is what is so crucial. Jackie had indicated to me previously that I belong in her life. That's a great, great, deep honor. But even more crucially, it's a source of a great satisfaction to me. Now, there is no way that I can be caressing Jackie without sex rearing its ugly head. So we'll both handle it. But in my experience, you handle things far better when they are out in the open than when you deny them and refuse to admit them. Also, in my experience, I will handle sex far better and I am far more resistant to using sex inappropriately than I was when I was so deprived of human contact.

By meeting our deprivation in the most appropriate ways that we can find and still accepting our mistakes, we become far more free. It's like the symphony again. When the drums get quieted down to a reasonable level, then we can hear the other music and we find what a symphony really sounds like. It makes it so much easier for me to be holding Jackie like this, knowing that my needs have been and are well met. It is nice to have a larger degree of freedom than I used to have in this area. And it is nice down the road to anticipate an even larger degree of freedom.

Someday I shall be able to pass the test for the rabbis who codified the Talmud. The rabbis who the Jews put in charge of this very special task had to be the kind of men who could be at their rabbinical studies and if a naked young woman walked through the room, they would look up, see her and return unfazed to their rabbinical studies. Someday, if I could adequately meet my deprivations I would be able to be such a man. That's not a mark of somebody without feeling. It's a mark of a person who has feeling but the feeling is in balance with all of that person's other feelings. The whole symphony is playing in harmony. So this is the crucial thing I find.

"Jackie, do you want to say something?"

"No, it feels good."

"Thank you."

Okay, that's what to do about it. At least, that's what to do about meeting our needs through touching the people around us. To me, though, there's something far bigger than touching involved in touching. Important as touching is, I don't believe there's enough touching in anyone's typical day—unless they give massages—to make a big dent in our deprivation. I think that when we're afraid to touch people and the door to touching is closed, I think there's a terrible wall between us and the world, that shuts out all kinds of emotional contact with the world. So then we're really shut off.

I think when we work on getting the door to touching open, we can then touch the world, our brothers and sisters, both with our hands and bodies, but we get our emotions opened up too. So I think our touching is a physical expression of our attitude towards the world.

Our unwillingness to touch friends more than three times per hour tells me much more about you and me than our touching. It says we are closed off emotionally to what our friends can give us. Are we aware of this? Probably not. Is the goldfish aware of the water? Are we aware of the ocean of air we live in? No. I don't think we become aware of the shallowness of our emotional and physical contact with the people around us until the pain gets so bad we're forced to pay attention. Always our big ego is lying to us, saying, "It's not me who's the problem, it's everybody else."

As I said earlier, our second big obstacle to meeting our needs for love and sex is our self-centeredness and our fear of intimacy. We just saw how touching another person brings all the forces of the ego up to the surface, fighting to preserve our separateness. In all of our relationships, we hide ourselves. We try to manipulate and control other people's pictures of us, we try to make other people meet our needs like actors on a stage. It's like we had written a play and we've got all the actors dressed just the way we want them; they've all got their parts. We're the producer and we're manipulating all those actors up there on stage. They're all doing what we want them to do. It's like the lady who said, "Jess I want my husband to do what I want him to do, when I want him to do it, the way I want him to do it." The husband feels the exact opposite. "I want my wife to do what I want her to do, when I want her to do it, the way I want her to do it." What is that problem? It's a very simple one. It's a god problem. We are god. We are playing the part of god, and we, in our infinite wisdom and majesty, know what is right for ourselves and everybody else in this whole world.

Now, in my experience in the last few years, I've got enough trouble knowing what's best for me in any dimmest kind of way. No way can I know what's right for you. Long ago, I learned that I needed to get out of the god business. I still fail at that a lot each day and try to take back control of my life and other people's lives. But, any time I'm out of the god business, there are many advantages to me.

Some time back, one of my students came to me and said, "Jess, Willie left me!" I said, "What's wrong?" She told me her boyfriend, Willie had left her for another girl. "I want Willie back!"

"Does Willie want to come back?"

"No. But I want Willie back."

"Do you love Willie?" I asked her.

"Oh, I love Willie so."

"Then, why don't you let Willie go so he can have what's best for Willie?"

"But I want Willie back."

You see the self-centeredness? She doesn't love Willie. She wants to control Willie and the world to make her happy.

We don't see that we need to find what our needs are and then find good ways of meeting those needs. Rather, we go "man to man" on the people we pick out. I saw myself, to my horror, doing this in my college classrooms. I'd walk into a college classroom, and typically, the group would be about thirty students. I'd have them put their chairs in a circle so I could see them all. I found I would pick out a good-looking gal and a good-looking guy to go man to man on. "They're going to be my friends. They're the ones who are right for me." And I would conduct myself in such a way that I would literally go after those people, courting their favor, trying to make them smile at me, like me.

Meanwhile there were some other people in class, some boy and some gal, say, who desperately wanted to be my friends. But I couldn't see them. Very often, they were right at my elbow, saying, "I want to love you, Jess." Without being aware of it, I was saying back to those two with my actions, "No, no. Not you two. You other two are the ones I want."

That's what I call going man to man. It's like in basketball where when we play man-to-man defense, we each choose a man we will guard. It's our self-centeredness, our playing God. It's us deciding who it is who should be in our life. Having the misfortune of being very human, I would, of course, in my deviousness, pick out attractive girls and good-looking guys, popular guys. Those were the people I wanted to like me.

I got myself into all kinds of trouble before I finally came to a new understanding. Now the situation has changed, except in one way, because the women who respond to me are still exceptionally beautiful women. But that's because of one fundamental change. I have changed my definition of what is a beautiful woman. I used to go purely on surface beauty. Now I understand. A beautiful woman is someone who likes me. Some people don't understand that. They get kind of angry at me, because they think I have no standards and no sense of discrimination. But I do have a fantastic set of standards and a fantastic discrimination. The beloved son is never ugly. The person who loves me is never ugly; they're always very beautiful.

So something I have come to see is this very crucial problem, this business of playing god, because that's what our self-centeredness amounts to.

Why are we hiding ourselves? I think partly we're afraid of seeing we're not the all-powerful, all-controlling god we want to be or the animals that we're afraid we are. I think we have these two distorted conceptions of ourselves. I see it in the alcoholics I work with. As they lie there in the gutter, they think Jimmy Carter should call them up each morning and consult them on foreign policy. They're so sure that they could tell Carter just exactly what he should do.

I want to say, "You insane idiot, don't you realize that you haven't got enough sense to pound sand in a rathole? Your whole life is in tatters, and you're going to tell Carter how to run his foreign policy?" That's the egomania side and grandiosity in us, where we see ourselves as godlike, all-knowing. But the same man's mood would then swing over to the other side, and the next minute he would be deep in the throes of self-pity, "Oh, God, I'm worthless. I'm just a terrible person. I'm the most awful person in the whole world." And, of course, you're a little bit more inclined to agree with that at first. But it is equally untrue. Neither one of those extremes is true. The truth is somewhere in between.

There's a big part of us that doesn't want to recognize our egomania. When he's saying what a terrible person he is, he wants us to jump in and say, "Oh, no, you aren't. You're a beautiful person." Then he'll say, "Yes, I know that." I'm amazed at how we swing between being the giant of our dreams and the worm of our fears, yet refuse to see we are simply a man among men, a woman among women. We are all peers, equals.

I see our unwillingness to see ourselves as we really are as the biggest reason we run from intimacy, even when we have been well loved. It is such an appealing idea that we can give kids so much physical love and affection, body contact, that they wouldn't have any problems with their sense of identity. I used to believe this. But I don't any more, because there is a central flaw in that line of argument. You see, if by loving us enough as children, our parents could make us be good and have no problems, then in a funny sense our parents would have controlled us. By giving us all the body contact, all the loving in the world, they would make it impossible for us to have any problems. If you make it impossible for anybody to have any problems, you are controlling them. The person can't be free to work out their own destiny if you can love them so much that they can't have any problems and can't say no to God because they've been brought up so good that they've got no choice but to be good.

I've heard a lot of people argue the way the world should have been created was where we were automatically all good. We would all start out in the morning going down the street doing nothing but smiling and Boy Scout stunts all day long. If God would have known what he was doing, that's the way the world would have been created. But there's a chance that God knew what he was doing. There's a chance that by giving us our freedom, the freedom to say no and the freedom to say yes, that God knew what he was doing more than we can possibly imagine. I believe that I cannot have the freedom just to say yes. It does not mean anything outside the context of having the freedom to say no. Yes doesn't mean anything when no isn't the alternative.

What I have come to see is a totally different view of life. I grant the Zulu kids were typically far better adjusted, especially when the old stone-age tribal culture was completely intact. I'm sure they didn't exhibit many of these deprivation symptoms that we show. There's a sign of this from American Indian days. One of the early white men who went among the Indians before they had been disturbed much by our society told this story. One of the Indian chiefs was interested in the way white men reacted when they came to an Indian village. Their first concern was to grab a pretty girl and run off and have intercourse with her. The chief noticed this about white men and asked, "What's wrong with these men? Don't you have white women in your society?" So we have clues like that to suggest that all societies weren't as deprived for sex and body contact as our society.

As I see life, we are born in self and we have the opportunity in life to come out of our separateness and find wholeness in union with other human beings and in harmony with the universe and God. Each of us can come to God in our own way and on our own time. And this God is the higher power, God as you understand him. Or you can simply call it order in the universe, with or without reference to God. I find that people who come into contact with a higher power that means good things for them in their life, all experience the same kind of healing and rebuilding in their lives.

I see our self-centeredness has no relationship to anything that you and I ever did or any accidents of birth or upbringing or what have you. While the deprivations we have endured will make our task more or less difficult, to me those deprivations are not decisive, they don't control us unless we allow them that power. To me, the higher power I understand has given us the strength we need if we will but ask for help. I know that sometimes it seems we've barely got enough strength to meet the test. But I believe the higher power has given each of us enough strength, despite the extent of our deprivations, to say yes to life. But we have to choose. The higher power I understand will not take that freedom away from us and will not force us to say yes to life. A lot of people say, "Well, the higher power is testing me here and testing me there and I'm being given all these trials to force me to say yes to God." That's not the way the thing works, as I see it. The system is already set up. It's already in place.

The trout can take two courses. He can live in the stream and fight the stream. Or he can live in the stream and use it to his benefit. Everything has been provided for him. All he needs to do is get in harmony with the stream, say yes to the stream. If he gets out of harmony with the stream, he will get his punishment from the stream, fast.

It's the same with us. Everything we need has been

provided for us. All we need to do is say yes to life. But if we won't say yes to life, it isn't God that's going to punish us; he doesn't need to. We're going to get punished all kinds of ways by life. It's just like driving down the highway. If you persist in not paying attention to where the road is, you're going to get messages from the bumpy shoulders. You're going to hear from the ditches, and fence posts and telephone poles and cliffs and lakes. No one needs to step in and punish you if you don't drive your car right. The conditions plus the other drivers will punish you plenty.

Well, the same way in life. If you want to persist in saying no to life, we don't need to invent any punishments for you. In fact, we couldn't think of punishments as fiendish as what life will hand out if you and I persist in saying no to life and denying life. So this is the issue: Are we going to say yes to life or not? Are we going to get out of our self-centeredness into relationship with other people?

And then, as I said earlier, we run from intimacy because intimacy is the true mirror that shows us what we are and reveals our self-centeredness to us. The sexual relationship is the deepest and truest mirror of all.

A lady novelist whose name I can't recall, about ten years ago wrote in *Saturday Review of Literature*, "No one has ever written about those desolate things that happen in bed." And why do you suppose not? Again, it goes back to the fact we all have this feeling that we're inadequate, we're terrible, we're awful and we think this is why we're having all our problems and we don't dare admit it to anyone else. So we use these flights from ourselves. We want to run away. We say, "I'm not the way the other person sees me." And the answer is, "No, we're not the way the other person sees us. We are as we see ourselves in that mirror."

One way we run away is we try to figure out what everyone else is doing and conform to that. We're all dressed alike. We look like we were stamped out by cookie cutters. The guys wear ties that narrow and widen with the swing of fashion. The gals' skirts go up and down with the swing of fashion. We're all like a bunch of high school kids.

In my day in high school if you didn't have a Gant shirt in a strawberry or navy blue color with a little loop on the back edge of the collar, you didn't dare to go to school. There were differences, like some guys wore a thin belt and some an extra thin one, but everyone tried to look alike.

Every one of us were created fantastically unique, a once-in-a-forever lifetime event. Never before in history has there been anybody just like you or me and never again in history will there be anyone just like us. Yet, like I say, we run around because of our fear of being different, all looking and acting the same.

Hell, you could slip any one of us husbands in bed with a wife and it would be a week before she even knew there was a difference. It's just about that bad. And unfortunately the opposite is just about equally true. The husband is too passionate or too unresponsive and the wife has too many headaches or is too sexually demanding.

A sign of our uniqueness is when we really look and act and think and feel as different from each other as we really are, but yet through all that tremendous uniqueness there's a common thread that unites us. It's like the story Sydney Harris tells. He and a friend were walking down a street in Chicago. This black guy came down the street towards them. He had a hat with a big peacock plume and wore a great big purple velvet cloak. Sydney Harris' friend said, "My God, look at that! Isn't that awful?"

Harris said, "No, that isn't awful, that's great. Every one of us should dress that differently, just the way we want to dress." We're all dressed like we own stock in Conformity, Inc. If we don't wear the same-style suit, shirt and tie like everyone in our group wears, the whole world is going to collapse.

Now, I don't want to make too big a thing about dress, but it's just one of the ways where we look around us to see what everybody else is doing. We go to a dance and we've got to go late or wait until somebody else starts dancing. That's why it takes so long to get a dance going. By the time it gets going, we're ready to quit.

Now, in our sexual relationships we have a different set of fears that come out of our feeling of inadequacy. I had a friend of mine. He thought he was inadequate. We looked into it and by God he was. So he didn't have a problem. I did, though; I thought I was inadequate and I wasn't. I was just like everybody else. But we choose to feel inadequate because it serves our purposes; it helps us to hide out. Oh, poor little inadequate me. I'm not responsible for anything. I'm inadequate. Of course, you can't ask anything of me. It's just like down at your office or whatever work any of you are doing. "Will you do something?" "Oh, you know I can't do that kind of thing." What a beautiful cop-out.

If somebody says to me, "Jess, are you a good elk hunter?" I'll say, "Yeah, pretty good." If I say I'm inadequate, I'm not responsible for anything, but I'll admit that I'm pretty good at elk hunting. So they say, "Let's go elk hunting." And I say, "Okay, we'll go elk hunting." You can hold me to the fact I've said I'm pretty good. You can watch me to see if I pay attention to which way the wind is from. Do I have any sense of the needs of the elk and what kind of cover they prefer? When I see some tracks, do I know what to do? When I see tracks, do I follow the uphill track, because that's the way the bulls tend to go? If I do those things, you'll say, "By gosh, the guy does know a little something about what he's talking about."

You see, if I'm inadequate, I don't have to do anything. So it's a beautiful copout. I think that feeling of inadequacy is the thing that's given rise to all the lying about sex and all the silence about sex. It's just another reflection of our ego at work. The only way I can be inadequate is if I've got some idea of how I'm supposed to be. And where did that idea of how I'm supposed to be come from? It came from my big fat ego saying I should be some certain way.

Marshall Cook tells a beautiful story about down in Louisiana in the swimming hole. Everybody's skinny-dipping down there. There's a certain group of guys down at the swimming hole who spend their time walking up and down the bank. These are the guys who are really well endowed. All the other guys are in the water. But these "bankers" are walking up and down the bank. That's one of the things we run into. The guys in the water aren't inadequate; they just think they are because they've got the wrong idea of what adequacy is.

I was having a summer-school class and we had two young students in with all the older returning teachers. One of the two young students was a guy who really thought what I was talking about was great. He thought, "I'm going to be real, I'm going to be honest." We weren't talking sex specifically, just about life. A friend of his came to town from Missoula. They went down to the Haufbrau to have a beer. His friend was saying, "Boy, it's great to be single. Why get married when there are so many gals just hungry for you!" My student told me that he was about to say, "Yeah, yeah, I feel that way too," when he realized he didn't feel that way at all. He'd better be honest. He told his friend, "Hey, John, I don't feel that way. I've got trouble getting up the guts to ask a girl for a date, say nothing of scoring with her. I'm just scared of gals."

His buddy said, "You mean it?" And he said, "Yeah."

And his buddy said, "Well, I am too, but I was afraid to admit it."

One of the biggest things I see as a reflection of our sense of inadequacy is the talk that I hear from my students. I can see the same feelings in other people to the effect that "My parts aren't right. I'm too big or too small. My penis size isn't right. I'm afraid my vagina size is too big or too small. I'm flat-chested, or my breasts are too big." Nobody's got the right amount of anything.

In my college classes I used to do a little test. I was always interested in seeing how far I could stretch this. I would try to find the skinniest gal I could find, one who was like a toothpick. After I got to know her halfway decent, I'd say, "Hey, aren't you putting on just a little weight?" She couldn't have had more than an ounce of extra weight on her, if that. So I was always waiting for one to laugh at the joke. But none ever did. She always said, "Oh, my God, you noticed." To me it was a beautiful example of how far we will distort truth to be able to dwell on the negative side of ourselves. It shows how our ego is constantly at work telling us we aren't acceptable as we are. It was so sad to see some beautiful young woman who everyone else felt was just right, feel that she wasn't just right.

I know this penis-size thing is a tremendous problem for a lot of guys. Gals don't shower that much together, but guys do, so it's kind of obvious. What they never explained to guys adequately, as near as I can see, is the fact that what you see in the showers is somewhat deceptive, because most men's penises end up to be about the same size when the time for action comes. But the expansion ratios are somewhat different. What looks like a terrible disparity in penis sizes tends to average out. So about 90 per cent of men's penises fall within a two-inch variation. I've never heard of a man whose penis was too small to do what it had to do.

There is another problem here. Because of our terrible fear of talking of these things and the lack of information, it wasn't until recently that I ran across the very interesting fact that penis size has nothing to do with sexual satisfaction in about ninety-nine out of one-hundred cases. Everybody thinks, "Well, I'm the one-hundredth one, the exception." But size isn't important, because a woman's nerve endings are on the surface of the vagina, not deep inside. Good old Masters and Johnson have run tests that show a woman can't tell how big a man's penis is. Yet the classical picture in so many guys' minds is the sick picture of the locker-room myths where a guy who is built like a telephone pole is banging away on this gal and she is screaming for mercy and yet in sheer delight, both at the same time. That's got nothing to do with reality. In fact it is the opposite from reality.

I recently saw a collection of Ozark folktales called *Pissing in the Snow and Other Ozark Folk Tales*. What it is is the dirty folktales that couldn't be published in earlier collections. This guy who collected them had published five or six books and these were his rejects the publisher refused to use because they had contained one of the twenty-one dirty words. I read these folktales and a number of them had to do with guys with big penises and some of them with gals with big vaginas. Yet neither of those two are real problems. They are truly a myth. But they are handed down and perpetuated and never, unfortunately, canceled out by honest and real communication.

Our thought is we need sex education like this in our high schools. We think it would be great to send some sex educator into high schools and tell all the young boys of America the truth on penis size; it would be fantastically reassuring. The only problem is, who can you get to carry the message? I know I'd hate to have the problem of carrying this message to a sex-education class. I couldn't manage it. Say I tried to manage it with a group of seventeen-year-old kids. I'd send the girls all over into another room so I could talk to the guys. The minute I do that, of course, I've already got things half screwed up. But then I start talking about penis size and give them the straight story. But my voice would crack two or three times from my own anxiety and tension. Because of it, the kids say to themselves, "I knew the guy was lying." So the kids are right back with their inadequacy; only, now it's stronger, because somebody tried to reassure them and they knew he was lying. I would end up reinforcing their sense of inadequacy instead of taking it away. So it's a terrible problem.

Women seem to have much more of a problem with breast size than they do with vagina size. There are some very crude stories about vagina size. And again, from anything I've read in Masters and Johnson research, none of the stories have any basis in fact. It's no problem.

Both the penis size and vagina size represent to me our fantastic fixation at the genital stage of sexuality, where we have a childish view of sex where all we can see is what part goes where. We think those genitals are the sex instruments. And we've got our old ego telling us what we should be like.

"In fact," I told my Seattle group, "I'll give you an example. Do you guys want to see my sex instrument? Come on, now, don't shake your head, honey." So I stood up. "Now you see it. This is it. All 71½ inches of it from the tip of my toes to the top of my head. That's my sex instrument. It's ridiculous to concentrate on some small area of the body." I grant the nerve endings are especially rich there. If you make a map of the body in proportion to the number of nerve endings in each area like a population map of the United States, it would have the ten-inch circle around the genital area as over half the body.

Nevertheless, the whole body is the sex instrument.

Every pore in my body is a sex organ. Again, this emphasis on the genitals is just another reflection of our deprivation; it's a reflection of our very distorted understanding of our sexuality.

If sex was simply just one genital touching another genital, that would take away so much of what is available. But, again, so many people seem to be willing to settle for that. That's ridiculous.

Like I say, for gals the breast-size thing seems to be a bigger problem. A card from a gal at my Minneapolis seminar said, "In this day when big breasts are held up to be the big thing and I'm flat-chested, how can I possibly accept that?" The answer is, breast size has nothing, absolutely nothing, to do with sexual love. There have been all kinds of odes written to all kinds of different-sized breasts. The breasts of the beloved are never ugly.

Someone came back with, "Yeah, but I've got inverted nipples" or "I've got this and I've got that, you don't know me." Or "I've lost one breast to breast-cancer surgery" or "I've lost both of them." But, again, what does it really mean when we lose X per cent of our sexual equipment? I already lost part of my sexual equipment when I went bald on top. I lost more when I got all the scars on my chest from heart surgery. I suffered a loss when I had to have a pacemaker implanted in my shoulder. But I've got enough left in terms of sexual equipment. Let's not concentrate on the 5 or 10 or 15 per cent we've lost, let's concentrate on the 90 per cent we've got left, because that's more than enough.

It's just like the human body. You can cut out all kinds of parts and throw them away and it's amazing how well the person can live. It's the same with the sex instrument.

The only thing that's really crucial to the functioning of the whole sex instrument is the head and the heart. When those things are screwed up, no sex instrument in the world will work. But when those things are cleared up, any sex instrument in the world will work.

That's why I'm not talking about the problems usually talked about on sex. Here's a book on sex and I'm not going to talk a lot about all these mythical problems like impotence and frigidity and premature ejaculation and all those things. Because those things really aren't common problems. They seem to be but they aren't, for a very simple reason. There are all kinds of so-called frigid women who get away from their situation and they meet some guy and become unfrigid. Well, what's frigidity mean then? It means that in relation to the way they had been handled they were frigid. But when they were handled properly they weren't frigid. There are all kinds of guys who are impotent with their wives, but they can have sex with a gal next door. Okay, what kind of impotence is that? Our sexual problems have almost nothing to do, in my experience, with our sexual instruments, the genitals. Sure there are exceptions. For those exceptions you can go to Masters and Johnson and pay them two and a half thousand dollars and they'll probably solve that problem for you. But, for the bulk of us, there is no problem in the body, just in our heads and hearts.

This is the answer to sex in late ages. I don't know at what age sex becomes impossible as we typically recognize it. But once you see that the sex instrument runs from toes to head, then sex isn't ever impossible. A guy who's eighty-nine or 132 can have sex because his sexual instrument is still functioning beautifully, which is a totally different view.

It's like one of the ladies said last summer, "Hey, Jess, you're talking about sexuality, rather than just sex. This is what our marriage could use, a lot more sexuality and a lot less sex." But the answer is if you have a lot more sexuality you'll probably have a lot more sex, too, but the time together physically means so much more.

I see the same thing in sexual technique. When two people have gone through all the stages of sexual love that I'm talking about in this book, if they are even aware of what position they are in, there's something wrong. Two people going through all the openness to each other and the surrender I'm talking about are going to invent ninety-six new sexual positions that have never before been discovered on the face of the earth. Sexual position is not a problem. Anyone who claims it is is showing symptoms of a far worse problem. That's the problem we've got so much in this country because of our deprivation and because of our fear of ourselves and intimacy. We have held ourselves back and detached ourselves from our intercourse so much that we have become spectators at our own intercourse.

It's just like we're floating around in the sky there about a mile above our bed looking down at these people, one of whom is us. We're spectators at our own intercourse, and that's the problem. So to solve the problem we need, like the Hindu says, "To keep our minds on the fire at the beginning." We've lost track of the fire at the beginning. We've been so concerned about where we're going to that we've lost track of the fire at the beginning.

The sexual surrogates show us how bad things are. There was a sad thing about a lady out in California who was a paid sex surrogate for a sex clinic in Berkeley. There was a story on her and the clinic a couple of years ago in *Time*. A lot of people got on her for being so immoral, yet here was a lady who was helping guys who hadn't been able to have any kind of sexual experience. She was calming this guy down and talking to him and they're pleasuring each other. She was finally able to tease out of him a sexual performance he'd never been able to produce before.

I know that, for many people, reading about her offended their sense of morality. But I don't trust most of my moral judgments of other people. To me, most moral judgments are heavily based on appearances, not truth and charity. Here was a woman who I think was doing something very helpful for this guy. Now, if what she was doing was wrong, she's going to have to answer for that in her own way. To see people get on her, to me that was a cheap shot. The sadness, though, is that it takes a sex surrogate to bring this sexual performance out of this person. Yet you and I, typically, are the partners of that husband or wife. We think we are loving them. Look what that says about us. You see? And look what that says about the kind of bad heart we have towards the partner.

One of the people in the June seminar said, "My wife likes to have sex in the dark. What can I do to get her out of the dark?" I made some flippant, irreverent comment about taking turns, one night in the dark, the next night with the lights on. What I would say now is to wait for the lady to get over her fear of being seen. So what if it takes twenty or thirty years. That's the person we claim to love. If so, why aren't we more understanding?

Can self-doubt and love go together? Not very well. To me, the more self-doubt there is, the less love there is. It's like a glass of water; the more water in it, the less air. You can't have a lot of both. So that's why we have to try to get rid of it.

One gal was telling how, in her husband's case, she was afraid to wake the guy up and have sex with him. She knew he'd probably want it, but she was just hesitant to wake him up. But I think, again, it's self-discovery she was more frightened by. It's much easier for us to imagine sex and fantasize how it would be than to face the realities of a real sexual experience.

I think our attitude is our key. We can concentrate on our fear or we can concentrate on our hope. There was a beautiful article in the *Grapevine* about a guy who came into Alcoholics Anonymous at sixty-four. He had a year of sobriety. He found in AA answers he'd looked for all his life. Not only was he sober, but AA was showing him the way to an abundant living that he hadn't even realized was on this earth. He thought these things were only in heaven. But what did he do? He didn't curse the sixty-four years he'd spent in the darkness. He thanked God for the year that he had. "I thank God," he said, "that there is a life before death." He didn't say, "Isn't it awful that I just have so few days left to live this new way?" He said, "Thank God I've had the year and I've got these days."

How do we get in such a mess? Did conditioning do it? Well, I hope you don't feel by now that we're in this bad way because we've been conditioned by society. This attitude is all around us, but it is all around us because everybody else has been so terribly deprived. People don't want us to see us touching, because they want touching so bad yet they can't get it and they hate it when we do it. But we can't run our lives by what other people want from us. We've got to run our lives by the light that we get to guide ourselves. That's the only light we can run by.

Anaïs Nin speaks of this from the standpoint of women. She says, "If we think that men did this to us, it sounds like a legitimate thing at first. But if you think about it, it says that men have that much power and I am consequently so passive that I would allow this or let it be done to me." She saw that it was no one who did it to her.

That part of the women's lib argument is so ridiculous to me. The idea that men are so smart and have so much control that they can set things up so women are completely controlled and conditioned shows no understanding of how limited conditioning is. I also can't believe men could ever get that united and that successful at pulling the wool over anybody's eyes. Sure, there's all kinds of bad feeling and fear towards women by men. But I'd guess there's some of that on the other side. I think both men and women need to see how we and our big fat egos are contributing to our own problems and work on them.

I'll close with the lines from the great Indian poet Tagore. He said, "Who was it, prisoner, who forged these chains of yours so carefully?" The prisoner said, "It was I who forged these chains of mine so carefully." To get rid of them, we've got to be willing to take them off. It helps us to be willing when we see that if we don't take off the chains we have forged for ourselves, we stay dead to life. Then our ego has won its battle to stay separate from that other special soul we are meant to share our lives with.

CHAPTER 4

Let's Get On with the Business of Dying: Our Escapes from Love and Sex

What do we do when we have a terrible need for love and sex but we're afraid of losing our separateness and risking getting close to people like those who earlier hurt us so? Simple. Most of us find an escape that helps us run away from life and ourselves.

When we choose escapes, we choose death. The more escapes we choose and the more we lose ourselves in our escapes, the more we hasten our death but, even worse, the more we kill today.

Most all of us recognize the truth of that, but we need our escapes so badly it seems we almost can't help ourselves. But we can. Because most all of the escaping I see myself and others doing isn't so complete that we won't admit deep down what we're doing. So there's the hope. We don't need to give up all our escapes right away. No one can do that. But we can peek out from under the covers of our little escapes and consider starting to get on with the business of living instead of getting on with the business of dying.

One problem we have in giving up our escapes is that our whole society seems to be filled with people who are escaping. That isn't really the case; it just seems that way to us. If you were a bank robber and were pretending to be a fine, upstanding citizen, who would you hang out with? You'd go hang out with what seemed to you to be fine, upstanding citizens. The problem is some of them are pretending too. They may feel they are very inadequate people, so they are pretending to be fine, upstanding citizens. In the bunch are some people who really are fine, upstanding citizens. Obviously they don't need to pretend to be anything.

In your new pretend role, when you're picking your buddies at the Rotary Club, who will you pick? Without realizing it, you'll pick the ones who are pretending and you'll stay away from the ones who aren't pretending. So the pretenders will be attracted to the pretenders. Because those are the only people you'll be attracted to, you'll come to the conclusion that everybody in Rotary is a pretender. That's just like the alcoholic who feels everybody drinks, because all he sees is people who drink.

So when we're escaping, we set up a society for ourselves full of people who are escaping and pretending the same way we are. At the same time, there are all kinds of other escapes going on in different ways in our society.

Now, if you were the bank robber pretending to be the fine, upstanding businessman and you saw someone who was a bank robber pretending to be a counselor who was helping people, would you squeal on him and blow his cover? Probably not. It would be too risky. If you squealed on him, there's a grave danger that he could recognize another pretender real well and would squeal back on you.

So all of us in the escaping game are drawn to others using the same escapes. We feel everyone is escaping, because that's the only kind of people we're attracted to or are attracted to us. We usually don't do any more than complain a little about the escapes most other people use. About the only exception is if people are younger than us or way older. We feel safe that they won't understand our escape, so we yell at them for their escape.

We yell at the kids for using drugs to escape and we're on alcohol and tranquilizers. They yell at us for using moneymaking and materialism to escape and then turn around and want a big check every month because we owe it to them.

Meanwhile, back at the rest of society, there are a bunch of people we're not attracted to, because we can't understand them. They're people who, by and large, aren't escaping much. They're doing pretty much the same things we're doing, but they're doing them out of love and because those things are right for them, rather than using them as an escape.

Two guys are working side by side in a bank. One's hiding out from himself, pretending to be a fine, upstanding citizen. The other guy is whistling and happy being a banker. Same with telephone linemen, teachers, auto mechanics, anything. One woman is pretending to be a mother to hide out from her feelings she isn't a woman; another is a mother because she loves it. A dad is pretending to be a husband and father because he's afraid he's really a homosexual. Another dad loves being a dad and shows it.

Just as you can't convince the drinking alcoholic that everyone isn't as fascinated by alcohol as he is, so you can't convince some other kind of escaper that everyone isn't escaping just like they are. The hope, though, is in the fact that life has usually already shown them that their escape isn't serving them very well. So they're ready to think about putting it down. But then they often get scared and quickly pick up their escape again.

When we wake up and start getting out of our escapes, we usually don't do that quietly and gracefully. We usually start yelling at other people about their escapes and even criticize people in the escape we just left. People who are sleeping in their escape don't like noisy people waking them up, so they retaliate or run away and leave us by ourselves. Then we yell at them for doing that: "Why don't you stay here so I can yell at you?"

It takes us a while to understand this and to see that yelling at people about their escapes is another escape. Freedom from escape means letting everybody else do just what pleases them while we calmly and quietly go about meeting our own needs. Even this will disturb some people who are sleeping, but that's just the way the cookie crumbles. If someone wants to get disturbed at my fumbling attempts to find my being and be it, that's their privilege. I can't let myself be caught up in that either, although I do need to see that much of their irritation is caused by my fumbling and awkward *attempts* at being me, rather than *being* me. I see that the calmer and quieter I am about being me, the less waves I make and the less trouble I cause.

Let's look at the common escapes and see if we can find ourselves in one or more of them. For me, I don't have much trouble identifying with escapes. I've used so many and they are so real to me it's like I invented each one. If I was in an "I hate people" escape, I find I've jumped into an "I love people" escape and the new one is maybe a worse escape than the old one, because who would think of looking for me there? I fool even myself. I'm learning that the relatively escape-free life is very difficult to find for a tricky rascal like me.

My wife, Jackie, in the book she just finished, talks about her addictions, her escapes. I found myself patting myself on the back because I didn't have one of those more spectacular addictions. But then I looked more closely and saw that one of my big addictions is hurry sickness. I always go to bed with a sense of what's not done and I get up with the feeling that I won't get done today any but the most essential parts of what I have to do. So I'm always in a hurry. The only way I get so many of the enjoyable things done that I do for myself is to take the time away from the other things on the grounds that this is more important. That had been *some* improvement, because I've done many more things with members of my family and my friends than I would have done otherwise. But always there was the time pressure of hurry.

My hurry sickness isn't a very spectacular addiction, but it has been killing my body, shortening my life and, most of all, robbing me of the sweetness of the day.

My addiction is so clear to me now, because there is so little reason for it any more. All I need to do is stop taking on new obligations until I get my piles of overdue work cleaned up by doing the jobs or admitting they don't need to be done. In a fairly short time, I could be in a situation where my work and my personal life are without piles of things to do. I don't mean that I won't always have lots of things I'd like to do. But there is a clear difference between that and the way I'm still letting the press of my life put me in a hurry situation where I think I have to find the shortest, fastest way to drive through town or to do some other job. But even talking about being free of my addiction scares me, because I've needed it so badly and used it so long to avoid facing me. Here's just another example of looking for inner guidance, surrendering to what is, and changing the things I can, looking for progress, not perfection.

What's the oddest escape of all from the need for holding and touching? The oddest escape of all is holding and touching under the guide of sex when there isn't really any feeling there. So the sex addict has the oddest escape of all, the person who is using sex to run away from body contact. It's like a guy was a bank robber. So he gets a job as a bank guard. He's guarding this bank, knows all about it, goes out to lunch, slips on his costume, comes running back in with his stocking cap over his face, holds up the bank, runs out the side door, goes around the corner, throws the money in a little box he had there, tears off his costume and comes running in the other door, saying, "I heard there was a robbery here. Who did it?" Who would think of looking for him as a bank guard? If you're running away from sex, who would think of looking for a person trying to escape sex and body contact and all these delicious feelings? Who would think of looking for that person in one who has a lot of sex, the sex addict?

What would be kind of humorous if it weren't so sad is that we've got all these sex addicts telling us, "Hey, you guys, when it comes to sex, let me tell you about it. I'm getting so much. I'm the one who really knows." But that's just like letting the skid-row wino tell us about wine tasting. He hasn't really tasted wine; he gulped it down so fast he was half drunk before he stopped gulping. Yet he's going to tell us about the delicate tastes of wine? And the sex addict is going to tell us about sex? In fact, in the worst cases, that of the extremely promiscuous person, they are a person who isn't able to get anything out of sex. That's why they're promiscuous. They're just repeating a routine over and over again, seeking something they can't find. So the more promiscuous they are, in a sense the less they are getting out of sex.

But it's so weird, like I say, that the person who has such poor credentials for something would ask us to follow their lead. There is a lot of this today, where these folks are trying to tell us what sex is really like.

The truth of the matter is that there is a big difference between the current "fashion" as sex is presented and what people want. According to the current fashion, most everyone has sex with most everyone else and marriage is some old-fashioned thing no one believes in any more. Yet the surveys show that over three fourths of single people—unmarried, divorced or widowed—feel that marriage is the desirable way to live together and a necessary first step to raising a family.

Well, then, who are the people who are drumming up the noise about the current fashion? Are they just some media weirdos? No. It's you and me who are the customers who have set the fashion. That fashion of preoccupation with sex can't exist without customers. It's the sex-starved, body-contact-starved part of you or me that buys pornography of all kinds, movies, stories, etc., and is fascinated. Yet, another part of us sees and appreciates the need and value of permanent relationships.

That split part of most of us can be looked on as a great sadness. Your big buyers of expensive pornographic literature are your well-to-do businessmen. Many of them undoubtedly have at least a nominal church affiliation. But I don't see this split in us as a cause for despair; I see it as a sign of hope, because each of us can build on the good and get the better results in the life we want.

I think the big demand we could make on anybody who wants to tell us what sex should be for us is, "Hey, let me look at your life. Let me look at your ability to establish and maintain relationships."

The week that Jackie Smith was in Bozeman, she was able to see the state of my relationships in the different areas of my life. Some of them are terrible. Some of them are pretty good. Some of them are great. But that is reality. Now, typically, the sexual athletes, in my experience, haven't got anybody around them who was around them more than six weeks or six months ago. They're like gypsies. They're just bouncing from one deal to another. Now they hold up their bouncing around as a good result; they say, "Well, it isn't crucial to stick with a relationship." But, for the results I want, I can't conceive of bouncing around being good for us. No society I've ever seen, not even the nomads, lived without roots in their families or tribes.

Also, I have looked at some of the psychological

profiles of people who are the sex addicts, including the wife swappers and the swinging people. There are some weird things about them, just on the surface, without going deep within. For example, if you're a swinger and go to some swinging deal, it's forbidden that any telephone numbers be asked for or given out. I'm sure it's more anonymous by far than Alcoholics Anonymous. In swinging, not only do many use just first names, but they use a fake first name.

That's just one indication of the transitoriness of the deal. When you look at their psychological profiles, the sexual swingers typically are people who are very shallow in their relationships with other people; they don't experience or feel very much. So, when you see that, it isn't very surprising that it would take several bombs going off for them to feel something. Then you see, like I said earlier, why the genital part of sex has to be so big, because it takes something that big for them to feel. It's like a person who's terribly hard of hearing. When he goes to the symphony, all he hears is the drums. They're the only thing that's loud enough for him to hear. So would it make sense for us to listen to him tell us what a symphony sounds like?

I feel that it would be wise for us to start to widen out our sensitivities and sensibilities. Then we can tune in all the tones and subtle shadings of the music and we can appreciate the whole spectrum.

The promiscuity we see so much of is best understood, as I said earlier, as the inability to experience bodily pleasure. And this is what some of the promiscuous gals that I've talked to report. They have sex a lot, but they don't get much of anything out of it. Now, I have seen a number of promiscuous gals healed by their promiscuity, or at least healed *of* their promiscuity. What was the difference between them and the others? Simple. They seemed to be able to benefit in some way from their experiences. One young gal I

ran into in my teaching was a good example of the
hopefulness seemingly hidden in some behavior that
was very hard for her to handle. Her role as a freshman was being "it" for gang bangs. The fraternity
boys would be lined up outside the door, one, two,
three ... up to twenty and slam, bam, thank you,
ma'am. That isn't a lovely kind of sex life. It isn't the
kind of thing most mothers hope for their daughters.
But what's interesting is that she progressed from
that to one-night stands. I was in touch with her
during most of this, because she was a student of
mine. She was telling me, "Jess, if a guy doesn't ask
me to go to bed with him on the first date, I figure he
must be queer." She went from that to where she could
go with a guy at least a week before he would sicken
of her and her possessiveness and clinging.

I followed this gal along as a friend during her
school year. She got so she could go with a guy for a
few months. Then, lo and behold, at the beginning of
her senior year, she was going with this guy and she
really liked him a lot. She was running a restaurant,
and one night she started a fight with her boyfriend
and went out with one of the customers.

She came to me and said, "Jess, why the hell did I
do that?" I said, "Honey, I think you were probably
feeling like you didn't deserve him and you were probably trying to screw that deal up because you didn't
feel you were worthy."

She said, "By God, I bet you're right." So she patched
it up and she ended up marrying the guy. I would just
guess from what reports I've had that they are still
very happily married. I'll bet she is a lot better wife
than many of her sorority sisters who had their nose
turned up at her.

That's a beautiful example of promiscuity where,
because she was open enough to learn something from
her sexual activities as well as her other activities,
she was gradually healed and became a different per-

son. As a freshman, she had no control. She was like the alcoholic; she had no sexual control. She changed to a person who had a higher degree of sexual control than most of her sorority sisters.

The year I had my first School of Life,* in Bozeman, which is held for a week in the middle of July and the middle of January, I found an amazing thing happened within me. On the morning of the third day all of us were together, I told my students how differently I had been feeling since they came to see me. I felt so good. I hadn't had the munchies once, I had almost lost interest in food at mealtimes, I was so filled up with them being there. And I was needing less sleep. After six or seven hours, I woke up feeling more rested than eight hours usually makes me feel. When I asked them if they had been feeling the same way, about half the people at the school raised their hands.

I realized what gave all of us our different feeling was that a group of like-minded people who had come together from all parts of the country were opening themselves up just by being there and that we all felt more whole because of it. Our feeling of wholeness and getting out of our separation was what was making us feel so good. It wasn't anything special we were saying or doing, because the first few days of school are pretty quiet, with most of the people just sitting and listening and not opening up too much to anything but the people they came with.

This goes back to sex escapes in this way. By taking away the terrible loneliness, the pain of the loneliness is gone. So the source of most of the need for the escape is gone. It's hard for someone with an obsessive escape to realize it isn't necessary, but I see it clearly.

Overeating is a way we escape from the pain of our separateness. That escape is particularly troublesome to us because it is so obvious and socially so unacceptable. But those of us who have to have something in

---

* For information, write School of Life, P. O. Box 249, Bozeman, MT 59715.

our mouths to ease the pain aren't held back by a little thing like social disapproval. I had a heart attack seventeen years ago, yet for sixteen years I carried around about twenty pounds of harmful fat that added to my risk of dying. I lost the same ten pounds twenty times, but I couldn't keep the weight off. My pain was too great.

I finally got enough wholeness in my life to do something about my diet. Last June (1978) I tried being a vegetarian under the influence of the Polarity Health* folks, led by Jefferson and Sharon Campbell. I lost twenty pounds and can eat all I want. A baked potato tastes better to me than the steak used to. And I feel so much better, and the weight didn't come back. But also, my pain has gone away enough from years of working on getting some wholeness in my life so I can finally resist my desire for fudge, ice cream, candy and all the other sweets I used to eat so much of. So the real answer to eating as an escape isn't just stopping; you have to get at the root of the pain, which is the separateness—the lack of wholeness.

The most socially acceptable of all the escapes is work. We can be a workaholic to run away from the world and to numb our pain and everyone will think we're really a great person. Yet we suffer from a double lack of love for those around us. We are running away from the people we love, and since our work isn't done out of love but is being done out of escape, our work is poisoned and that poison affects our fellow workers and the product of our work, as it is felt by the people who use what we do or make. Yet we think because we work fifteen hours a day we're really doing something great.

Very few in business understand the sickness of going home with a full briefcase every night. One man who did was Jack Cornelius, the former manager of the Batten, Barton, Durstine and Osborn advertis-

* Polarity Health Institute, P O Box 86, Olga, WA 98279

ing agency branch office in Minneapolis. One evening, he saw John Bowie, a friend of mine, working late. He said, "John, is there any reason you can't get your work done in eight hours like the rest of us?" That was a rare insight.

But when you talk to one of us workaholics, we defend what we're doing as being for the good of our country or the good of our family. "I'm just doing this for my boys and girls at home, so they won't have to suffer like I did from not having things." Meanwhile, at home, the wife and kids are suffering from a far bigger loss than of some junk in the garage. Even if it's high-priced junk like Rolls-Royces, it's still junk when it tries to take the place of love.

People argue, "Jess, if it wasn't for us workaholics, what kind of a world would this be?" It would be a much nicer world, because all the work would be done out of love instead of fear and hate. The part of this book that came out of my love is the good and useful part. The parts that came out of anger, fear and pain are the flaws in the book.

Wouldn't it be nice if all the people who were bankers, garage mechanics and teachers were working only because they loved their work and not because it was an escape? Have we got too many in any line of work who truly love their work?

The fact people are so sure no work would be done out of love, that only pain makes people work, shows their blindness and their escape. They don't even realize there is such a thing as people doing what they're doing out of love.

Another escape that is very socially acceptable is serving others. This is such a devious escape. It's like the sex escape as an escape from closeness. Who would think of looking at our teachers, our counselors, our ministers, or people in the welfare agencies to find people who were escaping their pain at not being able to get close to people? But you just talk to the people affected by those helping professions and you'll find huge loads of pain they received when they went seeking help from the helpers. Much of the escape of helping others comes out of our need for power over others. We feel we are so inadequate that we couldn't participate on an even basis with people. We have to feel we are doing something for them to make us feel good. I watched a man who was renowned in his profession do this. He would help new people who came to town, because they needed help. But the minute they got to the point where they tried to help him back, he ran away. There is also a lot of controlling in helping others, because we can keep the person from getting too close to us.

Also, as my friend Wally Minto of Alpha Awareness* says, "It can be especially destructive to play the game of helping others because we always need to be needed. If a person we're helping wants to stand on their own two feet, we don't want that because we need them to need us."

There are a lot of structures in our society that have been built up by us and others as we seek escapes from ourselves. Oddly enough, one of the worst structures is government. Much of government is designed by us to take away responsibility from us for our actions. We don't need to do something about poverty, sickness or other problems. We'll have the government do it for us. "Oh, the poor this and the poor that. People are doing a terrible thing to them, and government, not us, has got to solve the problem." We'll throw enough money at the problem and we'll solve it.

People start throwing money at the problem. There's a whole group of people in this country up and down the pay scale who know how to get government money. They get in between the money that's being thrown at the problem and the problem, and the money sticks to the people who are in between. Very little of it gets to

* Alpha Awareness Tapes, Books and Training, Drawer G, Susanville, CA

the problem. But those folks are telling us it does get to the problem. And the money keeps coming. Pretty soon we've got so many people that the money is sticking to that they are a huge voting bloc and they say this problem has a fantastic importance and we should keep throwing money at it.

I had a lot of real do-gooders in my classes, especially the nurses. They were just dying to help other people. "I've got to help them. I don't want anyone helping me, because then they'll get close to me and I'll feel good and they'll be in my debt." And all the time, these people are saying of the ones they're claiming to help, "They need me."

It isn't that there is anything wrong with helping people when we do it for ourselves and admit it. What is a problem is, as mentioned earlier, when we need to be needed. When we have this deep need and don't admit it, people have to get sick or in trouble so they can need us. If everyone is happy and feeling good, we feel terrible, because we aren't needed.

One of the most common escapes from love and sex is helplessness. I remember the story of an alcoholic. He had gone through treatment and came out not drinking but still had his terrible desire to drink to take away his pain. When he finally caved in and took his first drink, he knew what was going to happen and felt very hopeless. His thought was, "well, let's get on with the business of dying." He didn't see any way out for himself—yet. But he later found a way out. There was a tone to a few of the questions on the cards that were written by my students in Seattle of: "What can I do?" That's helplessness, partly. To me, it was kind of obvious what you should do almost right from the beginning of my talking to you. But, you see, this idea of helplessness serves our purposes. It's like our sense of inadequacy, "Oh, woe is me, what can I do?" Our big escape is helplessness. "Oh, I can't do that." What we mean is "I won't." Have you ever heard a person say, "Oh, I can't do that, I can't do that?" Eventually, sometimes, if you crowd them, they end up saying, "I won't." They say, "I can't be nice to that person. I won't be nice to them." And the steel comes into their voice.

I used to think neurotics were very weak people. They cried a lot and told how they were such pushovers. They wrung their hands a lot and complained, "Oh, the world is doing everything to me."

I see now that neurotic people aren't weak. They're some of the strongest people I've ever seen. If you don't believe that, you just try to make a neurotic do something they don't want to do. One of the things you can try to make them do is give up their neuroticism. They'll show you a strength and a cunning and a power that makes a steel trap look like a marshmallow.

"Oh, poor little old me. I just can't do it." The real "I won't" behind that is angry, and because it is angry, depression is really frozen rage. A psychological term that's commonly used for depression is learned helplessness. That may be true, but that isn't the aspect of depression that's interesting to me. What's interesting about depression to me is frozen rage in people who are 100 per cent pissed off that the world isn't going the way they want it to go. They're mad. They cover it over with this "Oh, woe is me, I won't say anything or do anything." But their anger and frustration at not having their way is written all over their faces and bodies. So they have a lot of pain and frequent headaches.

What are some of the other escapes we use from sex besides depression? Alcohol and drugs is a lovely one. Alcohol for the guys and drugs for the gals. Now once in a while we find a gal muscling in on the guy's act and becoming an alcoholic. Once in a while we find a guy muscling in on the women's act and becoming a pill-popper, a pill-head.

But it's such a fantastic escape. All you need to do is crawl into a big bottle. All the worries go away—for a while. Then, pretty soon, it takes more and more of the big bottle to make the worries go away, and soon you are addicted to the big bottle. It doesn't make the worries go away, they even multiply a hundred times over.

Often, the alcoholic goes to the doctor. In trying to take him out of the big bottle, the doctor puts him in the little bottle. All of a sudden the guy's got two problems, the big bottle and the little bottle. Then it's really hard to get unaddicted from both of them. And I've seen a lot more people beat the big bottle than beat the little one.

So the ladies, they go to the doctor and they get the little bottle. The doctor says to himself, "Hey, there's nothing wrong with you." But he doesn't dare tell her that, because if he does she'll go to another doctor. So he gives her some pills. He doesn't have the time to talk to her, she probably couldn't or wouldn't tell him what was wrong.

But if he did find out what's wrong, there's usually nothing he could do about it anyway, because she won't let him solve her problem and he doesn't know how. Besides, in a way, he's using his doctor's suit as an escape, so why will a guy who's escaping into a doctor's suit take away an escape from a lady who wants to escape into a little bottle? There's collusion between the two and he puts the lady into the little bottle. Pretty soon she needs a bigger and more reliable source of supply, so she develops a new ailment so she can go to a new doctor and get another source of supply. Before too long she's got a regular trapline of five or six doctors she visits regularly to maintain her supply of little bottles—Mother's little helpers. Meanwhile she's yelling at her hippie kids to not take drugs, because it's bad. And the Valium gets shipped into our big cities by the boxcar load so we can go around like zombies who say through half-closed eyes and a dazed expression, "I feel fine. My life is just great." Then we laugh at the kids for being on drugs. It's so weird.

"But," they say, "I'm taking doctor's medicine on doctor's orders." What a clue that is! Like I say, here's this doctor escaping and then here's this customer of his escaping. But she says, "He's such a cleanie. He would never do anything like this to me." Baloney.

Our whole society is just loaded with structures that let us escape from the very thing we shouldn't escape from, because everybody's got pain. Our pain goes off, and instead of looking for the source of the pain and solving that, we just want to get rid of the pain. It's just like when a fire alarm goes off. What do we do? We don't like fire alarms. We don't like the noise. So we go and cut the wires. It's a beautiful way to handle the problem, very intelligent. Oh, we've got big heads, we have. It's like Nikita Khrushchev said, "There is an old Russian proverb: The horse has a very big head, but he is not very smart."

So this is what we do with our great minds. We go and cut the wires to the fire alarm because we don't like pain. And we've got a whole bunch of people who are willing to take pain away from us.

There's another way of escaping pain. It's called marriage. Two groovy people, a gal and a guy, get married and they're going to have a great time together. The honeymoon lasts three days up to two weeks. Usually a week is about as long as a honeymoon should last, because most people don't want to allow more time than that. Then the guy goes back to work and gets lost in his job. The woman gets lost in something else and they're both escaping from each other. It's just beautiful, just fantastic. Pretty soon the guy isn't coming home hardly ever. He's dedicated to his work. The wife has got her work or activities or kids or something or somebody else. Everybody's escaping from everybody else. It's just like the monkey that got raised in the cage where he couldn't be touched or touch others to meet his needs.

As soon as the intensity of sex wears off and loses the power it had to temporarily break down our walls, we all tend to push away the physical and emotional contact we need. But we're all in cahoots with each other. I've got my escape and you've got yours; I'm not going to try to take your escape away from you. Why should I? If I try, you're going to strike back and try to take mine away.

I'll tell you another escape. That's running around the country talking to people. I told my audience in Seattle, "This speaking can be a real cop-out, because if I came to very many of these places, I could start believing my own publicity. You people say such lovely things to me, I could start thinking, 'Boy, I'm some kind of giant.' All I need to find out what kind of giant I am is just go back to Bozeman, Montana, for a day or two. My wife isn't interested in listening to my fancy ideas, and my kids aren't interested in listening to my fancy ideas. My friends aren't interested in listening to them, and my neighbors aren't interested in listening to them. I end up talking to my horse. That isn't very satisfying either, because he doesn't give me a lot of grins and a lot of support, like you guys give me. You've really made me feel good here today with all your affection."

Somebody asked on one of the cards handed in to me, "How come you're coming here to tell this to us?" The answer is very simple. I wasn't there to save those benighted folk. I might have given them that impression every once in a while, but I wasn't. I was there frying my own fish. I was saying a book so I could get a set of tapes to write most of this book from. If you want to hear what I said so you can get that

extra feeling the voice carries, you can order the tapes.*
If I hadn't been saying a book, I'd have at least been
there making money.

Another escape has to do with the issue of responsibility. My friend Walther Lechler is a psychiatrist
from West Germany who taught at my first School of
Life, for people who want to learn more about living
in harmony with the people they love. He says there
is a very simple reason for our problems. He talked
about inadequate enculturation, or the poor teaching
we receive on life in our society. And then, of course, I
would add to that the lack of body contact we get, our
ego problem and all these other things. But he said
our poor teaching is all well and good, but it's past
history. Why do all of us stay that way? As an answer,
he wrote out the words "social stupidity" on the black-
board. One of the gals at our school really objected to
that. She said, "I'm really a very intelligent person;
I'm not stupid."

I finally said, "Diane, just exactly what do you call
it when you know what it is you're supposed to do, you
know what you have to do to save your life, but you
don't do it? What better name is there for that than
stupidity?" She finally had to agree that I had a certain point.

Walther proceeded to point out that if you stayed
stupid, it is your fault. It's not your mother's fault,
your father's fault, your grandmother's fault, your
husband's or your wife's fault, your boyfriend's or
girlfriend's fault—it's your fault. Well, you don't hear
much of that in psychology or society today. It is your
and my fault if we stay the way we are and don't
change the things we can change. That is not appetiz-
ing news to people, so there aren't many who are
carrying that message.

I say to you the same thing I say to me: "If I stay

---

* Jesse Lair Tapes, set of eight Seattle sex tapes, $40.00 P. O. Box 249,
Bozeman, MT 59715.

this way, it's my fault." It's just like one of my students who was only nineteen years old who said, "For what I did yesterday, shame on my parents, and my past. But if I stay that way, shame on me." What is she saying? She's saying, "If I stay this way, it's my fault." Isn't that simple enough? isn't that real plain?

So there are lots of escapes. They are all designed by us and others to help us escape responsibility. That's beautiful. There's only one mistake I can make: That's rationalizing that these things are good for me. I can argue that I should embrace these escapes on the grounds that they are so common, everybody does it, what can you expect, look at my training, look at my conditioning.

If you want to see what our escapes have done to us, all you need to do is look at one of the saddest facts I can offer you. In the little town of Vilcabamba, Peru, there's a man named Erazo who is 132 years old. When Grace Halsell went down there to interview him in this town where there's lots of people over a hundred years old who are active and full of life, she found that for him and many of the other old people, their fondest memory was lying in bed in the arms of their loved ones. Halsell went out to visit old Erazo and he propositioned her. So here he was 132 and life hadn't died in him yet.

What is so terrible about that story is it says the genetic capabilities of our bodies have a hundred and thirty-two plus years in them, and look what we've done. By the time I was thirty-five, I had nearly destroyed my body by attacking the weakest link in it, which was my congenitally small heart arteries. I attacked my body so vigorously that I nearly killed myself by the time I was thirty-five and had my heart attack. That's only one fourth the life span of an Erazo. I could have destroyed myself in one fourth of the time Erazo lived. And in the process of destroying myself, not only do I die in one fourth of the time that he lived, but I'm miserable for the whole thirty-five years.

At the time of my heart attack, Erazo had lived four times as long as I had, and all those years had real living of life in them—living in harmony with his fellow human beings. He didn't have a perfect life, because he, too, was born lonely and he, too, had to come to the God of his understanding. He, too, had had to get in harmony with life. And he, too, I'm sure, spent a lot of time saying no to God.

But even his long life-span does not say to us what the maximum is for man. The maximum life-span must be in the vicinity of one hundred and fifty to two hundred years, because Erazo certainly did not live perfectly. Now the geneticists say that those long-lived people in South America and Russia and the fact that they live in these little spots is not due to heredity. They say some small percentage of it might be due to heredity, but it would be under 10 per cent; 90 per cent of their long-livedness is in the way they handle the instruments they were given at birth and the way they handle each other's instruments.

In those places, babies are loved and held, and adults live in harmony with each other. People make their principal occupation spending time with each other, socializing and visiting. They attend the festivals. They work some, enough to eat. But it doesn't take much food and they don't eat much, because they just need to feed their real hunger, not their false need to be putting something in their mouths. That's another reason they live a long time; they aren't fat.

They're also not like us in the amount of things they have. We're like a squirrel gone crazy, who, instead of piling up enough acorns for the winter, just keeps on piling up. We get enough acorns for the winter piled up and our fellow squirrel says, "Let's run and play." But we say, "Oh, I've got to have more acorns piled up." We already have this idiotically big pile of acorns, enough for ten winters. We spend all of our time piling up acorns. Then we're so tired, because we spent the whole summer working. We missed all the game playing, so in the winter we're mad. The next summer, we're still so mad and so separate that we'll pile up twenty years of acorns. Asinine. We do this in the name of our own particular rationalization. We're putting by for our old age, we're providing for the tough times to come, we're giving the kids a better way of life than we had. It's all a lie. We're doing it to run away from ourselves and life. All we need to do to see what terrible harm we've done, again, is to stand up naked in front of that full-length mirror. The wounds we have inflicted on our body are there for us to see in scars, tensions, fat.

My sex instrument has a scar that runs from my throat to my belly button, where they did heart surgery on me twelve years ago. I've got three scars on my chest where the chest tubes were inserted for the surgery and a big scar on my left shoulder where they cut in the blood-pressure indicator for my heart surgery. In 1970 they opened me up for the tumor surgery and said, "You've got cancer; you won't live to get back to Montana." They opened me up from the belly button to my groin. For years those scars were very red and very livid. In January of 1977 I had to have a Pacemaker, and that's cut into my left shoulder. The scar is still pretty fresh and red. And also from breaking my elbow as a kid, there's a big scar on my left arm, and that arm is very thin and very weak.

Through my shoulders there is a tremendous amount of tension. I used to think the fact my shoulders were so square was a fantastic thing. When I would buy suit coats, the tailor would have to keep cutting out material from under the collar in back because my shoulders kept pushing the cloth up into the neck. I thought, "Wow, that's really masculine." I find now that's really terrible. My shoulders were so tense because I was figuratively carrying the weight of the world. My shoulders should have had some slope to them. That's the way a man's shoulders should slant. That's what happens when you aren't tensing up to fight the world. I'd tensed up my shoulder muscles so long that they had almost rigidified into bone. There was no flexibility to them. You could press on my shoulder muscles and they were hard, constantly, almost like bone. I couldn't get my shoulders down to where they normally would be. I'd been, in a sense, fighting off imaginary foes and going to battle in foolish battles that didn't exist.

We laugh at Don Quixote tilting at windmills. I've gone into foolish battles that make Don Quixote look like the wisest man in the world.

So my sexual instrument shows the ravages my choices in life have inflicted on it. Most of the damage, including my need for a Pacemaker, had been done by the time I was thirty-five. When I went into the hospital for my heart surgery, in 1967, before I came to Montana, I had a spell where I passed out from too low a pulse. I got sick, the blood rushed to the stomach and that robbed the heart part that did the timing of the heart, so my pulse dropped and the blood pressure dropped some more in a vicious circle. The Pacemaker corrects that. So all that damage, I had managed to do by the time I was thirty-five.

Now I'm in the process of trying to reverse that and trying to make my sex instrument a better instrument, physically, for all of life, from the top of my head to my toes. I have found that I can do a lot of things now that I couldn't do ten and fifteen years ago. I've had some people say some nice things about the progress I've made. People look at pictures from ten years ago and say, "Hey, you're looking younger now than you did then." It's a nice feeling. I think it's true. But even more important, I feel younger than I did then. Recently I went in to buy a sport coat and found that my shoulders had loosened up so much they weren't square any more. They had dropped nearly two inches, so the new coat fit just fine with the shoulder slope that was built in.

What I see is that I've already had some taste of what I was talking to you about in the definition of love, which is not welfare, not growth, not development, but healing where that which is not whole and that which is not straight and that which is not good becomes whole and straight and good to a much better degree than before.

I have seen plenty of evidence very satisfactory to me that the damage to our instruments is not irreversible. Not only can we take the resources we have left and squeeze out a far longer period of time from them, but we can also undo damage that has been done. We can get a healing, and I've experienced some of it and I believe there's more of that healing that I can experience.

I'm not going to live as long as Erazo. I don't know that I necessarily would even want to. Most of my friends have been just as hard on their bodies as I have been, so at about the age of seventy-five or eighty I'd have to acquire a whole new batch of friends. But that's not the point, how many days we live. The point is what we do with the days we have. But the lesson of old Erazo is so instructive to me and it gives such a lie to the idea we've got a good society. We've got a terrible society. We've probably got the worst society ever invented. We've got a society that would make the cannibals look like a bunch of Sunday-school teachers. And that's what you and I are living in. So, partly, that's a sign, to me, we've got to pick our way very carefully along our path.

But we've got the best society that each of us can provide for the rest of us because of our deprivations and other things. I'm not going to wait and try to reform society by yelling at you and me and trying to change our institutions. Sure, I'll do a few things to work on improving and changing things in society. But the prime component of society I'm working on is this cat, here behind this Bic ball-point pen. Yet, what happens as I decide to seek more harmony is I vote for a different way and if any of you decide to vote for a different way, then our society becomes a different society and we start being easier on each other—and being more straight with each other.

I had the beautiful experience of going into a growth group that I had been a member of for a long time, and as I came into that room of men and women I had opened my heart to and who had opened their hearts to me, they weren't men and women any more—they were just people. It was such a beautiful experience to transcend what I thought was a fundamental barrier between us, that of sex, being a different sex. It was such a fantastic feeling, and I've had that feeling a lot since then. These are not men and women we are surrounded by. These are hearts, and it's just the costumes they wear, their bodies, that have their sex. Those costumes are of no consequence. What counts is their hearts. And their age has no consequence. What counts is that we are heart to heart with no boundary between us. We are all equals, we are all peers. You see? And this is so crucial. To me it comes when we accept responsibility and freely and honestly admit that we are and what we can do. Then we aren't having to cop out behind these inflated ideas of what we are and what we're supposed to be. We've got all these funny ideas of the way it's supposed to be, and I don't measure up to that.

As we free ourselves from our escapes we can say, "Hey, with this instrument, weak and imperfect as it is, I will do the best I can with the time and resources available to me." That's what counts. To me, that understanding is essential for us before we can say yes to life. We have to get rid of our crazy perfectionism and ideas like: "I will do this thing that you are talking about only if and when my instrument is of sufficient quality and size and scope to handle the particular difficulties that I have." That's a cop-out. We have to accept just what we are before we can move on and do anything with what we have.

But, you see, the minute we accept what we are, then we can start. When that first book of mine was in the window of a book-store at Carroll College, which is a Catholic college in Montana, an old priest made them take it out of the window, because he thought the title, *"I Ain't Much, Baby—But I'm All I've Got,"* was negative. He didn't see that that's an overwhelmingly positive title, because the minute we say, "I ain't much," then we've got something. We've got what we've really got. That's better than pretending we're what we aren't. When we're pretending we're what we aren't, we don't have anything. So when we say, "I ain't much," that's a powerful, overwhelming first step. It's 90 per cent of the way to "Ain't I a wonder," rather than being negative. It's so much better than saying, "I'm nothing" or "I'm great" or "I'm something that I'm not." So this is why it is so necessary here to see these escapes and to see what they really are—which is a big lie. We aren't down at that office working for our kids, we're working to run away from our wife and our kids. She isn't going out to the clubs and the PTA just to build a better America, she's doing it partly to run away from the husband and the kids. The kids aren't smoking grass just so they can have these groovy experiences, they're also doing it to run away from their folks and their brothers and sisters—and from each other. The big people are using their own drugs to run away—alcohol and pills. I don't want any of that junk in my system.

To me, anything that interferes with my hearing the delicate music of the symphony is something I don't want any part of. What I see as so crucial is that I give up this lying and see life as clearly as I possibly can see it for me. Of course, that means giving up seeing the other person's problem. I've got 20-20 vision as to what's wrong with you guys. But, again, what a terrible escape! So what I have to do is to see my escapes as clearly as I can and get free of them by being willing to release them and being willing for them to release me.

How do we recognize our escapes? In all the talking I've done about them, it should be obvious how to find our escapes. Escapes have these qualities: They let us be intensely preoccupied so we don't need to see our pain. They are so close in and seem so natural to us it's as if they'd always been there. That makes them hard to spot, because they're so close to us. It's like looking for our glasses when we've got them on or they're pushed up in our hair. An escape is really in control of us, not us in control of it. And an escape is something we defend violently when it is attacked. When we are doing something out of love and it's questioned, we're pretty calm about it. But question an alcoholic's drinking and he isn't calm about it. Or question an overeater's eating. Or a workaholic's working. Or a helper's helping. They all get real loud fast. So we just use that test on ourselves and see where our hot spots are. Where the hot, defensive spots are is where the escapes are.

The answer to finding escapes isn't in what we escape to. There's nothing that's bad for us by itself. It's the use we make of it. Trout fishing used to be an escape for me. I came to Montana on vacation with my family and, twice a day, I went trout fishing come hell or high water. I spent a good part of my time intensely poring over catalogs, preoccupied with what I was going to buy. It was a great escape. I grant it doesn't sound like too harmful an escape, but it was. It separated me from the people I was with during the time I was preoccupied.

I'm now free of the trout fishing escape. Do I still go? You bet. Five to ten times a year, a day comes along where the weather is nice, the fishing is good, one of my sons or a friend wants to go and there's nothing else that needs to be done, so we go fishing and have a great time. I really have a lot more fun than I used to have, because I'm not so intense and I can enjoy the day more. All those hundreds of preoccupied hours where I was obsessed with trout fishing are freed up for really living in those other moments.

The biggest problem in escapes, though, isn't finding out what they are. We all have a pretty good idea of that. The problem is rebuilding our lives so we don't need escapes so much. We won't really put an escape down until we've got something better to take its place. That's what this whole book is about, and all my other books: seeing our basic problems and doing something about them. As we do that, the need for the escapes and the escapes just drop away.

Ashley Montagu is working on a book called "How to Grow Younger." He says one clue to growing younger is to get rid of our adultish ways. But the answer is not *acting* younger. There's no value in youth as such, just as there is no value in age by itself. In fact, I wouldn't go back and live my time from ages ten to twenty or from ages twenty to thirty or from ages thirty to forty; I wouldn't go back and live those over again for all the tea in China, or even forty to fifty. I'm happy with this year I'm now living.

So the point isn't youthfulness as such. The point is staying young in the sense of maintaining a non-adultish stance. An adultish stance is the part of us

old people where all we do is complain about Carter
and our taxes. Both of them are myths; they're fictions.
They are ridiculous things to waste a lot of time on.
We can vote as wisely as we can on election days, but
in between times we had better get on with living.

Montagu says there are four things a person has to
learn to do. One is they need to learn the ability to
love. We've already talked about that. A lot of the
writings on deprivation mentioned earlier comes from
his research. He put that stuff together, in a way that
was just overwhelming, in the article called "A Scientist Looks at Love."* He made his point on our need
for love so strongly that it was amazing to me that
anybody could ever read that and then go on their
merry way without being affected. So a person needs
to learn the ability to love; they need to learn the
ability to play. Montagu spends time doing a Russian
dance routine he loves, and he does ballroom dancing.
He's got a face that just radiates life, and he's seventy-
some years old. He says we need to learn the ability to
work. And then last, and most important, he says we
need to learn the ability to think critically. What I
think that is, is the honesty about one's self that I see
in most growth groups.

In my growth group, I see myself and other people
learning to be a little more honest about our own
behavior and quit kidding ourselves so much and quit
asking other people to do our work for us and solve
our problems for us. Like one lady said, "I came into
this group for the first time, laid out my spiel about
what a mess I was and sat back waiting for all of you
to fix me up. What did you do? You just listened to
me, told me you were glad I was there and then went
on to the next person." That's perfect, because after
five years of that, it dawns on each of us, "Hey, number one is going to have to fix up number one by
getting some help from the higher power."

* Phi Delta Kappan, May 1970, p. 463.

I don't mean that we are self-sufficient. I cannot live by myself alone. I can live six days without water, six weeks without food, but I can't really live a day without love. So I can't live by myself alone. I can live only through the cooperation of some other human beings, the ones who have a special fit with me. But, like I say, I'm the one who has to see what my needs are. I'm the one who has to reach out to get them met. I'm the one who has to pick the people I reach out to so my needs get met, instead of sitting back like a little baby crying, "Why doesn't somebody do something for me?"

So that's it for escapes. Like I say, we've got a country full of escapes. I'd just as soon get as far away from escapes as I possibly can, because I've had my belly full of them. I've studied these two old communities where people live so long, like the one where Erazo lived. Two books have been written on them, *Los Viejos,* by Grace Halsell, on Vilcabamba, Peru, and *How to Live to Be a Hundred,* by Sula Benet, about the community in the mountains in southern Russia.

What's so interesting about that community in Russia is that the people there have a tradition of social eating which is just fantastically well developed. In fact, one of the things they teach their children, right from their early years, is that you must be able to eat seven suppers. Yet the people there aren't fat. What they do is they eat just a little bit and they eat very slowly as part of the ceremony of meeting together. The big thing is their feasting, which occurs when two or more come together. Anytime this happens, one of the group takes charge and they are called the toastmaster. Children are trained from the time they are eight or ten that if company should come to the house in the absence of both of the parents, one of the children should be the toastmaster so somebody in the house can receive the person or people coming, be the toastmaster, sit down, present the food, and talk with the company. That is night-and-day different from anything we commonly experience in this country. And yet those people live to be a 100, 110, and 120.

Overeating in that society is one of the worst sins there is. As I recall, there is no obesity, or almost none. An obese person is scorned the way we would scorn someone who is sexually promiscuous—or worse. So there is this tremendous emphasis on the social side of life. Work fits in its proper place as one of Montagu's four things we need to do but it is in balance, in harmony with the rest of life, rather than, as for us, an escape. In fact, the interesting thing about these two societies is that there are no escapes of any consequence that I can see in the societies. The people in the society don't need much in the way of escapes.

Because there is so little escaping, there aren't the results of the escaping, which is the destruction of the body, and worse yet, the destruction of the emotional life. The thing we suffer from so in this country is the big head, the smart head, this great big head and this little, stick-figure body. The head will tell the body what the body needs and the head will order the body around. The head will tell the body and the body has no vote in the matter, no opportunity to communicate with the head at all. The head will say, "I'll keep the body in strong, muscular shape." But the head will not give the body what the body truly needs, because the head doesn't like love.

It's like one of the cards at the seminar said, "How can I love somebody when they might be taken from me?" That's the head talking. We should love who we have, while we have them. Then love somebody else. But the head's not going to give the body what it needs. So we need to find a way to let the body have its say and also the heart and the soul, so we can change from this big distorted head into what we really are, which is a little head and a big body and soul and all in harmony. Then the head is truly clear and truly able to meet and serve its own needs. The most basic of those needs is wholeness, real emotional closeness with others. We'll talk about that next.

CHAPTER 5

Learning to Love— Friendly Love

A good example of how friendly love is related to sex came to me from Father Richard Rohr. He's a great priest. He's got a commune in Cincinnati, Ohio, and he's got a set of tapes called "The Spiritual Family and the Natural Family." You get them from the St. Anthony Messenger Press, in Cincinnati.* He tells about the young people in their commune. What they do is they live in families of six to eight people. He said he didn't learn anything about religion until he went to live with six people. He was a fantastic preacher of the Old Testament. He knew Bible up one side and down the other. He has an eight-tape set on the Old Testament that's so good, he sold thousands of sets at about sixty dollars a throw. Fantastic preacher. But he gave up that kind of preaching to big crowds and went and lived with six people. He found he had a lot of trouble, because the people he lived with kept arguing with him. They couldn't get along with him. He was mad at them and they were mad at him. All his lovely ideas like just exactly what the meaning of Job is, all those lovely ideas, just went down the drain. He couldn't make them work in his daily life. So then he began to get to work finding out how those ideas he had preached on so eloquently could work for him in his daily life with six other people.

One thing he found was the young folks would come in the commune just boiling with sexual desires. Then, for the first time, the people around the young folks were really loving them in a celibate way, hugging

* St Anthony Messenger Press, 1615 Republic Street, Cincinnati, Ohio.

them and showing affection and really listening to them and talking to them. Their sexual urges went way down. They didn't go away, but they went way down. So he saw how much friendly love or celibate love had to do with putting out the sexual fires. He saw that loving celibately was a tremendously powerful thing to get rid of some of the driving power that our sexual deprivation gives sex over us. So young people and old people, too, were coming to the commune and finding that warm, powerful celibate love was taking away their obsession with sex.

It's a beautiful example of what I'm talking about here, how celibate love or friends can moderate this terrible desire we have for sex and get sex in its proper proportion and then it can be like the drums in a true symphony, where all the instruments are in their ideal relationship. Then we're free people.

A young woman who came into Alcoholics Anonymous told me a chilling story. She and her gal friends would barhop a lot on weekends looking for guys for free drinks and sex. One Saturday night, one of the gals in the group said, "Hey, tonight let's get some married men." Someone else said, "No. They're too easy." What a sad comment on the shape most marriages are in, when all a gal needs to do to get a married man is snap her fingers and she's caught him. That's a sad, but good, example of how we have so little control over sex at first that we had best start learning friendly love with members of our own sex.

The whole point of this chapter is that what we really need is wholeness, closeness with another person or other people. It's like the story I told in the last chapter on how I felt so whole right in my first few days of the School of Life. Because of feeling so whole, my urge to eat went away and my whole body relaxed.

We need to experience, in our own lives, this feeling of wholeness. As it is, sex has such a strong hold on us, we can't believe there is anything else in life. We can't believe our needs for sex aren't the problem. But as the commune story shows, what we need isn't sex but wholeness. Also, if sex was the only need, what would there be in life for all the physically handicapped people, the seemingly homely people nobody wants, the old single people. But it's not that kind of world, where there's no answer for anybody but people living in a sexual relationship.

Our deprivation has also so exaggerated our need for separateness that only sex has enough force to temporarily smash down our being alone. But as soon as the sexual fire is out, we're right back being alone. We need to see that we're looking at the world through the wrong end of the telescope. Sex isn't the only thing, it isn't the biggest thing—wholeness is. We can get wholeness into our lives if we will only put down our separateness long enough to let the love of a few people into our lives—and keep sex out of it until we can get a better perspective on the part sex should really play in our lives.

We need to create a set of experiences for ourselves like in that commune down in Cincinnati, where we are loved and held and listened to for our souls, not our sex. When we feel a part of life, we see we are valued for what we are, rather than for something we do, like sex. Then we see that sex isn't the root of relationship, it's just one of the flowers. And there are other flowers of relationship for the people for whom sex won't be a part of their lives, for it isn't just priests who are celibate. There are a fair number of people in our society who won't, in their lifetime, have a continuing sexual relationship. For them there is some other blossom than sexual intercourse.

It is a mark of our deprivation that we have so much trouble understanding that. I'm asked, "How can people live without sex?" What I want to say to them is, "If sex is so great, where are all the happy people?"

We're caught in a vicious circle. Only sex is strong enough to bring us close to one another. But sex, used for all-purpose closeness, loses even that power. Then we're in worse shape than before, because now we've got nothing to bring us closer to one another and we've blunted the tool of sexual expression we might need later on.

Hard as it is, there is no answer but opening our hearts to the people around us. Much as we hate it and fear it, we need to reach out, go join the brother or sister and find the wholeness we need through friendly love.

There is a lot of criticism today of both the older generation and the younger generation for their selfishness and narcissism. There's no question, to me, but that there's a lot of self-preoccupation. The question I have is about the reasons for it. A common argument of the Freudian analysts is that we parents have relinquished our roles and the younger generation has refused to be involved and responsible. It's too complicated a discussion to get deeply into at this point except for one aspect of it. I see all our generations—the youth, the parents, and the grandparents—as having a pretty clear sense, deep down, of what they would like to do and want to do. I don't think the problem is that any of us have chosen to run away from our problems. I believe we are temporarily incapacitated and can't live the way we see we would like to. For generations, babies have raised babies who grow up as babies to raise babies. The knowledge that each of us has of our shortcomings and deficiencies compared to our own ideals is very hard for us.

I just can't conceive that any but a few of us might be so pathologically sick that we make our self-destructive choices without any pangs of remorse and sadness. I feel that the opposite is the case. The deficiencies in living that I and my friends show come from the same awkwardness and ineffectualness in social relationships that the monkeys showed who were locked up in the cages. It's the same awkwardness and ineffectualness that the kids raised in emotionally impoverished homes show. I see in myself and so many around me large parts of the "affectionateless character" Bowlby talked of earlier. So that's where I think our problem came from.

It's like two auto mechanics in a garage. Both are doing poor work and are about to be fired if they don't do better work. One man is highly trained and clearly shows he has all the skills but isn't using them. The other man, it turns out, bluffed his way into the job and hasn't really learned all the skills he needs. You can see that the manager of the garage needs to take two different approaches to the two men. One needs to be jacked up and told to do his job or get out. The other needs to be told to solve his ignorance and learn to do what he hasn't yet learned.

To me, this is the problem. I don't think it's like some of the Freudians say, where we know how to do the job, we're just choosing not to do it. I think we haven't learned to do some of the most crucial things we need to do.

That's why I'm stressing learning to love on a friendly basis first. Then we can't use the intimacy sex temporarily gives us to kid ourselves into thinking we did something on our own. We didn't. Sex did it for us, temporarily. As we learn to love people of our own sex, and as we learn to love people of the opposite sex without sex, we really learn what intimacy is. Then, ideally, after we have made a good bunch of friends of our sex and the opposite sex, we just marry the best friend we have of the opposite sex.

For the baby in us that still demands instant gratification, that process sounds like a long, slow one. It is. But I haven't seen any quick way out of our problem. We can see the answer quickly, but it takes years and years to learn to love when you are as awkward and ineffectual at it as I was (and still am, to a degree). Maybe you're in better shape. I sure hope so. I see a lot of people in Bozeman who seem not to have all the problems at loving that I do. I'm happy for them. I'd like to be able to do those things they do, seemingly effortlessly. But learning to love, for me, has been a slow process. Sure, I know that the essence of my being is love. But my struggle has been, with the help of my higher power, to get that love into action.

It's like the chrysanthemum bud, and love is the sunshine. Sex isn't the sunshine; love is the sunshine. To me, whether non-sexual or sexual, love is the sunshine. And how do you open the chrysanthemum bud? Only love will open that bud, only the sunshine will open it. And that's what we are. We're like the chrysanthemum bud and we don't know really what we are like inside. Not until we get the sun of love into our chrysanthemum bud and it starts to open up, do we start to see what we are.

I told the people in Seattle, "What you see here is not what I am. What you see is me partway towards what I am. Just like the chrysanthemum bud is half opened or a little bit opened up, just a little touch of yellow is all you see. But it's on its way to opening up and becoming a flower. That's what love does in our lives."

While I'm talking about friendly relationships as being different from sexual relationships, all relationships really are sexual, because I am sex, we are sex. When I was relating with Hal in Seattle we were two men relating, we were two sexual things relating.

My genital nerve endings are a big part of my total nerve endings. There is no way you and I can move without being aware of our sex side. There's just no way, because our clothes rub against us and the different parts of the body are hinged in the pelvic area. As our legs move, the bones and muscles move in the pelvic area. We can't move without being sexual. And that's part of the problem. Because all relationships are sexual, we're constantly being confronted by this. To the degree we've got the sex part handled, to that degree can our relationship be a truly good and balanced relationship.

Handling these powerful feelings makes it terribly hard to handle intimate relationship with people of the opposite sex. That's so true that in our culture today the word intimate or intimacy primarily means having sex with someone, rather than emotional closeness. In my experience, this is why we need quite a bit of celibate loving, especially with members of the same sex, before we do very well with members of the opposite sex. All these powerful sexual feelings really come alive when there's a member of the opposite sex involved. Then, like I say, one real big tendency is for us to jump right into intercourse as a detour to try to cut off the developing emotional intimacy. What a sad thing, to use sex to cut off intimacy!

Some of my young college students were able to see this. In fact, they first brought it to my attention. In one of the first classes I taught, a young gal told me, "Neither my boyfriend nor I were virgins when we started going together, so we started having sex almost right from the start, but there were a couple of big things that divided us. We were using sex to avoid getting into those things. Now that I've been in your class, I can see that. So I kicked him out of bed. He feels kind of rejected, because he doesn't have the class, but we're working on what's really dividing us."

Okay. That's a nineteen-year-old girl talking. She's a lot wiser than many ninety-year-old girls. But it doesn't matter when we come to this knowledge. The important thing is that we come to it. It doesn't matter, when we get there, whether we're nineteen or ninety.

I'm loving the easy ones, because I'm on a life-and-death mission. I'm loving the easiest ones I can find. To me, that business of loving the hard ones, that's the world's sickest game. That way we automatically know we're going to get rejected and nothing's going to work. We're not going to get any love into our life, and therefore we won't be faced with seeing ourselves clearly. If there are no loving relationships in our lives, we can keep on wandering around in this morass of confusion and not see ourselves clearly.

The reason people avoid close relationships so desperately is because they will see themselves as they really are. I've seen the same thing in hunting camps. Here's a hunting camp and all these hunters are great rifle shots. They were born great lovers and fantastic shots with a rifle, especially from the back of a running horse. As for myself, being a practical sort and not a very good rifle shot, I'm always playing it safe and checking my rifle and zeroing it in and then checking to see that it didn't get knocked out of zero. So I'm inclined every once in a while to paste up a target and go back a hundred paces and get me the best rest I can and see what I can do to hit the target. From a rest, I can put my shots in a two-inch circle. But what I've always been struck by is, when I do that, there are a lot of guys who don't want to join me. Those big talkers a lot of times won't shoot their guns when somebody else is watching. There's too big a gap between their big talk and what might be their performance. They're very unsure and feel inadequate.

So they won't lay their rifle up against a tree and touch off two or three shots to see what kind of a circle they can shoot. "Aw, she's just fine." Then, the next day, they miss. I don't mean I don't miss; I miss plenty too. But they keep missing, typically. Some hunting guides have a rule that guns have to be checked to be sure they are zeroed in. In some cases the hunters are so reluctant to face their own shooting, the guide has to check the zero of the gun.

Why is this? It's very simple. They don't want to know the exact state of their rifle markmanship. Now, I know the exact state of my rifle marksmanship. At a hundred yards, when I'm shooting without a rest, I've got trouble keeping my shots in a two-foot circle with the big rifle I shoot. Consequently, I don't shoot at anything offhand if I can possibly avoid it. I'll sit down, lay down, kneel down, get a brace on a tree or use a stick. I'll use every help I can get. But this guy doesn't know he shoots such a big circle standing up, because he's never had the guts to find out about himself.

Same thing with our personal relationships. I know what I look like in a relationship. When I'm in a relationship with a guy, I'm a real prima donna. I'm constantly thinking, "Hey, is this guy doing enough for me?" I'm constantly second-guessing. I see all kinds of terrible thoughts running through my mind that are nothing like the thoughts a perfect person would think. But, despite all the trouble I have with myself in the relationship, it still beats the alternative which is not being in the relationship.

When I'm in a relationship with a gal, I see that I'm a sex-crazed maniac, and I don't like to see that, either. So you've got two choices: you can hang in there and see the truth about yourself or you can cut and run and not ever have to face the truth about yourself. See the advantage of not having friends? See the advantage of rejection? It cannot only confirm your vague, general bad impression of yourself, but it can keep you from ever seeing your real weaknesses and your real strengths, just exactly like the guy who won't shoot his rifle in front of other people. He won't even shoot it by himself. You go away and leave the target and say, "Oh, I won't watch." And he still won't shoot, because he doesn't want to see. He can't bear to see that his myths about how great he is aren't true. On the other hand, he's afraid his sense of inadequacy is so right, because he's felt it being confirmed so many times. He's fighting this phony war all inside himself, where he can't get any real help. It's self-perpetuating. This is why it takes such a desperate crisis to drive us out of that pattern. As we go deeper into loving relationships, we see deeper into ourselves and it's a continuing cycle.

Another way to be spared this self-knowledge is to have our relationships nice and shallow. Even if we have some relationships, we'll keep them shallow, we'll bounce around from one person to another. Before my heart attack, you could have asked someone around me if I had many friends. They would have told you, "Why, he's got lots of friends." I had a hundred friends to avoid having any. "I'll take you off the shelf and we'll go to a hockey game and I'll come back a year later and we'll go to another hockey game." "You and I will go fishing together and I'll see you next fishing season." What a beautiful way to protect myself. "Jess? Oh, he's a guy with a hundred friends." That's a tough thing to have said about you.

I don't claim a hundred friends now. I claim five. And I'm not doing that great a job with two or three of those. Now, sure, in a sense my two students in Seattle from the School of Life, Bob and Archie, were friends of mine, but I don't use that word friend as carelessly any more as I used to. In the friendship sense that I'm talking about, I have five. And I mean that. I'm not kidding. Because my life depends on it. I'm not going to screw around lying about it to myself or anybody else.

I infuriated one guy. He came out to see us from the old days. He believes in instant friendship. He even makes friends on an elevator. I told him I couldn't be his friend that way. He said, "Well, you have to be!" I said, "No, I don't have to be." I forget just why I was so mean about it with him, but I just didn't feel like pussyfooting around with him. I just wouldn't give in

to his idea that I was going to be his friend in the way
he wanted to be my friend, so he quit being my friend
in his way. I was sorry there was a misunderstanding,
because he felt rejected and went off in a huff. I would
handle that differently today, but that's how I handled it then. Today I wouldn't even try to talk about
something that wasn't appropriate for the two of us to
be talking about.

"When to love the porcupine?" I think I've answered
that question. Porcupines are professional unloved ones.
They're good at it. I think the people who want to be
unloved in this world should stay unloved. And stay
unloved and stay unloved. Let the pain get worse and
worse and worse. Finally, when it gets super bad and
they're sick of the results they're getting, then they're
going to give up being unloved. I'm not going to inter-
fere in the beautiful order in the universe and go
around attempting to love the unloved. People argue
with me on that and say the people escaping into the
game of being unloved don't want to be unloved. I
think people who think that don't realize how hard it
is to keep pushing love away.

Like I said, I'm on top of Everest and I've got two
hours to get off the place. I haven't got time to screw
around going over and having a little conversation
with somebody who feels unloved so I can make them
feel loved. Better men than me have tried that and
failed. This whole universe is love. To manage to feel
unloved in the midst of that love takes a real professional.

But they say to me, "You should do this." Sorry. I've
got a wife and children down at the bottom of Everest
and it's important to me that I get off the mountain.
But they say, "What about me?" I say, "Come on
along." "I don't want to do it," they say, "I can't!"
What they mean is "I won't! I won't." Self-will run
riot. And a dumb Norwegian like me is supposed to
save someone from something like that when God

Himself won't step in and change that person's life until the person will surrender and ask for the help of the higher power and invite God in? When God won't break down their door and enter their house uninvited, why should I presume to, or even worse, see myself as powerful enough to do so? No. All I do in those encounters is act out another chapter in their little game of "rescue me." Then, when I fail, as I must, they just smile inside and say to themselves, "See? He's not so hot. I knew he couldn't rescue me."

At this point, I'm sure you're questioning, "What can loving five guys have to do with sex?" That's a fair question. I think loving five guys and being in harmony with most of the people around me during each day has a lot to do with sex for two reasons:

One reason I've just discussed at length and that is because in the security of a celibate loving relationship we can see ourselves so well as we really are. The second reason is the world of celibate loving is the world we move in all day long. When I have been in good or loving relationships all day, it's a different kind of person who comes home to loving than before, when there was no love in my life during the day. What came home then was a battered hulk who had been hiding from love all day and creating my own rejection.

Most of us start loving sexually before we really start loving in a friendly way. Most all of us, especially as younger people, are so removed from each other that it takes the tremendous power of sex to crash through our walls and make us finally open up. These are the high school romances and the college romances. We go into one romance and it's so deep and breaks up and we go into the other romance and it's super deep and it breaks up and then we go into the next. Typically, most of the younger people I knew when I was growing up and the young people I know now are not good at having friends. When I talk about my five friends to my college classes, it kind of goes over their heads. Most of them don't know what I'm talking about. It's only to adults that I can talk about five friends, people over twenty-three to twenty-five. You usually have to be at least that old before five friends makes any sense. Some of the younger people think it does but, typically, they move away from their so-called close friends and most of them never write to their friends or hear from them again, except in the most casual kind of way. Well, to me, that's good evidence that there wasn't truly the kind of deep friendship that I'm talking about.

So, for most of us, if we could have learned to love celibately without sex before we loved with sex, it would have been a much better deal. Then we could have picked a sex partner who was a friend, rather than picking a friend from among our sex partners. We could have had a bunch of friends of the same sex. I could have had my five guy friends where we really loved each other a great deal. I've got a ring on my little pinky finger that Bob Hickman made for me. He's a dentist, so he cast that out of gold from people's teeth, including my own. It's a beautiful thing. The design of it has a lot of little holes in it. Each of those holes stands for a hole in my personality. The holes go on around the ring in an endless procession of holes. My personality is somewhat like a Swiss cheese, full of holes. In fact, if you took the holes away, I used to have the feeling, there wouldn't be hardly anything left. So the ring is very symbolic and shows that Bob Hickman and I are friends. And then there's Gerry Sullivan. Those are the two I see the most. And then there are Jim and Dave and Kenny and some of the others.

Ideally, in the days of my growing up I would have had such deep and close friends as these. And then, partly from that experience, I would be able to finally have a few women as friends and be able to be close to them. I would need to learn friendship from men, because even in this hypothetical and ideal world the sex deprivation in me is so powerful that it makes a tendency that any time there is an intimacy and a closeness developing between me and a woman that I would want to jump in the sack with her, which is a lovely way to shut off the developing closeness and intimacy. It takes quite a while before you can handle your deprivation well enough so that you don't jump in the sack with someone to cut off your intimacy. Or so that you don't want to so badly that it's just about as much a distraction as jumping in the sack with somebody because your mind is just obsessed with the desire that you want to.

But then, after I had had a number of women friends and found that I could establish close female friendships, I would then find one of those close female friendships, that I would then like to take into the sexual area, because this person and I were such fantastic friends, we had so many things in common, we had such a deep feeling for each other and we had such a shared vision. We also had what only an across-the-sex relationship can give us, which is some extra vitality and warmth because we're opposite sexes and the oppositeness of us adds a dimension and flavor to the relationship that a same-sex relationship doesn't have. The oppositeness of us adds something very important.

Only then would we say to each other, "Hey, let's add a third dimension to our friendship, which is the sexual expression, and go the deepest way we can possibly go into friendship."

Now, that's an ideal scenario, and while I know it's happened a few times, I've never seen it happen. But it's a nice little illustration to show you what might be.

Oddly enough and fortunately enough, there is another pretty good system operating here, and a lot of people got lucky and some people got luckier than they knew. I started going with Jackie when I was twenty-one and she was eighteen. We got married a year and a half later. I did all of the right things for the wrong reasons. I got real lucky. I see a lot of other people who got real lucky. I was doing the process backwards, completely backwards. But I did get lucky enough, and as I see, there is a kind of miraculous business of selection of the mate where there is a tremendous rightness. We don't realize how many hundreds and almost thousands of people we screen out before we pick the one person for us.

I was in a high school where there were over four hundred kids in just the senior class alone, so that's two hundred gals, and there were the two other classes, one a half year ahead and one a half-year behind. So I looked them all over and decided which of those I would like to date. At college I maybe knew two or three hundred gals well enough to say hello to and thought about which of those I was attracted to or was attracted to me. On the ski train where I met Jackie there were three or four hundred gals. We went into this dance hall, this friend of mine and I, that night. I picked Jackie's friend to dance with and he picked Jackie. By the next day we had things straightened out. So there was a tremendous selection process.

Then, you date a gal once or twice and you say, "Hey, she's not for me." Of the maybe thirty, forty, fifty gals that you might have had some contact with, there were five or ten that you went with some, and of those maybe five that you went quite a bit with, and there were maybe two or three that you were serious enough about to think of getting married, and of those you married one. So there is a tremendous screening and it's no surprise that beneath the surface of our hormones screaming and our emphasis on external beauty and background and the kind of house they live in, there's that still little part of us that can recognize mutuality. That little part of us has its way much more than we realize.

This is the point that I made earlier where I see a lot of young people who aren't able to hold a marriage together, where, as near as I can see, those two people have great reasons to stay together. They are tremendously well suited to each other. But they don't seem to have the resources they need to call on to hold that marriage together.

But most of us, hopefully, made the right choice if even for the wrong reasons. Then we're kind of working at this business of celibate love backwards from this ideal sequence I mentioned to you.

In my case, in my forties and my fifties I learned celibate love. Now, I'm not going to tell Gerry Sullivan I love him. It would bother Gerry. But I do love him and he loves me. Now, he isn't going to tell me he loves me, either, because he couldn't say something like that. And it's good that he can't. That's beautiful. A lot of us confuse talk with the real thing. People run around saying, "I love you, I love you." What's that worth? I'll tell you. That and ten dollars will get you into the basketball game. It isn't worth anything. "But," they say, "I'm loving you so." And I say, "I'm sorry, but I can't tell that."

I've had people who loved me and I could always tell when they did, because I could feel something. But those other people are satisfied with their cotton-candy idea of, "Oh, what a lover I am!" Until they face the truth of themselves, they couldn't love their way out of a paper bag. They've just got a beautiful system of self-deceit operating. But that's fine. They tell me they love me and that's great. When I'm with somebody I love, it's like I'm in a warm room with a stove and I can cuddle up to it on a cold day. That's the kind of love that does something for me.

So I think we need to learn that, despite the fact most of us are having sex in our lives, we still need to learn to love without sex before sex can find its best place in our lives. So a big place to work at improving sexual love is non-sexual love, friendly love.

The biggest thing, and we've got into it already, is only we can meet our needs. Only *we* can meet our needs. If there is anything that would be lovely, it would be if people would recognize that they're the ones who are going to have to meet their own needs instead of asking other people to guess at their needs and meet them for them.

We get in these little guessing games: "Guess what I need and then give it to me. Oh, no, you're wrong, I didn't need that. Oh, no, you're wrong again, I didn't need that. Keep on guessing, because if I really mean anything to you, you'll guess what I need and then you'll give it to me."

Instead, there's an opposite and very lovely system. My students in Seattle saw demonstrations of it in the touching we did. They saw people who needed me come forward to meet their needs. Like lovely Katherine (who I put on a touching demonstration with at the beginning of the second day); she was touchingly honest about herself. I said some things to her that would blow a battleship out of the water. But instead of hauling off and hitting me in the face, she said, "Hey, Jess, you're right, and I love you for it."

This meeting our own needs is something we really have to learn, we have to get ahold of. It's like I said, we're in the same desperate situation as if we were trapped on top of Mount Everest and a sudden terrible snowstorm came up. We haven't got a week to get off Everest. We're going to get off in the next few hours or we're going to die. We can't rush, because if we rush we screw up. You all know what happens when you rush, right? If you hurry, you're all thumbs and everything goes wrong. So even though we're in a desperate emergency, we need to see that there's enough time. We'll use the time we've got to the best advantage, and we won't rush. We know there's only an hour or two, but the first few minutes we'll just sit down quietly and say, "Hey, what should we do?" We won't rush off saying, "We've got to do something quick." We don't have to do something quick. No, we don't have to do something quick.

The first thing we've got to do is sit down and consider as many alternatives as we've got. We'll say, "Let's just take five minutes and see what our alternatives are." And we'll take every alternative that we can think of in those five minutes and we'll say, "Which of those alternatives sounds best?" And we agree that alternative six sounds best. "Everybody agree to that?" "Okay, we'll take alternative six." And then we'll take our time putting alternative six into operation.

One thing I've taught my sons is to do this in the mountains in an emergency. Everybody says nature is so beautiful and lovely. But Mother Nature is also a killer. She'll just wipe you out like swatting flies. Not out of vindictiveness, but when you violate one of Mother Nature's laws she stamps on you just like a foot stamping on a bug. So I've taught my kids that when we're in an emergency in the mountains you make good use of whatever little time you've got. One of the first things you do is to be as calm as you can and figure out what's the best way to get out of this pickle, the quickest and surest way to get out, rather than just starting to do something. I've seen that that's occasionally made a difference.

To me, this is the case in our lives. Of course, I've had such an advantage on you in that respect, because I was nearly killed three times, and it helps me know that I'm not going to live forever. You guys have the misfortune, most of you, of thinking you're going to live forever. You think you've got an endless amount of time, and that's too bad. It's like the immortal saying of Dustin Hoffman in *Little Big Man:* "When you should have died and didn't, you ain't ever the

same." Two or three times, I should have died and
didn't, and I ain't ever been the same.

I saw an airline stewardess in the lobby one of the
mornings in Seattle. She looked so drug out. I said,
"Hey, it looks pretty tough, hun?" "Sure does," she
said. "Well, just remember, this is one of those days
you looked forward to when you became an airline
stewardess." "But that was so long ago," she said.
This is one of those days that, in 1970, when they told
me, "You've got cancer and you've only got three weeks
to live, and you'll never make it back to Montana,"
this is one of those days that I wish I had then. It
turned out they were wrong and I didn't have cancer
and the tumor went away and I did go back to Montana. When I came home, I sat there in my living
room with the tears running down my face in grati-
tude and joy. Okay, if this is one of those days I was
wanting so bad, why don't I act like it? Why don't I do
something with it instead of goofing it away?

We need to see that we need. As my friend from
Germany, Walther Lechler, says, "I exist, I need (because we exist we need), I am entitled." If each of us
could see that we exist, we need, we are entitled, it
would do so much to make us better lovers—of life, of
the people around us and of our friends. But we have
so much trouble admitting to our needs and seeing
that we are entitled to having our needs met. We
wouldn't starve a dog. Yet each of us is usually starv-
ing ourselves in vital areas of our own lives.

When we talk about being entitled to have our
needs met, most of us think that there is a limited
amount of what is needed to meet our needs. We think
we can't have all our needs met, because then someone else would have to go without. When we are so
mixed up about our needs being met, I see that we're
usually making one or more of these three mistakes
in our attitudes: First, we think we aren't really worthy, we aren't entitled to have all our needs met

unless we do things to deserve it. We see we can't do those things, so we don't deserve to get our needs met. Second, we don't see that most of our real needs aren't material, they are non-material or spiritual, because they are things like happiness, contentment, peace, health, etc. We think of our needs as being mostly material, like money, houses, cars, etc. We don't see that when those material needs are met, we would still need to have the non-material needs met, because we realize lots of millionaires and famous people are miserable too. On the other hand, when the non-material needs are met, the real needs we have for material things are very easily met. Third, we think that the things it takes to meet our needs are all limited, like things in the material world. We think, if our needs are met, someone else has to go without.

There is only a limited amount of gold; if someone has it all, then there's none for anyone else. But the non-material, emotional and spiritual needs work from different laws. The more happiness I get, the more you have. The more contentment and peace you have, the more I have. So, for our most basic needs, not only is the supply not limited, the more you get your needs met, the more the supply in that area is increased, rather than diminished.

Here's an example of how differently things work on the nonmaterial or spiritual plane, compared to the material plane: Take the spiritual ownership of land. A number of years ago, I was sitting down in the Grand Tetons. I had walked back off the highway two or three miles trout fishing, and I was sitting up on this hill. It's a place I had fished quite a bit in the years we had gone to the Grand Tetons. I realized that while the taxpayers owned the land (or maybe this happened to be a spot of private land), that I was the spiritual owner of that land, because I was the one who was using that land and respecting it and paying attention to it and being careful with it, like the

Indians. In the spring of one of their final years as
free people, back in the 1870s, the Indians were having so much trouble with the white man they thought
maybe what was wrong was that they had offended
Mother Earth, so that spring they took off their moc-
casins and walked barefoot on the ground, because
they thought even the footprint of the moccasin might
have been an offense. That was their respect for the
ground. Down in the Tetons, I was respecting the
ground too, not quite that well, but I was respecting it
nevertheless. So I was the spiritual owner of that
land.

The fact I was the spiritual owner of that land
didn't mean that everybody else in the whole world
couldn't simultaneously be the spiritual owner of that
land. In this spiritual world there is no limit. The
opposite is true. The more peace, contentment or joy I
have, for example, the more you have. In the spiritual
world, the more you have, the more I have.

That is on the spiritual plane, and it is important,
because when we know that in the spiritual area
there is an unlimited supply, then we see that the
more I have does not in any way diminish what you
have; it increases what you have. So when it comes to
getting the true things we need in life, which is not so
much houses as it is love, tenderness, closeness and
peace, we don't need to be bashful and hang back.
"Oh, I can't take anything for me, because there are
all these other people here to take and there won't be
anything left for them." It's like an endless banquet
table stretching into infinity. Everything we need is
on that banquet table, and all we've got to do is just
walk up and sit down and eat and we don't need to
worry if there is going to be room for everybody,
because there is room for more than everybody. We
don't understand that, because our thinking is so limited and finite. We get the material plane mixed up

with the spiritual, and we don't understand anything about the spiritual plane.

As I told the class in Seattle: "All you need to do, and our Sunday-school teacher here reminds me of it, is if each and every person sitting here in this room was Jesus, think of what all the rest of us would have. You can imagine the feeling in this room. But, you see, the truth of the matter is, putting it in the Christian denominational sense, each one of you are Christ. Each one of you has the essence of everything within you. The only problem comes from what you and I have done to ourselves. We have so obliterated and smoke-screened that essence of us under a conformity of trying to dress and act and think and look like everybody else in the world because we are afraid of what we are, both the majesty of what we are and humanity of what we are, we have so cloaked what we are, that there is not that sense of our divinity.

"Now, there is a great sense of that divinity in this room for me. You people are paying a deep and powerful respect to me and I appreciate that. That does a lot for me. But, if you were able to pay the attention to me that you could pay if each one of you understood in the deepest kind of way how unique and precious and valuable each of you are, there would be a totally different feeling in this room. The walls would practically burst with it."

This issue of having our needs met is so important because it makes the difference between dependency and true friendship. If I come to you with most all my needs met, I'm with you for the sheer joy of being with someone as beautiful as you are. But if I come to you because only you can meet all my needs and save my life, that's a dependency. In those cases, you're meeting a need of mine. But I'm sure you can all see the fundamental difference between the two. That's why dependency is so different from need. When I'm meet-

ing my own needs, one of which may be through being
with you, it's very different from me coming to you
and begging, "Meet all my needs."

So we've got to see what our needs are and meet
them. We've got to see that we are entitled. And
rather than saying, "Oh, I'm not entitled, somebody
else is," we are all entitled. We are all entitled to as
much as we truly need. Now, I don't mean that because I think I want something I should have it. I
might think I need six hundred houses to rent out so
that I can have a million-dollar income so just in case
things get really tough, then I've got at least a
five-hundred-thousand-dollar income so I can live like
I really want to live. That's not what we're talking
about. We're talking about something very different.
We're talking about having an abundance of the things
we really need, and that is an abundance of love, of
affection and friends and along with it adequate, even
abundant, amounts of food and clothing and other
material things.

In my experience, physical poverty, so much of the
time, comes because of spiritual impoverishment.
There's a lot of people who tried to solve other people's
poverty by throwing money at the poverty. But I've
seen that a lot of the people who are poverty-stricken
are fantastically ingenious at continuing and maintaining their poverty status no matter how much money
you throw at them. Why? Because of their discontent,
coming out of their spiritual impoverishment.

We see this in Alcoholics Anonymous so much. Some
guy is the ultimate of poverty-stricken, a guy with
shoes that don't match and clothes out of the bin at
the Salvation Army. One day, he finally surrenders
and walks into an AA meeting. The minute he walks
in there, he is on his way to prosperity. One minute
he was in the jungle, looking for a can to cook up in,
and the next minute he's looking for a place to park
his Cadillac. Now, I don't mean that material prosper-

ity is all that valuable, but once you get content in your heart you almost can't avoid being prosperous. Because when you are content in your heart, you can live on almost any amount of money, because you haven't got that burning desire to own everything in town. Once you get rid of the burning desire to own everything in town and everything in every store window, it doesn't take much money to live, because then all you've got to do is buy food and clothing instead of all this junk.

I've seen this so much in my own life. Once I had made even a small start at surrendering to life and gave up my foolish striving for money and fame, the world started to shower me with a bunch of material blessings. Some of them I hung onto. I spent the money on myself, and my family and I enjoyed it. But I go down the street and there isn't a shop window that's got anything in it I want any more, not because I have everything, but because most of my wants have gone away. It used to be I wanted everything in every shop window on the street.

So we've got to see that we exist, we need, and we are entitled. And we've got to see that only we can know our needs and only we can meet our needs.

Now, I can't convey to you in any way the extent of our deviousness in avoiding recognizing that we should give up trying to manipulate other people to meet our needs instead of us learning to meet our own needs directly. I came to Montana State University to the College of Education. I'm a Skinnerian psychologist, a rat psychologist. I was using some Skinnerian words, and in the psychology field there's a big prejudice, by and large, against Skinnerians like me as low people. This fine humanistic psychologist said to me, "I don't believe in manipulating other human beings." And by implication he was saying, ". . . like you do."

What was he doing? He was manipulating me. How was he manipulating me? By punishing me or using a set of words he found offensive. There is more hidden manipulation like that in the ways we work with other people than you can imagine.

Now, I contend that Skinnerian psychology, in the way that I'm talking of applying it, by and large, not only does not manipulate but frees you from manipulation. I reach out my hand in whatever love and friendliness I can command and say, "I need you." Okay, now Katherine indicated that she needs me back. I say, "Hey, I'm being rewarded. My interests are being served here, Katherine." And she's saying, "Yes, mine are, too." And I reach out and Carl (who I worked with along with Katherine in the touching demonstration the second morning) comes to me and indicates very clearly that, as I'm meeting my needs through him, he's meeting his needs through me. How can there be any manipulation in that? Especially when I say, "Hey, Carl, you're free to stay or leave." We don't need to make a fuss of this, but Carl knows this and I hope Katherine does too. Carl knows that the minute he finds I stop meeting his needs, he will leave me. He'll say, "Hey, Jess, I'm going to split now." And I say, "It was nice being close to you."

You see what I'm saying? There can be no manipulation in that. I believe that love is like the butterfly that lands on the palm of your hand. It comes and lands and you glory in the beauty of the butterfly that had landed on the palm of your hand. Then, when the butterfly leaves, you don't say, "Come back, butterfly," or try to grab the butterfly and hang on, because that's very hard on butterflies. Or think, "if that butterfly leaves, no other will ever come back to me." Instead of doing that, you say to the butterfly, "It was lovely you came."

It's a lack of faith to think you have to hang on to butterflies or that they will never come back. I've never had a butterfly leave my hand that a prettier butterfly didn't come and land there, or at least another butterfly. So I don't get alarmed now when things get taken away from me, because I know that's typically so I can get something better. I'm trying, as much as I can, to completely release everything in my life so that anything can be taken away from me that isn't truly a part of my life, because then it will make room for something that is more truly a part of my life.

It is crucial to our loving that we move towards this openhanded attitude towards life and that we have the understanding of life that it has only the best for us.

Right here we run into another stumbling block. Most of you have a concept of your higher power as one that means the worst for you and dishes out punishment as to a naughty child. Or you have a view of a higher power that when things are going good that's a sure sign you're going to get zapped and lose it all. Then, on the final day, your higher power's big job is to sort out the sheep from the goats and throw you into heaven or hell. I used to have a higher power like that and, I tell you, she was no help to me.

But I now have an understanding of a higher power where she wants only the best for me each day. One who will give me whatever guidance and direction I need to get in harmony with life. That way, there's less need for getting me out of trouble all the time, as more and more now I can see trouble coming and avoid it. It's like the young gal about thirteen I saw at the Minnesota State Fair last fall. Across the front of her T shirt was the message, HERE COMES TROUBLE.

Now, the guidance I get isn't perfect guidance and perfect direction, so I don't always find the best path and avoid trouble. There's a limit on how much I can see. It's like the little light in front of me on the mountain trail in the black of night. I've got enough light to guide me in my path. I don't know where that path is leading, but I have learned that I walk mostly safely when I don't know where I go, which will probably be the idea at the center of the next book I write. I've got enough light to guide me. I don't know anything about where you should go. But I do know where I should go, because I can see this little three-foot circle of light.

Now, I can't see whether I'm in the Olympic Mountain range or the Cascades. And I don't know what's ahead of me and I don't know whether there's a cliff just ahead or not, but I know when I get up close enough, if there's a cliff there, there's going to be a path around it. And I don't need to worry about the fact I can't see very far ahead, although I sometimes want to scream, "What's ahead? What's going to happen tomorrow or next week or next year?" But through it all I've got a three-foot circle of light—for me.

The way I see life now and the way the right people fit together is just like two tennis players who find that each other is the ideal partner. Their games are matched, their time schedules are matched, their personalities are matched, they love to play with each other, everything is ideal. There's no necessity or attempt to please the other person. Their fit just happened, because their personalities were the way they were.

It's just like I said earlier. I used to come off as a kind of Sunday-school-teacher type who was really a great person at helping others and was interested in civic causes. But then I found I was surrounded by a bunch of phony bastards. The kind of people I attracted were people who pretended to be interested in my kind of civic uplift and dedication to excellence. Some of them were being phony and I was being phony. We really were phony bastards. And, of course, I was the worst of the bunch.

Then I realized what I truly was; that's an egotistical, cantankerous son of a bitch. I started to present myself just that way. I didn't attempt to please anybody. But there were a few people in the world who liked an egotistical, cantankerous son of a bitch. They came towards me. And it's no effort for me to maintain our friendship. I'm just being my natural self and they love it. And they're being their natural selves and I love it. So there's no effort in it. It's an absolutely effortless way, you see, because there's no attempt at pleasing them and trying to meet their needs. I'm meeting my needs, which is me being me. And I haven't been close to a phony for a long time.

In fact, as I mentioned to you, I was telling Gerry that I would like to improve my personality and get rid of some of my defects of character and he said, "Jess, go kind of easy. We don't want to lose the Jess we know and love." Now, typically, when we say we want to improve our character to the people we call our friends they say, "Well, it's about time."

You see what a compliment Gerry gives me? But, more crucially, you see how easy that is? How easy it is for me to be me? And how it's the hardest thing in the world for me to pretend to be somebody I'm not? Even worse, it doesn't work. When I pretend to be somebody else, I attract people who are pretending to be somebody else, and that's not who I want to attract. I want to attract people who like what I am.

Also, do you see how little faith and how much egotism there is and how little faith there is in the so-called God that you believe in when you try to pretend to be what you aren't? That's saying, "Hey, when God made me, she didn't follow the right recipe. She didn't know what she was doing." But I know what God was doing. God wanted an egotistical, cantankerous son of a bitch around, so he made me. I'm a perfect example of God's beautiful plan that there be someone like me on this earth. I'm going to pretend nothing. I'm going to be just what I am. The more blazingly I can be me, the better it works out, because then the more honest my advertising is. Before, I was doing dishonest advertising. I was advertising a product as one thing that was really another. Now I'm trying to get my advertising just as honest as it can be, so I can present my product as clearly as possible as it is, because my life depends on it. I need to present myself precisely as the higher power made me and as I exist at this moment on the way to more of a perfection. The higher power wants us to be able to progress towards perfection. As I present myself at this moment moving towards perfection, the more I attract into my life the people I need, those who like me as I now am.

Many of you have all these goodies for me about how I'm supposed to save other people. I keep having to tell you, I'm sorry, but I'm not good at that business. Like the guy in Richard Bach's story "Illusions" says, I resign from the Messiah business. I didn't like it. In "Illusions," the guy's life got cluttered up with a whole bunch of people bothering him while he was trying to do his mechanic's work. So the guy just says, "I quit." And they said back to him, "You can't quit being a Messiah," and he says, "Yes, I can, too. I quit." And he went back to being a mechanic.

Okay, that's beautiful. I refuse to be a Messiah. I didn't go to Seattle to save the unwashed people. I went so I could write a book. I was frying my own fish. Now, some thought I came to save them. I wasn't able or wanting to do that. If their getting saved depends on me, they are lost. If you're looking for a Messiah, you'd better go down the street and find one, because you aren't going to find him in me.

The only good I'm going to do for anyone is for those of you who freely, on your own volition, decide there's some part of my personality that you can relate to and freely choose to need me back.

When there is that free choice, look at the freedom there is for both parties. The minute you don't like anything about me, fine, I didn't promise you any-thing. "But," you say, "I don't like what you're doing."

I say, "That's tough. That's beautiful. Go find yourself a better deal. Wonderful." And if they say, "If you keep acting like that, you aren't going to have any friends," the answer is, "No, that's not true. I'm going to have a few friends and I don't need a lot. In fact, I can't handle a lot." They say, "Well, you're sure a slippery, ornery old so-and-so, aren't you?" And the answer is, "Yes. Yes, I've learned. I've had some hide barked off me by people setting their hooks in me and I didn't like that." I got sucked into those sick games because I needed sick games. I can't really call it sucked in, because when I needed something how can I call it getting sucked in? I went and found them.

But, by and large, I've stopped needing to find sick games. Why? A big reason is because I've got some celibate friendship. I used to be sitting in those university classes and somebody would be hassling me pretty bad and I'd actually say to myself, "I'm really hurting here. These students are climbing my frame with spurs on." And, of course, I'd see that I'd caused the trouble. But they were helping cause it some more. But then I'd say, "Hey, Jess, if Gerry loves you and Vince loves you and if that really means something to you, the fact that these people are giving you a bad time should not bother you that much. If it does, it's a matter of your trying to please everybody, and that's no respect to people you claim you love. So Vince and Gerry love me. The fact that this person doesn't love me shouldn't shake me up."

You see, if it does, I'm saying that Gerry and Vince's love doesn't mean anything. Their love is inconsequential. This kid who hasn't known me more than a few hours, what he feels of me counts more in my mind than Gerry's feelings do. See how stupid that is? Yet I was trying to be just instant plastic, trying to make myself into any old groovy form so they would like me. That's a little bit egotistical, a little bit self-centered, a little bit controlling. I'm deciding how that person should feel. "You shouldn't be angry at me. Just because I'm obnoxious and narrow-minded and angry, you shouldn't be angry back." The hell they shouldn't. If they've got any sense of themselves, they will be angry when it is appropriate.

So that's how I see celibate friendship operates. The deeper I get into being loved by guys, the stronger hunk of faith I've got in myself and in this creation, this unique creation that I am. When I first took a look at what I was, I was like a little kid. I wanted to run and hide under the covers like I'd seen a ghost, because I was nothing like the god I hoped to be. I was more like the animal or beast that I was afraid I was. I was so sure I knew how God wanted me made and that was just perfect, you know. I was supposed to be absolutely perfect and perfect according to my idea of what perfect was. That's how God wanted me made. Well, I didn't want to consult much with God about the matter. It's taken me a long, long time to see that maybe God knew what he was doing and maybe I didn't, that maybe my idea of how I wanted to be perfect wasn't such a great idea, after all.

In my third book, *"I Ain't Well—But I Sure Am Better,"* I talked about learning to have five friends and called the process mutual need therapy. I've found now some new things to add to mutual need therapy as characteristics. Mutual need therapy is pretty much the process I've been describing where two people who really have a feeling for each other get so much for themselves as well as benefit each other in the relationship.

When I talked about mutual need therapy, I felt there were a lot more people saying, "Sure, I've got friends like that," than people who really had friends like that. So I found a couple more characteristics of a mutual need relationship that make it tougher to claim and help us see our relationships more clearly.

What characteristics do two people in a mutual need relationship have? Number one, their faces light up when they see each other, their faces light up when they see you. This is also how you can tell when somebody is a prospect for a mutual need relationship. I could look around the room in Seattle and I could see some people that, if I were living there, I could have a mutual need relationship with. Anytime I looked in Sherry's direction, for example, she just lit up. There were a number of others, but she was a very notable example. While her face really lit up when she saw me, I can't believe it lights up that way when she sees everybody. I've got a suspicion that once in a while there's someone in her life where, when she looks at them, she does the opposite of light up, which is darken down.

Number two. They have no program for my improvement. Now, that's a tough hurdle to jump over. Most everybody has a program for my improvement. Like my language, it's a little bit of a difficulty for some of you, but some of you say you like the way I put things out.

I'll never forget the Methodist minister in my class a long time ago. I said to him, "Gee, Ben, I'm sorry, but I occasionally use a bad word." He said, "Jess, think nothing of it. I worked on a Northern Pacific railroad crew. So I've heard language you haven't ever dreamed of yet." Ben was a minister, and I just loved him for that, because it was such a beautiful compassion on his part to put me at ease that way. He had no program for the improvement of my language.

Number three. They like us the way we are, which is kind of the same thing but a little different flavor. They like us the way we are.

Number four. They joy in our presence. It's even stronger than they like us the way we are. They joy in our presence. Every once in a while, Gerry will say, "Gee, Jess, you know it was so great having lunch with you today. I feel so much better." And of course, I say, "Same way, Gerry." So we just sit there having a good time. I remember the other day I said, "Gerry, we've been having lunch now ten years. What are we going to talk about the next ten years?" He said, "Don't worry, we'll think of something."

But we don't need to think of anything to talk about. Gerry and I aren't what you'd call quiet individuals. He's got an I.Q. about ten times my weight and he's quick. I'm always glad he's on my side in an argument. In the last year or so I've noticed things are getting quieter, there are longer quiet spells in our time together, and it's no problem. In fact, it's a little better.

Number five. They look us up if we don't look them up. I had a beautiful example of this in Seattle with Jackie Smith the first day and Bob Smith the second day. I tried to call Jackie and Bob the night I got to Seattle, but I couldn't reach either of them. But Jackie showed up and Bob showed up. They look you up. So you aren't always taking the initiative.

Now, in a relationship you must not ever count times. There was a person in my life who was always saying, "I went there last. They've got to come here this time." What a tremendous sense of inadequacy that is! In some of our relationships we will be in a situation where maybe as much as three fourths or four fifths of the time we will be taking the initiative in that relationship. I do refuse to take the initiative all the time. But, other than that, I will understand that there's something in the nature of that relationship that I might take the initiative most of the time. I also want to see not only that they will take the initiative part of the time but I also want to see the other qualities I mentioned in that relationship.

Gerry is a good example. I call him maybe three times, at least, for each time he calls me. But that's partly just the nature of our schedules and other things at this time.

Number six. They stick with us. This is what I see in so many relationships. If you move away from them, you see that the relationship wasn't what you thought it should be, because the person doesn't stick with you. Or you get into trouble or you do some unpopular thing like molesting children and they don't stick with you. Really. I once heard that. I think it was asked in a Sunday-school class. If you found your friend had molested a child, what would you do? It was used as a discussion topic, and it's a good one. If I found one of the five friends had molested a child, we'd have lunch tomorrow, just like we'd had lunch yesterday and the day before. He might talk to me about it. But I wouldn't spend any effort or energy trying to help him, trying to give him something. I don't believe in giving people things. If you want something, ask for it.

When we go from friendly love to sexual love, how will we do? Perfectly? No way. Perfection, that's for gods, and we aren't gods. We're imperfect. So we'll do imperfect things. We are terribly immature. All of us are sexually immature, partly because of our deprivation and partly because of our lack of experience. You go through immaturity to get to maturity. What other path is there to maturity?

But we most often ask for perfection from ourselves: "I'll learn to love people sexually, but I don't want to make a single mistake, because God told me, 'Make a single mistake and you'll go straight to hell.'" God didn't say that at all. God said the exact opposite: "Because you will make mistakes, I'm here to take care of forgiving all the mistakes." But the person says, "No, I know God didn't really mean that, he wanted me to be perfect." But who's that talking? It's the big I, the ego; that's what wants to be perfect. And who's being God in that matter? "I" is being God, not God. I need to get out of the God business and let God be God and I'll be Jess. It works a lot better. Who would ever want a Norwegian God?

It's just like riding a bicycle. If any of us insisted that we ride a bicycle perfectly the first time we got on it, who would ever ride a bicycle? If anybody wanted to do any physical thing perfectly the first time they did it, thread a needle, learn ballet, whatever, who would ever do anything? But when it comes to sex, we say, "Well, I'm going to do it perfect or else. The first time. No mistakes. I'm not going to make any mistakes."

When you learn to ride the bicycle, you fall off, skin your knee, get hurt, run home and cry to mother. "I'm not ever going to ride that dang thing again. Too hard." But then the kids want to go out and play. And if you don't get back on your bicycle, you aren't going to get to go along. So you get back on the bicycle. And you get better at riding the bicycle.

I remember how high that bicycle seemed as a kid. I had to get on a sidehill to get my leg over. I could hardly reach the pedals. Everything about it was hard. It was an uphill struggle. But it got easier. I can ride a bicycle now pretty good.

There aren't very many of us who are supposed to be celibate, from what I can see, but, whatever, it doesn't matter. Both kinds of love, in the highest state, call for surrender. The celibate lover who hadn't surrendered sees their celibacy as a burden and a pain that they are putting up with for a God that values suffering. But I haven't seen any sign that the God I understand values suffering, and if that person is wrong and God doesn't value suffering they're in trouble, because they've won all these Brownie points that they can't cash in. They come to cash in all their suffering trading stamps and the booth is closed. Kind of funny, isn't it? A whole life misspent and they

thought it was well spent. All their suffering and pain
and all their do-good actions don't count and the booth
never existed. And here a bunch of hell raisers are
enjoying heaven along with them.

An opposite view was held by old Pope John, who
was so sweet. When he was forty-three years old, he
said, "The reward for my past forty-three years is the
past forty-three years." I know what he means. I told
the people in Seattle, "I've got my reward for this
morning here with you, this morning. If some of you
are saving suffering trading stamps, there's a danger
that's a false god."

The Popes have those fancy red shoes, the soft silk
slippers, but John had hard soles put on his so he
could go out and see the people. At Christmas, he
went to the jail to see the prisoners, because he knew
they couldn't come to him.

When he was a bishop, he heard that one of his
priests was having trouble, drinking too much. John
went to the priest in the bar and said, "Father, I
would like to go to confession to you." So they went
out on the street and the big bishop, John, said his
confession to the little drinking priest. To me the
stories about old Pope John show us celibacy at its
most loving and most surrendering, where celibacy
isn't a burden and suffering, but a joy. If a man like
John had decided to give up his celibacy and become a
sexual lover, imagine what a lover he would have
been.

For sexual love, that same kind of surrender yields
the same results. The reason, in my experience, that
most people haven't got much out of sexual love is
there wasn't much surrender in it. It was like two
people having sex through a partition; in fact, two
partitions. You know, two people are carrying their
partitions around with little holes in them. They put
the partitions up against each other and they have
sex through the two holes in the partitions. Then they

say, "I'm not getting much out of this." Isn't that a big surprise? And guess how you get rid of the other guy's partition. "Throw yours away first?" Right.

Now, eventually, if the other person doesn't want to get rid of his partition after twenty years of waiting, then maybe get another guy or gal. But you take down your partition and wait for twenty years first. Because for those of us who are married, you and I made a vow, "For better or for worse," and the other person has been living up to that vow too, as well as they could. Let's make sure we really get our partition down. Let's not kid ourselves that it's down when it isn't. Let's really get it down and wait. And the higher power of my understanding will provide all good things for us in the higher power's time, not our time.

My students used to tell me, "Oh, I have just this little problem of impatience." I used to think that was a little problem, because I was impatient too. I still am some. But I see now that lack of patience is just a different version of being God, because it's saying I want things to come to me on my time, not God's time. Because I know what I'm doing and God doesn't. I know when I need this and God doesn't.

It's just like Father Rohr says: "I don't value enthusiasm; I value fidelity, sticking with someone, laying down your life for them."

How does the need for body contact get met if we decide to stay with celibate loving through choice or by necessity? I don't know just how body-contact needs get met, but they seem to have gotten met for Pope John. I don't think anybody in his right mind would want to argue he was like some of those Popes way back who tended to father a lot of children under the vow of celibacy. Pope John wasn't that kind of Pope. So he got his body-contact needs met in celibate love, obviously, because he was such a sweet person. And you can't be a sweet person if you're obsessed with sex and full of hungers and screaming that your needs be met. You're an angry, cantankerous, bitter person when that happens. So, obviously, his body-contact needs got met some way. It was probably like in the commune in Cincinnati. When the young people got lots of loving attention, and hugs, their sex needs quieted down. I'd guess they quieted down in a few people so much that they saw their needs for love were finally being met and they then chose the celibate life because it was right for them and they saw they could make it work in their lives for good instead of for suffering.

So you don't need to choose sexual love or celibate love on the basis that you have that huge body-contact need, because it can be met either way.

It looks to me like surrender is the key, whether to a higher power or another person. But it was said, "As you did this to one of the least of these brothers of mine, you did it to me." So maybe surrendering to a higher power is the same as surrendering to another person. And maybe surrendering to another person is the same as surrendering to the higher power. Let's talk about that.

CHAPTER 6

Surrender in Sexual Loving—The Messy Business of Carrying on a Personal Love Relationship

All loving takes surrender, but sexual loving takes the most surrender. Like I mentioned earlier, surrender in sexual loving is where, instead of making love through the holes in the shields, we take the shields away. You'd be amazed how much nicer we fit that way. You'd be amazed at all the things that there are in love that you didn't know when you were making love through the holes in the shields.

I mentioned earlier the legend that man-woman was one creature with two heads, four arms and four legs. Man-woman had such a beautiful time on earth that the gods became angry and split them apart. Ever since then, the two halves, the two halves that belong together, have been looking for each other. But that's where it takes surrender, so we can find that part that was cut away, the special half, the woman half that was cut away from this particular man in an intricate shape like a jigsaw puzzle. There has got to be just that right match, and then, boom! Now, the only way you can find if there is that fit, you see, is to completely surrender so all the different irregularities can meet the other and find if there is the fit they've been seeking. What we're talking about fitting is souls, not just bodies; but the way the other body fits and feels a part of your own body tells you something about the soul fit, too.

The idea that somewhere out there, or right next to us in bed, is a woman or man whose soul fits ours is a lovely ideal. But to get to that ideal we've got to go through the messy business of carrying on a series of personal love relationships. "He leaves his underwear in the middle of the floor and I squeeze the tooth-paste tube in the middle." This series of love relationships starts with our first puppy love and ends when we sense we've found our soul mate. But because we're often so busy being God along the way, we're usually pretty repulsed, horrified, and fascinated by some of the things that go on in the backseat of a car.

One of the big problems we have is a denial of all kinds of feelings. We don't want to look at what we see as the dark side of ourselves. Those are the things we hide. We spend a lot of our precious energy keeping those hidden things hidden and keeping people away from us so they won't see our particular skeletons in the closet. And there also can be a great denial of our feelings of anger and pain when we try to achieve peace instead of love. Surrender helps us in all of this by letting us take all the things in us and around us as they are. We give up the struggle against the world, and then we're free to change the few things about us that we can change and really need changing.

The more friendly relationships we have, the more we see sex is not the big thing we thought it was. It only seemed that way because we had no other way than sex to meet our needs. Once we get other ways to meet our needs for emotional closeness and body contact separate from sex, then sex can fall into its appropriate place in our lives. But as sex becomes just what it is, instead of being a crude attempt to get something else than sex (body contact and closeness and status and power and relationship), sex begins to be realized in its true nature, just for itself. It can become a far bigger thing than we ever hoped or thought it would be when we had sex loaded down with extraneous burdens and foolish, misled hopes.

It would help us, also, to be sure to approach sex

and surrender with as open a mind as possible, free of as many of our old beliefs as we can manage. Most of our old ideas were part of what caused our problem.

One of the most widely held misconceptions about sex today, with no evidence to back it up, is about sexual frequency. The general belief is that the more sex we have the better. That's just crazy. There's no evidence I've seen that supports it, and I see a lot of things that oppose it. If the more sex the better, then all our prostitutes would be smiling, happy women instead of the saddest, most depressed, highest-suicide group in the country.

There are an awful lot of people having a lot of sex who are plenty depressed and unhappy. There are some very happy people who believe the less sex is used between husband and wife, the more energy they have available to turn upwards towards a shared vision of God, a higher ideal. The Shakers, whose furniture I make and so admire, lived completely celibate lives. Husbands and wives who came in became celibate and had no more children. This meant the community had to continue to bring in outsiders or gradually die out, which it did. The fruits of the Shakers' lives that they left behind are beautiful fruits.

I'm not urging celibacy on myself or anyone else. I'm simply pointing out that there isn't any evidence for the idea the more sex the better. The wide acceptance and endorsement of that idea, is, to me, just another sign of our deprivation. And it's a good example of belief that we had best get rid of. Oddly enough, if you'll get rid of that belief, your sexual frequency will probably increase if that's what's appropriate for you.

There is a substantial trend today to show how much men and women are equal. I believe in total equality before the law, I believe women should have every legal and employment right that men have. I believe ERA would be a good idea. I believe women have important contributions in the world of work and should be completely free to find their own spot that lets them make their maximum creative contribution.

I believe that a relationship between a man and a woman needs to be equal legally, but it cannot be equal emotionally for a simple reason. I believe women are very unequal to men. They are stronger emotionally than men, their bodies are more durable and they handle their feelings much better. About the only advantage I see men having is in bigger muscles and being more inclined to philosophy, if that's an advantage.

In our attempt to give women legal and job equality, we must watch we don't extend the equality into areas where it isn't appropriate. We can be equal but still different.

Jefferson and Sharon Campbell of the Polarity Health Institute* have some ideas that are very helpful to me in seeing what it means to be a man. As Sharon says, "After years of trying to deny my womanhood I was finally forced by my pain to look at this body God gave me and ask myself why I was given a woman's body." Jefferson talks of the process he went through as he came to some of his understandings of what it meant to be a man and what he learned from Sharon about what it meant to be a woman:

"At first there are certain things the other person has that we want. That's what attracts us. But out of our giving to each other comes spiritual love. Giving sex to the other when we don't feel it, is a service. It's very improbable that two people are at the same place sexually at the same time. So they give out of a good feeling for each other and the other knows that. They see that sex isn't just gratification, it's part of a more positive way of being together.

"Then, when sex is being used to conceive a child,

* Polarity Health Institute, P. O. Box 86, Olga, WA 98279.

it's totally different. You see that the energy is very much in the upward direction, not in a sensual way. Then you realize what sex is really for.

"The reason we have so many sexual desires is that we are so sexually stimulated. We end up getting so totally involved in sex that we don't understand what we are doing and we get very unsatisfied in the results of our sex. Today, we feel that if a woman is not like a man and a man is not like a woman, that's bad. But that's the problem. We need to learn what is to be a man and what it is to be a woman.

"I have male energy and female energy both in me," says Jefferson. "The female energy in me is latent, but I need to accept that female energy to me. Man is outward and has outward drive. We see that every time he ejaculates. Woman is more inward. She only ejaculates once a month. So they need to understand each other.

A man and a woman have some days where they are relating beautifully, as if they were truly one. All of a sudden he starts to feel he is losing her. In a few more days, he feels he's lost her for good. But then she starts coming back to him. A man thinks that's his cycle. It's not his cycle, it's the woman's cycle.

"Man is like the sun sending all its energy outward. Woman is like the moon taking in and reflecting back that energy. When a woman stops reflecting, the man wonders where she went. She's right where she was, she just isn't reflecting at that time.

"At the woman's elimination time, emotions are coming out. Man learns this, not from another man, but only through being with a woman. He cannot experience this through himself.

"In a man like Pope John the divine energy is inside and that's neuter or neutral. We can't get to this through our maleness or femaleness.

"The woman has all the power, because male energy is always moving out where the woman receives energy.

"If our path in life is to be celibate, that's great. We don't have to get married, but we do need to accept and make peace with the opposite energy. This is the happy celibate."

I see this last paragraph is the answer to Sister Theresa of Calcutta's and Pope John's happiness. They were both well aware that the opposite sex was out there. And they were aware and accepting of what that energy was. They just didn't choose to get involved with it at the sexual level. The unhappy celibate is the person who hasn't made peace with their own sexual energy and the sexual energy of the opposite sex. I mention Pope John and Sister Theresa so often because they are so well known and such good examples. There are equally as good examples of happy celibates in your own community.

I mention Sharon and Jefferson's ideas here not because I feel they are right or wrong but because they provide us an additional perspective on the relation of men and women which we can use if we find it useful to us. We don't have to believe it or not. We can just use it. If it works for us it's shown its usefulness. There are no words or theories that can come even close, I feel, to describing the relationship between men and women. But, when we admit the limitations of any theory, we can then go back to the theory with an open mind and see if and how it might be useful to us in improving our relationship.

Up until about three years ago I was having lots of problems in my marriage. I was having the feeling of lack of love, coldness and anger. Three years ago I finally began to face my own contribution to those problems. I saw that my fear made me run from problems and that I hadn't really faced those problems. I saw that while I claimed to believe in my marriage, I hadn't been willing to be myself in that marriage. So from that day on I resolved to fight, with all the power in me, to be me in my marriage. But I surrendered the marriage when I accepted that I didn't need the marriage. It it wasn't mine, it would go away. If I worked at being me and the marriage was truly mine, it would stay.

It was just over a year ago that I found Sharon and Jefferson's ideas on man and woman and marriage. They were a real help to me, primarily in helping me see where I was harming my marriage and why the things I had earlier started doing differently were working better.

When you carry out Sharon and Jefferson's Polarity ideas into marriage, you get this theory: Man's job in the marriage, because he's outgoing, is primarily to be responsible. When he is responsible, the woman can be receptive. Woman's job in the marriage, because she takes in energy, is primarily to be receptive. By being receptive she will reflect some of her great power back to the man so through her reflecting he can be more responsible.

At my mention of women being receptive I can just hear many women saying, "That's not fair for me to have a different role." So please understand my point. I'm not saying the idea is true or false. And I can't decide for a woman what her role will be. All I can do is choose a path for me. I find that there are very few ideas available to me on men and women relating to each other.

The current idea is that men and women are equal and the same. I believe they are equal, but I can't see that men and women are the same. To me, they seem very opposite in so many ways except for their souls, which I can see are the same. But I'm not debating the issue. I want you to hang on to your beliefs, whatever they are. I don't want you to agree with me. But I'm not interested in having you correct my views as being wrong in some of your eyes. My views are neither right nor wrong, they are simply more or less useful to me. And I'm seeking as useful a set of ideas as I can find, particularly in this important area.

The idea that really helps me is the idea that I need to be more responsible. I saw that it was like I was a little baby when I had my heart attack, at thirty-five. I was almost completely irresponsible. Sure, I put on the mask of responsibility, but I wasn't really responsible. I earned money for the family, but even there I was irresponsible by spending too much on the ego things like a big house that made me look good and spending on my hobbies and by being so much in debt.

When I started in search of what I believed in, I began to grow up. At thirty-five to forty-three I went through a fairly blind childhood. From forty-three to fifty I went through adolescence and early manhood. I think I started being a man three years ago, when I finally took responsibility for my irresponsibility in my marriage—my central human relationship.

When a man is irresponsible, it really scares a woman, because then she has to try to do his job for him and through him. It's like working for a dumb boss. You have to shut off his dumb ideas, feed him good ideas, and do it so carefully he doesn't catch on. It's almost impossible for the woman in that situation to avoid taking over the husband's responsibility and telling him what to do and just how to do it. Then there's a big mess where each person is trying to do the other's job for them.

I feel that as I began to act more responsibly in all the areas of my life, I finally gave Jackie the freedom and space she deserved and needed. I paid more attention to Jackie's needs, to the children's needs, to our financial needs, to taking care of things around the house. I did all these things for me, not for Jackie. I did them because I owed it to myself to be responsible, so I could feel good about what I was doing. This kept what I was doing from being a trade where I was doing things for Jackie and she had better do them back for me. I was doing something for myself that made me feel good about me.

But, as I say, as I became more responsible, Jackie was finally able to get out of the role of trying to carry my responsibility, which she had been partly forced into by my irresponsibility. I say partly, because there's a part of all of us that escapes into trying to do the other person's work as an escape from doing our own work.

There are a couple of interesting secondary effects to the Polarity ideas. As a man and a woman develop their primary roles, they become more able to develop their secondary roles: the more responsibly the man acts, the more able he is to let the woman take more responsibility and he can reflect that energy back to her. The more receptive and reflective the woman is, the more responsible she can be and the more the husband can receive her leadership.

From all that I've observed, it doesn't work very well the other way, where the woman tries to take complete responsibility first and the man tries to be completely receptive first. It depends on individual personalities to a degree, but we're looking for a general principle that applies to most everyone, at least to a degree. It's like acceptance. The best way I've found to get acceptance is to give it first. Then I usually find I get back the acceptance I need.

Another thing is that as I become more responsible, then my emotions can come out more and I get a better understanding of both my own and the woman's emotionality. I can be more tuned in to her so, day by day, I can pretty well tell where she is at in her cycle.

When a woman starts being more receptive and she accepts her emotions and cyclic form, then she isn't so frightened of the emotional part of herself and she can be more responsible.

To me, this leads to true liberation, which comes not from denying a precious part of ourselves but by accepting it all. Women aren't only women, they're men, too. And both sexes need to accept that. Same for men.

Women are basically more nuturing than men, although men can nurture too. But women have breasts, which physically express their nurturance. We've got a lot of research that shows the emotional and nutritional importance of breast-feeding for the baby and the added emotional bonding for the mother. But, for a variety of reasons, partly the babyishness of us men, women are hesitant to face their nurturance. There are some sad things that may be resulting from this besides the decline in breast-feeding.

One in five women today get breast cancer. Many are more worried about breast cancer than dying. One piece of research shows that through a psychological test the night before the breast biopsy, 70 per cent of the breast cancer can be predicted just by the woman's attitude towards life. If she feels hopeless and helpless, it's more likely her lump will be cancerous. Another finding is that women with breast cancer are more likely to have mixed feelings about being a woman.

Many of our present trends make it more difficult for women to express this nurturance. When a husband and wife on the farm would butcher a pig or kill some chickens, they were both expressing their nurturance of the family. When the husband gives money grudgingly to the wife, she goes to the supermarket and grudgingly pays high prices for TV dinners that come home and get shoved in the microwave for a few minutes. There is a real enslavement of the woman, and she feels degraded at not being able and not knowing how to give that nurturance to her family. It isn't that there's anything intrinsically wrong with TV dinners. The least little personal touch of doing something to that TV dinner with love can change the whole thing. But we are caught up in a vicious cycle where we are impoverished and we live with an impoverished person and we can't even find good examples around us to follow, because the people around us are impoverished too.

Monkeys raised in cages, deprived of touch, are hostile, awkward and ineffectual as mothers or fathers and raise monkeys more hostile and ineffectual than themselves. It would be a vicious, downward cycle if it wasn't for the fact that we can be transformed. I don't know if a monkey can have a spiritual awakening. But I sure know people can have them. I've seen hundreds of lives turned around that looked hopeless. Just go to your local skid row and look at the alcoholics. Then realize that maybe half those guys will have a spiritual awakening someday down the road and will rise up from where they lie and drink no more and turn into fine human beings. That's a miracle. It's the kind of miracle we need. And one place you can go to find that miracle is in the arms of the loved one in surrender.

I've gone into these ideas in much detail at this point because we can't surrender unless we have some sense of what we're surrendering and what we're surrendering to.

We also need to look at surrender itself, so we can get a better understanding of that process.

What is surrender?

Living in ego means constantly wanting what you don't have.

Surrender means constantly appreciating and being grateful for what you do have.

Ego is when we constantly think we know what's best for us.

Surrender is when we see that the great stream of life, the higher power, God as we understand him, knows what's best for us.

Surrender is the prayer of release and the prayer of attraction. I release all things that are not a part of my inner perfection, and all those things release me. I am attracted to all things that are a part of my inner perfection, and all those things are attracted to me.

Living the surrendered life is like being a butterfly, a soul in full flight seeking the beauties of life. Like the butterfly, we start putting our trust in the present good thing instead of hoping for the next good thing. To get that attitude, we need to seek a new vision, a new hope, a new spirit. Sometimes, the biggest obstacle to the next thing God wants to give us is the present thing God has given us. We put so much trust in what we've been given, we won't put it down so we can receive the new thing.

We need to see that we are with a loved one now. When we don't pay attention to her feelings or his feelings, it turns them off. Then all the sex problems follow. There's a story about the Garden of Eden where Adam was bored and God created woman for him. A while later God came back and asked Adam how things were going. Adam said, "God, what's a headache?"

That story is missing a part. It's missing the part where Adam was with Eve and they were making love and it was great. Afterward, she wanted to talk feelings, but he didn't want to hear her and went off to work. That turned her off. Then the headaches started.

There are two kinds of living. One is fear-oriented and the other is love-oriented. Fear and love can't exist side by side. That's why we need to get a new attitude towards life, to get rid of our fear, before we can get in a surrendered relationship where we expect joy and love, rather than pain. When we expect pain, we can't let our centers meet. If we want our centers to meet, we have to find a higher ideal that protects us; we may be hurt but we'll never be harmed.

For a lover there is no death. For a non-lover, every

minute is a death, because, every minute, something is being taken away and the self they so love is a minute closer to death and annihilation. But there is really no need to try to hide ourselves, because every one of us knows everything about everybody.

It's very easy to tell by looking at a person if they are leading a love-oriented life. Their face usually shows a good expression, ranging from calm content to a mischievous delight at the pleasant surprises the day is constantly offering. You cannot joyfully embrace a person in the deepest of all ways without joyfully embracing the world all day long and being open to anything that happens. And you cannot embrace life all day long with love without embracing the men and women in it and most of all, in the deepest way, the one special man or woman in it.

This is why infidelity can't work, because it is selective and it is a concealment. You can't be deeply open and also conceal. And this, too, is why loving a woman or a man and loving God is the same. It doesn't mean you have to love a woman or man to love God, but it does mean that by loving this special creation of God in this deep way you can't escape loving God.

That's why it was no surprise to me when a survey of one-hundred-thousand women showed the highly religious ones as being most satisfied with sex in their marriages. The leap of faith that is the ladies' lane to religion is very close to the letting go in the sexual relationship. It's the same surrender of self. When we have a high ideal, we're surrendering, too, and then it isn't so hard to surrender to the old duck we're in bed with.

Before we go to intercourse, let's look at touching again, because now maybe we can see some problems in our connections with people we couldn't see before. Especially, look at the lack of surrender in so much of all our touching.

There are many bad experiences people have had

with touching. Because of our deprivation, touching is so hard for us to handle that some people almost won't let anyone touch them unless they are prepared to have sex with them. They know they need the touching so much that they are almost helpless once they start touching. So they can't look at touching as just something that happens by itself and is a joy in and of itself. They are robbed of a precious way of communication.

Others show their deprivation with a "touch me not" reaction. They need touching so desperately they can't handle it at all. It makes their skin crawl to be touched. When it comes to intercourse, they want intercourse quick, to get it over with. For some of these women and men, intercourse relaxes them enough that afterwards they can be touched, even really want to be touched. But this is so unusual for them that the partner isn't aware of the sudden need and the sudden change. And the person needing the touch is so awkward and ineffectual at communicating their need that they can't ask for the touching they all of a sudden need and are ready to receive.

There are three ways I commonly see touching used inappropriately: the indiscriminate toucher, the caretaking toucher, and the hostile toucher.

The indiscriminate toucher is the one who says, "I'm a toucher." And they are. They touch people anytime they want, any way they want, without paying any attention to the needs and feelings of the other person. Their lack of attention makes much of their touching embarrassing or hurtful to the people where it is inappropriate. Because their touching is so mechanical, it doesn't do much for the person touched, even when it is appropriate.

Hostile touching is done by the person who won't own up to their anger and pretends to be touching in a good way but there is hurt in their touching. They are either too physical and cause pain or they are too

inappropriate and cause pain. A person who slaps you
too hard on the back, leans on you with their elbow or
pinches a child's cheek are examples of openly hostile
touching. A person who brushes your hair away from
your face, which is a very intimate touch and is sel-
dom appropriate, is an example of the more hidden
hostility.

The caretaking touch is given by the person who is
touching because it's good for the other person. A
mother or father can touch their children because the
mother or father enjoys it. But when they touch that
child because the child needs the touching, no one
enjoys that. I hear lots of excuses for this. One big one
is guilt. "I didn't touch enough, so I'll make up for it
now. I didn't touch them when they were little. Now
they can't stand to be touched, so I'm working on
them to get them over that." Can you imagine how it
feels for the child to be touched for those reasons?

There is a legitimate answer to touching. That is to
do it only for the sheer joy of being in close communication with someone. The basic rule I follow is to take
the touching I want, enjoy and need, but I concentrate
only on those who communicate to me they want to be
touched by me also. I concentrate completely on what
I'm getting out of it. I leave it up to them as to what
they are getting out of it.

People I touch so often say, "It feels good to have
you touch me or hold me." I need to accept that feeling, but I also need to be very alert that I don't cross
over a line and start touching to make them feel good
or because they need it or will like me because of it.
That's what it means to take, rather than give or
receive, where there is an element of control either
over the other person or yourself. So look at your
touching because it can give you so much but also it
can show you so much about where you're at in surrender.

When I talk about surrender, people ask, "How do

you surrender?" One of the best sets of directions I have seen on how to surrender is in the twelve steps of AA. The twelve steps have had the word "alcohol" taken out of them so they can be applied by people who don't have a drinking problem. Emotions Anonymous is a group that uses the twelve steps to apply to all problems with emotions.

Here are the twelve steps of Alcoholics Anonymous as changed for Emotions Anonymous, with only the two words "alcohol" and "alcoholic" changed in the first and twelfth steps. As you will notice, the first three steps are almost all surrender. The third step is complete surrender. Surrender runs through all twelve steps. And the eleventh step has a great surrender, where people meditate and pray "only for knowledge of God's will for us and the power to carry that out."

The steps are

1. We admitted we were powerless over our emotions; that our lives were unmanageable.

2. Came to believe that a power greater than ourselves could restore us to sanity.

3. Made a decision to turn our will and our lives over to the care of God as we understood him.

4. Made a searching and fearless moral inventory of ourselves.

5. Admitted to God, to ourselves, and to another human being the exact nature of our wrongs.

6. Were entirely ready to be freed of all our defects of character.

7. Humbly asked God to remove our shortcomings.

8. Made a list of all persons we had harmed and became willing to make amends to them all.

9. Made direct amends to such people whenever possible except when to do so would injure them or others.

10. Continued to take personal inventory and when we were wrong promptly admitted it.

11. Sought through prayer and meditation to improve our conscious contact with God as we understand him praying

only for knowledge of God's will for us the the power to carry that out.

12. Having had a spiritual awakening . . . awakening as the result of these steps we tried to carry the message and practice these principles in all our affairs.*

The twelve steps show one good example of surrender —what it means and how to do it.

When we talk about surrender, I see that it coincides with every religious teaching I've ever seen, not necessarily as the religion is practiced, but as it's taught. Instead of looking at the lives of the people who are pounding on me, telling me that I should join their particular denomination, I can go and look at the writings that they're talking about, and I find the writings to be on surrender.

I've come to see that surrender is vital, and as we surrender more we are able to establish a better sexual relationship, which is, for those of us who are not celibates, hopefully the best thing in our lives. And as we surrender, and deepen our sexual and loving relationship, we get closer to seeing and feeling and appreciating and loving ourselves, which relieves our starvation and deprivation and self-centeredness. As we do that, we start quieting down the drums so we can hear the rest of the symphony.

Now, part of the problem we've got today, as I say,

---

* For information on twelve step programs write. Emotions Anonymous, P. O. Box 4245, St. Paul, MN 55104;

Alcoholics Anonymous, P. O. Box 459, Grand Central Station, New York, NY 10017;

Overeaters Anonymous, 3730 Motor Ave , Los Angeles, CA 90034;

Parents Anonymous (for child abuse), 250 West 57th Street, New York, NY 10010;

Gamblers Anonymous, P O Box 59415, North Iowa Station, Chicago, IL 60659.

There are also groups of people, with emotional problems, using the twelve-step programs, who call themselves Neurotics Anonymous and Emotional Health Anonymous Look in your phone directory or classified ads Or write Emotions Anonymous for help is that there is so much said and written about sex and attitudes that just doesn't produce the results most people want deep inside, like, "Oh, we've got all these groovy times. We're having all these sexual relationships and then we have others and we're just looking for meaningful relationships and we're up front with our partners telling them what we're doing each day so it's all very honest and open. And all that old junk like marriage and commitment; that's all dead. We've found a new way."

The only problem is, as near as I can see, the people writing and saying that stuff are heading down a path that's got some very unpleasant results for many of them, because they haven't looked at the longer-range consequences of those attitudes and that behavior. To me, it's just like the research done on swinging couples. The personality profiles of people who choose being swinging couples are about the world's worst psychological profiles. I wouldn't want said about me what is said about swinging couples, which is that they are made up of people so flat in their emotional response that you have to set off a bomb—a sexual bomb—to even let them know something has happened. The only way they can have a sexual bomb go off is to have sex with new partners every day in new ways and you don't leave any telephone numbers and you use a false name so there's no emotional entanglement.

Now, I'd rather die right here on this spot than be described in those terms. But that isn't bad enough. As psychologists, we need to follow up on those studies five years later to see what's happening in the lives of those people.

I can guess what has happened to the lives of those people, because typically one or both of the partners finally get their guts full of the horror they are living and that probably blows apart the marriage the swinging was supposed to save.

I started teaching at Montana State University in Bozeman twelve years ago. During that time, I've been able to watch things. I've seen a lot of my students try out their bright new sexual ideas, like this one gal I was talking to just the other day. She is about thirty-two. She had all these groovy relationships in college and she lived with this one guy for a couple of years but then she married a different guy. Ten years later, she's just starting to get over being frigid. But, earlier, I'm sure, you could have asked her how living with her guy was going and she would have said, "Oh, I can handle this. I'm doing great."

Her girlfriend married the guy she had been living with for a couple of years. Both of the women were lucky, because they were able to stay married, at least they seem to be luckier than others. But, whatever the case, the gal that married the guy she was living with, she's been frigid, too, and is finally able to admit it.

What happened? Well, the big misconception I see today is the idea that sex is in the head and we've got it all figured out and there's no problem. And the great big head is going to tell the little bitty body just what to do, and the little bitty body is going to follow all the orders.

The only thing is, that is a fantastic conceit and it doesn't work that way. The body has a mind and a will of its own, and we'd better pay attention.

There's the beautiful story of the lady who came up to me after one of my speeches in the early days of Bozeman. She had followed me out of the room and she didn't talk to me until I was down the hall, so I knew something was up.

She said, "Jess, I've got a problem."

I said, "How long has it been going on?"

"About six months now. How do I stop?"

I said, "You can't."

"What do you mean, I can't!"

"If you could have, you would have. What's the story?"

She said, "Well, I'm sleeping with this guy." It's the other guy in her bridge foursome—a cozy arrangement. It's a little touchy to pull off, but cozy. You keep it among friends. "How can I stop?"

So I said, "Tell me about your relationships; tell me about your friends."

"Well, there's my mother."

"Can you tell her about this?"

"No."

"Then she doesn't count."

"I've got one other friend I can tell."

"Can you tell her?"

"Yes."

"Okay, go do so. What about your children?"

She said, "I've given them everything."

I said, "Okay, you've told me the problem. You are the poor, self-sacrificing woman who doesn't need anything. You just keep giving away from your cup that never needs filling. But finally the little girl in you nearly starved to death and she said, 'To hell with you, old lady, you aren't ever going to give me anything. I'm going out to play without you!' Your little girl is out running around playing because you nearly starved her to death and she said, 'To hell with you. You aren't taking care of me. I'll take care of myself.' And she's taking care of herself. And you aren't going to get the little girl to come home until you start doing something for her. So you'd better get to work."

As the years went by, I would run into that gal every once in a while, one place or another, and ask her how she was doing. Her first impulse was to lie, so she would tell me. "Things are going great." Then she'd repent and write me a letter and say, "I lied to you. Things are kind of tough." Later she said, "Well, things are lumping along, but I'm accepting it better." So that was an improvement.

About five years after I first saw her, I was auto-
graphing books at a bookstore. This gal came up to me
and I said, "Well, how are you doing?" She said, "Jess,
the little girl is back home and the bridge foursome is
still going on." Isn't that something?

This is to me the symptom of how we think these
big heads of ours are so smart and the old ego is
running things and to hell with the body, we haven't
got any body and to heck with this little, starved
person in us that's hurting for love and acceptance. To
heck with him. If I let him out, if I surrender to him,
he just gets me into all kinds of messy deals. And sex
can be a grubby, dirty thing and you can get hurt and
look bad and come up with egg on your face. And the
answer is, "You're right." It's just like riding the bicycle. You skin lots of knees on the bicycle. But it sure
beats the alternative of staying home and just pretending you're playing with the other kids.

To me, the people who write or talk about their
great sexual freedom, between the lines usually show
their great sexual guardedness and their lack of surrender. *New Age Magazine* had an article on love.
This gal was writing, and she claimed all kinds of
meaningful relationships, but she made sure that she
never left any clothes at the other guy's house. All of
a sudden she met a guy and the thunderbolt hit both
of them. It was different than anything she'd ever
seen. Pretty soon they had a talk about sharing his
apartment. The next thing they're all of a sudden
together and she's got all her stuff moved in and she
can't believe what's happening.

It turns out that they don't have a stove, for some
reason or another, and they want to get a real nice
stove. They go out to buy a stove and she really gets
shook about the buying of the stove. "My God! Here I
am. We're going to buy this together. What a terrible,
terrible commitment is involved, an entanglement, of
buying this stove together." So she starts throwing it

up to this guy. "What the hell's going to happen if we split up?" At this, he got mad and said, "If we split up, you can have the damn stove!" So they go and get the stove. Here's this lady who's so together, just so together, but over half a stove she makes a big hassle and to me she shows just exactly how together she is: not much.

So here's how we use this delicate instrument that we each got handed at birth—this delicate sexual instrument. It's so complicated that it makes the electronic tape recorder I use seem like a simple thing. Compared to it, our sexual instrument is like a huge computer. It's supposed to be in a dust-free, air-conditioned room, but we take it out in the dirt and the dust and throw rocks at it. And throw burning coals right in the middle of the circuitry. All the short circuits are sputtering and shooting sparks. And then, about five, ten or fifteen years later, we come to find a real wonderful, appropriate place where, by God, we could sure use that fine sexual instrument and the damn thing is just a mess of junk.

But, all the time, our head is telling us, "Oh, no, we've got a fantastic sexual relationship going here; we've really got something." Well, then, let's look at the results in our lives. How good are we at maintaining a relationship? How good are we at holding a family together? How good are we at being able to be on a talking basis with our wife and our children? How many friends have we got in our lives that have been there a while and who show some signs of wanting to continue to be a part of our lives? How much are we like rooted people, instead of like gypsies where one night we are next door to our best friend and the next morning our tent's gone and there isn't anything in the sand to show we were even there? We'll never make contact with that person again. Oh, there was a deep friendship there.

When I told that story in Seattle, the brother of a

friend of mine was with her and he thought, "My God, you're talking about me," because that same thing had happened to him just weeks earlier. A lady had kissed him good-bye in the morning, and when he came back in the evening there wasn't a single trace of that lady in his place. Every piece of paper that would identify her or leave any mark of her in any way was cleaned out of that apartment. He never saw her again and he couldn't track her down. I'm sure they were saying, "Oh, ours is such a deep, meaningful relationship. This is really something. It does a lot for us." Oh, heartburn! You see?

Most sexual loving is self-sexuality. It is simply using the other with the focus on the self, or even worse, most sexuality is simply self-hatred. "I'm worth nothing and I'll get into a cheap, rotten sexual relationship just to verify my low opinion of myself and prove that I am nothing."

Self-sexuality. It's an awful picture, a horrible one. The way some of the homosexuals get their sex needs met is to walk up to a toilet with a hole in the wall and there's some guy on the other side of the partition. What sadness, but there are often equally sad examples, in all our lives, of not being very loving to the loved one.

The partition example I used earlier came from that situation. To me, that and masturbation are the epitome of self-sexuality. There doesn't need to be any other involvement. We'll take care of ourselves. Even if another person is involved, they might as well not be, for all they are truly involved. They are just like the piece of liver used by the adolescent Portnoy. They simply are an object. And it isn't just women who are sex objects. There are men who are sex objects, just as there are women.

In the Fleming's book *First Time*, where prominent people tell about their first intercourse, there are a number of cases where the women and the men both admit that when they decided to find what sex was like they grabbed the first person they could find and pushed them into bed. To me, when the other person, female or male, is a sex object, it amounts to almost just a mutual masturbation with both people completely separate.

Despite how wound up I can get about the extremes of self-sexuality in its different forms, nothing is pure bad. I've never seen any sexual loving so bad there wasn't at least a little good in it. Because there's at least a little good in even the least lovely of our sexual loving; hopefully, most of us can start there and tease our way to the situation where we get a lot more good into it and from it.

So when we start out, there's very little surrender to the other person, because surrender is like ballet; it takes time and practice and experience and learning to feel, before we can be good.

One of the questions a pretty young gal at the Seattle seminar came up and asked me was, "Jess, does a person have to be destroyed before they can start learning?" And I said, "No. If we did, then we would all have to die before we could learn our first lesson and we'd be dead so there's no way we can learn it."

A lot of people have learned some lessons from my experiences. I've learned some lessons from other people's experiences. So we can learn without being destroyed in every area.

The main thing I've seen about all sexual loving, no matter how bad it looks, and to me this is the light of hope in this mess, is that any time any part of our nakedness touches a part of someone else's nakedness, there is inevitably some openness and surrender. It is impossible to have sexual intercourse without there being a small element, at least, of surrender and maybe quite a bit of surrender. So all we need to do is pay attention to what is there and follow that to more surrender. As D. H. Lawrence says in *Lady Chatterley's Lover,* there's no such thing as bad intercourse. It ranges from good to heavenly.

The surrender we feel when we are naked and open is very frightening, and we attempt to detach ourselves from what our bodies are doing. We become spectators at our own intercourse. That's such a common phenomenon in this country. We become so detached it's just like we were lifted above the bed, watching our own intercourse. After a while, we are so detached we can't get to be a part of it. Then we need to resort to externals, like positions, rigs, pornography, sex fantasies, as turn-ons. So the partner is not the turn-on anymore, but the external thing is. He's having his fantasies about who he's having intercourse with and she's having hers, so there's a whole big crowd in the bedroom. "She's being attacked by a huge stud horse and he's in bed with twenty-six gals in a harem. So there's twenty-nine things in the bedroom, plus all the previous people each person had intercourse with or fantasied with. That's a lot. It's kind of hard to keep the head clean when all this commotion is going on in the bedroom. Again, that would be exceptionally funny if it weren't so terribly sad. (At this, most everybody in my group in Seattle was nodding their heads, and nobody was shaking his head.) Yet despite the mess our sex fantasies create in our heads, there are articles that counsel you on the advantages of sex fantasies. That's the most asinine thing I've ever heard of.

Earlier in the day, I had been holding a girl named Jay who had come up front with a question and to be held. So I was holding Jay. Here was this lovely thing. Assume that things were such that we were both free in a responsible way to make a commitment to each other and then to have intercourse together. If being with her didn't mean enough, so I had to think of some old movie actress as a sex turn-on, I ought to have my head examined.

And you can say, "Well, you can understand that for me with her, but on her side of the matter, here she is in bed with this beat-up devil." But, again, if she doesn't feel that it's really important to be with me, why, then, we don't belong together. Or, you argue, "Sure, that's fine the first few years of sex, but then it starts getting dull." True, in a way. But that dullness doesn't come from the partner. It comes from us. We're unwilling to go any deeper and be more open so we can go to richer loving. We usually don't stay as deep in intimacy as we were at first. We back up and rebuild up some walls around ourselves we had taken down under the warmth of fresh love. So our dullness tells me about me, not about my partner. She would be a very exciting partner to someone else, at least for a while, and then they'd have the same problem too.

So, to me, sex fantasies not only aren't important, they're a symptom of a terrible problem. The great expert on Tantric sex, Bhagwan Shree Rajneesh, counsels us goal-oriented Americans not to be so goal-oriented in sex. We aren't interested in going on any trip unless we know where we're going. We've got to know the destination and the time of arrival. We set out on our vacation like arrows zipping right to the spot in the fastest possible time, no chance to even stop and go to the toilet. When we get there, we rush madly about, having a good time. Immediately after having our good time, we get in the car and rush madly home, not stopping to go to the toilet again, just like an arrow.

We have goalitis, which is something like colitis— it's a real pain. And in sex you see this. Rajneesh, who has a column in *New Age Magazine*, says, "In sex, keep your mind on the fire at the beginning. If you concentrate on the fire at the beginning, not wanting to go any place, there will be no embers at the end."

That's one of the causes of spectatoritis—people have got all these goals in sex and they've got a list of the places you've got to get to, and if this doesn't happen in this way, it's disaster. That's ego, not surrender. I can remember that, at first, for me and the other kids of my generation, just to be laying down with a gal without any clothes on, the idea of that was enough all by itself. But, hell, just a few years later, we get angry because ninety-six things straight out of *Joy of Sex* didn't happen in five minutes. It's ridiculous to escalate like that.

In the Zen tradition, students spend years and years learning a couple of things, one very similar to keeping the mind on the fire at the beginning, which is the knack of doing something the two-thousandth time yet retaining much of the excitement and feeling of the first time. Suzuki talks about it in *Zen Mind, Beginner's Mind.* He says that we are full of joy doing something the first time. Then, as the act is repeated, we become an expert. In the mind of the expert, there are very few possibilities, because he knows what will happen and what can't happen. So he has narrowed the possibilities way down. But in the beginner's mind there are many possibilities. So we need to see how we can keep the beginner's mind which is big-mind, so life can continue to be, as it really is, filled with many rich possibilities.

Now, we're really bad at that. We climb Everest once, okay, we've climbed it, to hell with it. Now what are we going to do. It's the tallest mountain in the world, so we might as well blow our brains out, because there aren't any taller mountains to climb. And all other mountain climbers should commit suicide too, because the tallest mountain has been climbed.

In my first book, I told the story of a friend and student of mine. "Jess," he said, "you say to do what we like to do, just follow our nose and it will work out." And I said, "Yeah, Jim." And he said, "What can I do? What I really love to do is ski and rock-climb." I said, "Well, Jim, I don't know, but why don't you follow your nose as well as you can and see what happens?" So, by gosh, he got a job with the ski patrol that winter, and the next summer got a job teaching rock-climbing at an Outward Bound school in Minnesota. He went on and became head of the ski patrol and had his own rock-climbing school.

I saw Jim when I was skiing Big Sky, and skied with him. I said, "How's it going, Jim?" "Well," he said, "the ski-patrol thing is going great. But rock-climbing isn't going good. I'm having a bad time with it." I said, "What's wrong?"

"Well," he said, "damn it, it's just a hassle." I said, "Well, you're doing something wrong, Jim, or it wouldn't be a hassle."

He said, "Now, Jess, I want you to understand, I'm doing world-class-type climbs. One of the climbs we were aiming at was just done for the first time, but there are four other of these world-class, non-attempted climbs left."

I thought about that the next day and the day after that, and I think I know what the problem is. When he's telling me about being a ski patrolman, he's telling me about how much fun it is to go downhill. And I think rock-climbing has got to do with about how much fun it is to go uphill, and not his big ego. So I think Jim's ego got into his rock-climbing and done poisoned it to death. I don't know whether he's ever going to be able to go back to rock-climbing just for the fun of rock-climbing—the way it was when he was a beginner.

I've got a pair of big elk horns off an elk I ran into last fall. But I didn't get those big elk horns because I looked for them. I took whatever kind of elk I ran into, and this particular one, the tenth year I've hunted elk, happened to be a nice one. But I don't care if I get a big one or a little one next year, or none. I'll take whatever kind of elk that God gives me. And if I go to my grave without ever getting some gigantic, seven-point or ninety-six-point elk, why that's just lovely. I've had a lot of fun elk-hunting.

But I've noticed that any time my big ego gets involved in something, why, that's poison, that's the end of her right there. I think that's what happened to my friend Jim, on his rock-climbing. I find that it's hard for me to handle any kind of recreation that's got a score or conspicuous goal attached to it. I hung up my golf clubs after my heart attack, because I couldn't handle my feelings about my own score. That was seventeen years ago and I'm still not to the place where I feel I can go out with those clubs and just enjoy the day and the fun of swinging the club. I can feel I'm getting close. I almost went out this summer. But I'm going to wait until I feel good about it before I even try, because I've got plenty of other things I love to do. But that's how my ego works. (After I wrote this, I tried golf again and found I could play it just for the fun of it, so I joined the country club and I'm having fun with golf; I'm not frustrated with my game, I'm happy with it. So far, I'm not even keeping score.)

In skiing, especially when we get good enough to handle most any kind of slope, all there is to do is go downhill having a good time in the snow. But Jim's rock-climbing magazines have all these ratings and grades for climbing, like scores for golf. So there is plenty to fire up the ego. That's hard to handle. So I think that's what moved in and poisoned rock-climbing for him.

There's a point here that people miss. They say, "What's wrong with a score?" The point is, nothing is wrong with a score. It's what we do with it. A world-class climber can climb for the love of climbing while he's taking new, unattempted routes. The guy he's roped up with can be making the same climbs as a way of taking a scalp, getting his name in the magazine. The problem is our ego and how it fits in.

Making love is just like rock-climbing in the way the ego can rise up and spoil it. The more ego the less surrender. The more ego the less open we are to the loved one. When it's all ego, it's just two people in self-sexuality. When it's no ego, the two people merge into one and, that moment, experience themselves, each other and God.

So goalitis and ego are all hooked together. I've got to get someplace. And what's the place I've got to get to? It's got to be a fancy place. Unless there's this kind of performance and that kind of results, it isn't good.

To me, we drastically misunderstand sex, and I think the misunderstanding comes out of our deprivation. To us, our sex is too much concerned with genitals and too little concerned with the rest of the body. This is my sex instrument, from my toes to my head, all 71½ inches of it. How I take care of my whole sex instrument makes a difference. When I see that my whole being is my sex instrument, then sex doesn't ever have to end. I don't know when some parts of sex will stop, but sex doesn't ever end until this instrument ends—the total instrument ends, from the top of my head to the bottom of my toes. To me, when a man would lose a feeling for being in bed with a warmhearted woman, no matter what happens in that bed, the guy might as well be dead anyway.

Again, it's like the Tantric thing. The old guy in South America who's 132 years old gets in bed with a woman and he has a good time, because he has his mind on the fire at the beginning. He doesn't have a destination. So it's impossible for him to have a bad time. How can you have a bad time when you haven't got any destination? How can you have a bad time when you're already having a good time?

So there's no end, then, to sex as I understand it now, because all of me is the sexual instrument. But, again, it's a sign of our sexual deadness that only when the bomb goes off is there enough feeling so we can appreciate that something happened. Now, the funny thing is the more surrender there is in our lovemaking the more bombs go off under all kinds of circumstances and in response to all kinds of stimuli instead of just one.

How weird it is that some fantasy of a body, some sexual fantasy, is more of a turn-on than a real body. How much it tells us that our head has taken over and is out of balance with the body. Again, it's because we're so concentrated on the genital side of sex.

In the book *First Time* there's a kind of amusing little thing by Loretta Lynn where she talks about her first time of sex and how little enjoyment she got and what a letdown it was. She spent years without having any satisfaction out of sex, because nobody told her about her clitoris and where it was. She had asked all kinds of doctors why her sex life wasn't better. They weren't able to tell her, and that tells me a lot about doctors.

People go to doctors with their sexual problems. That's just like going to a bank robber and giving him the money you want to retire on. "Here, bank robber, I've got some money to entrust with you. You're the person I most think of to leave it with." Because most doctors I know anything about have about the worst sex lives of anybody I've ever seen. How can you work sixty to seventy hours a week and be real depressed and have a good sex life? Half the doctors in a big survey admitted their marriages were very unsatisfactory. But doctors have got the world's greatest dodge, you know. They're being God to run away from life and their wives and everything else. And then people go to them for sexual advice.

So anyway, Loretta Lynn went and asked a bunch of doctors what was wrong with her sex life and none of them ever thought to tell her about her clitoris.

When she finally did find a doctor who told her about her clitoris, she found out it was in the wrong place, geographically. It was too far north to get in on the action. So she recommends that the clitoris be relocated further south so it can get in on the action better. But now Loretta Lynn has found out about all this and she's pretty well solved all her problems. One of my students at the sex seminar said a better name for the clitoris was "the little man in the canoe." But call it what you will.

Then Sherry Hite came along and she was fixing to start a little war. She loaded a questionnaire with leading questions as well as she could, sent out one-hundred-thousand copies and got two-thousand back, which was a little bit of a distorted sample. To the distorted questions, she found out that a lot of the women hated men because men wouldn't give women what they wanted. What women wanted was for men to stimulate their clitoris, and because men weren't doing this, why, the women were unhappy. I wanted to say to the gals who were angry about this, why not ask the guy instead of wanting him to read your mind? Any gal who thinks a guy is going to be able to read her mind is really dumb. I suppose there are two thousand out of a hundred thousand women like that, but that's pretty dumb and pretty sad, really.

In Hite's book she also starts lobbing the hand grenades at other women. One of the women is Marie Robinson, who wrote a book called *The Power of Sexual Surrender*. In it, Robinson argues that while a clitoral orgasm is on the path to sexual maturity, it is not sexual maturity. Marie Robinson is a psychiatrist who argues that a vaginal orgasm comes when there is more surrender and less of the ego and so is true sexual maturity.

Her viewpoint got hurt by Maribel Morgan picking it up, because so many women feel Maribel Morgan doesn't know anything. So there's a nice war going between Maribel Morgan and the women's libbers. Old Marie Robinson is about eighty now, so she's sitting there in the middle and they're reprinting her book like crazy.

But the gals are arguing back and forth about which is best. The answer, as I see it, is that it doesn't matter; this isn't a war or a race, it's a matter of individual progress. We like to move from one thing to another, and we'll take what comes. But I do see that the deeper the sexual experience, the more the whole heart, soul and body enters in, the more widely and deeply the experience pervades the whole body and soul. You see this clearly in the difference in feeling between self-masturbation and intercourse with the beloved person.

One of the things that's interesting to me about the argument is that Marie Robinson argues that surrender has got a lot to do with the question of vaginal orgasm. And I've got a suspicion, and I may be prejudiced against Sherry Hite, that Hite doesn't like the idea of surrendering to a guy. I don't have any spiritual light on her path. So I don't know where she should go or how she should go. I'm just talking to you ladies and guys who would read her book. It does have some interesting and helpful things, because she has a lot of comments from ladies saying what they like and don't like and how they feel. To me, anytime you're listening to how a lady feels, you're way ahead of the game. I'm not so interested in the editorializing Hite does from the comments on the questionnaire.

A guy and a gal in a recent Book of the Month Club selection went out and did a sex survey to show how wrong Sherry Hite was, and they found that 98 per cent of men want to please their women. Well, I have great difficulty believing that. I can believe that probably 98 per cent of the men *think* they want to please their women. But if the women I've talked to are any sign, I don't think it's quite that high.

I don't think it's as low as Sherry Hite says it is, but I don't think it's as high as the opposing book says it is either. I think, like always, the truth is somewhere in between. But, again, the point that we're making here is that statistics are interesting to read and argue about, but what each of us really needs to do is find out what our needs are so we can get our needs met.

When I gave the first sex seminar in Minneapolis, in June of 1977, I gave the ladies, all of them, permission to have orgasm. If they hadn't had an orgasm, they were to go home that night and have one immediately, with or without the help of their husbands. Some of them got mad at me, "Why should I have to do that for myself? My husband should be able to read my mind and know that I want him to do that for me, and I'm going to be unhappy at him instead." That's beautiful. They're entitled to that. If that's your need—to be unhappy—fantastic; you satisfy that need. It's a little bit, in my view, acidic. It tends to turn your face into a pickle. But if you want to have a face like a pickle, you go ahead. "Well," you say, "I have such a beautiful face; it isn't going to look like a pickle for twenty to thirty years." Then, you wait that twenty or thirty years while your face is turning into a pickle. It's going to be unpleasant for you while you're waiting, and it's really going to be unpleasant for you afterwards, because then you're going to have the feelings of a pickle and the face of a pickle, where right now you just have the feelings of a pickle, even though your face in its youthful resilience and beauty is unpickled.

Who's right in an argument on orgasms? I'm not a woman, so I can't know any more than what women tell me and what I read by them. Sex is just two people being together in a loving way all day long and in bed at night. How orgasm comes about may be special, but it's just a part of the two people being together.

A committee of psychologists have proposed a new set of guidelines on sexism in psychology. The last one of the guidelines says very clearly that psychologists are not to have intercourse with their clients. That's a long-needed statement, to replace the earlier one, which was not quite that definite. But there's another guideline that bears on our discussion of surrender. It says therapists are not to imply to women clients that vaginal orgasms are preferable to clitoral orgasms.

This is just another example of a deep mystery to me. As I've said before, I'm not a woman, so I can't say how women feel. But I am enough of a psychologist to know that if someone raises a problem with me about me and I get mad, I've got a problem. I'm a very competent woodworker, elk hunter and advertising man. If someone implies to me that I'm not, I don't get mad at them, I feel sorry for them for their lack of discrimination.

If a woman is completely happy with her orgasms, then there's no way her therapist's doubt about them is a problem to her. But if she says, "Yes there is, he's big daddy therapist and he shouldn't say anything that makes me unsure," she's got a problem with her view of her therapist and her dependence on him that she needs to work out. If her feeling is because she is so unsure about her own orgasms that the therapist's words are a problem to her, then she needs to look at her own unsureness.

I know that a therapist ideally isn't a mean person. But he does look for the hot spots to reveal them to the client, just as the therapist hopefully looks at his or her own hot spots to reveal them more clearly so they can be worked on.

What I can't understand is a guideline that says a therapist can't ethically talk in certain ways to a woman about something that bothers her. I think that works against the interest of the woman involved.

Most clitoral orgasms come about in one of four

ways: the man or woman's hand on the clitoris, the mouth, the body rubbing against it or the penis in the vagina. For men, most orgasms come about from the woman's or man's hand on the penis, the mouth, the body rubbing against it or the penis in the vagina. As near as I can see, for men some of those methods of orgasm are generally more pleasurable than others. For the life of me, I can't see what the problem is when the issue is raised about a vaginal orgasm being something for a woman to look at. Especially I can't see the problem when women like Marie Robinson, who hopefully have experienced both and worked with many women who have had both, say to women that they need to look at the problem.

It seems to me the the words "clitoral" and "vaginal" orgasms are largely code words in the same way "crime in the streets" was a code word used to talk against blacks. It looks like "clitoral orgasm" is a code word for orgasms produced by the man's or woman's hand or mouth, where the female experiences her orgasm separate from the male orgasm. It seems to me "vaginal orgasm" is a code word for the woman experiencing one or more orgasms as the man is experiencing his orgasm. It doesn't seem to me that the part of the woman's sexual area that experiences the orgasm is the crucial point, whether the focus of the woman's feeling is in the clitoris or vagina or both. The crucial point seems to me to be the question of separateness and surrender. By separateness I don't mean orgasms at different times. I mean that the sexual focus is on one orgasm at a time, rather than on both orgasms. I'm not talking about simultaneous orgasm. That's such a terrible idea because it becomes a goal, and both people commonly fail in pursuit of it and often fake to protect themselves and the other.

What I mean by being together is that both can have an orgasm or orgasms if and when they are appropriate for them. There is a lot of closeness and a

lot of surrender in this. I think that closeness and
surrender is the problem. I don't see that different
ways of having sex scare people; it's closeness and
surrender. That closeness and surrender is especially
hard when there are bad feelings between the two,
which almost automatically exist at times in a marriage
or other long-term relationship. Surrender doesn't mean
just surrendering to a man or a woman, it means
surrendering to most everything. But surrendering to
most everything does include surrendering to the man
and the woman. So often the feeling I find is "I'd
surrender to anything rather than him or her." So
that's where I think the problem is.

If surrender is the basic problem in this issue, I
sympathize with the woman just as I sympathize with
my own problems as a man with surrender. I don't see
anything that's harder to do than surrendering. But I
don't see anything I've done in my life that yields
bigger dividends than surrendering, either.

There are two parts to this issue. One part is an
individual woman's anatomy and physiology. Only the
woman involved can speak of that. But the other part
is surrender. The surrender problem looks to me to be
exactly the same for everyone and in almost every
religion or philosophy I've ever studied. I haven't yet
seen a person resist surrender without paying a big
price and getting results that most of the people I
know don't like.

This is one of the big paradoxes in sex—that two
people can have a shared ideal of some places that sex
will sometimes take them to but not have it as a goal
or an evaluation of their intercourse. They keep their
minds on the fire at the beginning and they both
surrender to the loving and each other as well as that
can happen, and intercourse gradually changes. How
fast and to what degree sex between them changes
and gets richer should be a matter of no concern
where each is thrilled with what they have at the

time. But the more thrilled each is with what they now have and the more grateful they are for what they now have, the faster things can change. So it is vital that we, at the same time, are able to understand and not resist an ideal, yet not try to reach anything but what we have today.

One huge problem in our sexual loving is our twisted sense of what's moral. One of the sadnesses we have in this business of what's moral is that we know that when God wrote the Bible, or whatever moral book you depend on, God didn't quite know what he was doing. So we change certain things and we put the emphasis in different places.

For example, the Christian Bible says that there are Ten Commandments. Now, God didn't know what he was doing in giving us the Ten Commandments. There is only one commandment:—thou shalt not jump in bed with thy neighbor's wife. Now, if I obey that commandment, I'll be a good Christian and go right to heaven.

There are a number of the other commandments that are either wrong or not necessary. The ones that are wrong are: Thou shalt not covet thy neighbor's goods. Everybody knows that's a good thing to do, and I'll marry any guy who covets all kinds of his neighbor's goods, because he will make such a good provider. And I sure never heard of any wife divorcing a husband because he coveted the neighbor's goods. I have heard of some women divorcing a husband because he jumped in bed with the neighbor's wife. I don't think, though, that I've ever heard of a woman divorcing her husband because he stole anything. So we have kind of twisted up the instructions of the particular Bible that we claim to have some allegiance to.

But that's all right. If we want to have some cobbled-up old religion that we made up ourselves and we are satisfied with that instead of a real one, that's fine. We can have whatever understanding of God we feel entitled to.

The bigger problem faces us when we come to judging our actions on this homemade moral basis. One of the big things we've got as to what's moral and what's not is we know very carefully what part of our bodies should not touch what other parts of other people's bodies. We've got a very accurate map. Like Father Rohr says, we could put up an anatomy chart, point out the parts, and this is untouchable, this is semiuntouchable, and this you can touch. And this part over here can't ever touch that part over there because God is really worried about that. That would really bother him. He would have real trouble handling that.

In the process of making sure that this part here does not touch that part there, we do some very, very unloving things to the other partner in the sex deal. But we know that doesn't bother God. We can be mean, and scream and bitch and yell and holler and be resentful; that doesn't bother God. It's the parts that are touching; that's what bothers God. We know that he didn't know what he was doing when he left us together in our nakedness and openness. He didn't set these things up just right. We know what limitations he should have specified. And when he said love one another as I have loved you, with great compassion and stuff, that doesn't apply to the dirty ugly stuff that can go on between a man and a woman. His idea of love one another doesn't apply there; it means something different, like general love, like I love everybody. I love horses and dogs, even though I whip my horse and spank my colt unmercifully at times when he's just being a colt. I really love animals, yet my horses won't come towards me; they run away from me. But I really love those horses; I really do.

I love people just the same way, even though they all run away from me and nobody wants to be around me. I really love the hell out of people except all the times when I run into a son of a bitch, you know, who nobody could love, and they deserve the treatment they're getting from me.

You see how we twist the teachings around? A person who has this distorted interpretation of their various religious or philosophical codes, they then turn around and use those distorted interpretations to guide their moral actions. And you wonder how come we're in a mess about sex. We're doing some of the most immoral things and calling it morality. And the sins of omission, all the truly loving things that we don't do but need to, to me they're the ones we are suffering for, and if there's a hell, which I have trouble believing, it's our sins of omission that are going to ride us right straight there.

One of the real interesting sins of omission is the iron virgin. The iron virgin is the girl who walks into my office and sits her big, tight fanny down in the chair opposite me and loudly proclaims her virtue, and how, by God, no guy is ever going to wrong her virtue. She's saving herself for Mr. Right. She lets me know in no uncertain terms that, despite the depraved nature of the men of this world, she has managed to hang on to her virginity.

I think, "You hard, cold lady." I've got nothing against virginity. Some of my best friends are virgin nuns and I love them. But they don't wear their virginity like they're flying the Notre Dame fight flag.

The iron virgin is so anxious to prevent sins of commission that there's a little chance that she's committing a whole bunch of sins of omission. For example, the iron virgin would not be like the Jewish lady I read about. Hitler was doing some very cruel experiments that are reported in *The Rise and Fall of the Third Reich*. To see what happened to German pilots who went down in the North Sea, captured Russian pilots were put in freezing water and left until they were nearly dead to see how much exposure a human could take and still live. Then they were plucked out and put in a room with a woman. The purpose of the woman was to warm up the guy. If the woman didn't warm up the guy, the guy died.

In this case it told of a person who had witnessed such a thing. This Russian flyer was put in cold water, plucked out and put in a room with this Jewish woman from the concentration camp. She used her body to warm him up and then stimulated him and had intercourse with him to save his life.

Okay, the iron virgin would not do that, because it would violate her sense of what is moral and appropriate to do. Because it is wrong to do that. We all know that; right?

So I quit using my own twisted moral rules on myself, because I have the same problems all of you do in the way I've distorted moral teaching in my own childish way. I quit using my own twisted moral ideas and I started saying, "Hey, I can't live that way. I'm in a desperate situation, like being in a snowstorm on the top of Mount Everest. I've got two hours to get off the top or die. All I'm interested in is what works and what produces good long-term results in my life—what produces peace and joy for me and the people around me." The funny thing I found was that the more I went in search of what had good results in my life, the more a bunch of guys who were moral teachers came to me and said, "Hey, Jess, you're teaching a true morality." But that isn't why I'm teaching it—because it coincides with the true morality. I'm teaching what I see working in my life and the lives of people around me.

I've come to see now that the only morality that I'm looking for in my life is what works and lasts. And I know that will be a true morality, incidentally, because the god of my understanding wants only the best for me, and what is the best for me is what works. So I find the simplest way for me to find what is the will of the god of my understanding is essentially to seek the best guidance I can get and to find what produces good long-term results in my life and in the lives of the people I'm involved with. If it produces, on a long-term basis, good results in my life and the lives of the people I'm involved with, then it is good for me. And then, incidentally, it will probably also be good morality in general if we want to concern ourselves with such, but I don't want to concern myself with such, because I'm a poor judge. I'll let the higher power judge me. I won't even attempt to judge myself, to say nothing of judging someone else.

What is important, I see, is my attitude. If I surrender to the will of the higher power as well as I can see it, I can make a ton of mistakes without having too many problems, as long as my attitude is being willing to be constantly corrected and to be given input. Being perfect isn't the answer. I'm not being perfect—that's God business.

Part of what I've come to see is that we don't really have a sex problem. We just think we do. When I was fifteen years old in Bricelyn High School, the idea of getting in bed with a naked woman, alone—that would be enough. If I was asked then, "What would you like?" boy, that would be fantastic. Okay, all we need to do is go back to being fifteen years old and, like my old Hindu adviser says, keep our mind on the fire at the beginning and don't have any destination. It would be amazing where we go. That way, we can start from a better basis.

So I don't have a sexual problem, because I don't have a lot of expectations any more about the way things are supposed to be and what things are supposed to happen. "If this thing and that thing doesn't happen, then I'm not as good as some other person. Oh, my God, I'm inadequate again" or "I'm not getting what I want; ain't it awful." So I can love on a better basis.

We see that our body is our sex instrument and our lovemaking starts each day at breakfast. The way we take care of our sexual instrument during the day has so much to do with the sex we have. Food, exercise, work, play—our sex instrument needs moderate amounts of everything. I've found, for example, I can't even touch coffee, because it gets me too high in a false way. I've recently given up even tea. And I wouldn't take a tranquilizer if you gave me the bank. I don't want any drug in me. A year ago, I tried being a vegetarian and I liked the results I got from that.

Then we surrender to what happens. A woman says, "I just want to be held and kissed." What she doesn't realize is that her husband is probably thinking, "Lots of times I just want to have intercourse without all the hugging and kissing." Those are both legitimate feelings, but they're both too much concentrating on where it's going to go. So the best way is for two people who claim they love each other to get in bed and love each other and take whatever comes. Then both people's needs are more nearly met, but neither person's expectations are ever met exactly, especially when they start out with a preconceived notion of how they should be met.

I see that much of what men are doing is an escape from surrender. I think that a big part of what is being written by and for women may also be an escape from surrender. Only in the most complete surrender possible can the two parts of the whole fit together, merge together and thereby bond together.

Surrender is such a problem for us, and here I see men and women as exactly alike; they are souls, not sexes, and they both have a surrender problem. Surrender is a problem because we have to give up being the stage director of the universe. We have to go from certainty to uncertainty.

There's a beautiful Zen story where the very proud samurai warrior goes to the Zen teacher. He says, "Master, is there a heaven and a hell?" And the Zen master says to the samurai, "Why, you fat samurai, I bet that rusty sword of yours can't cut butter." At this, the samurai becomes very angry and draws his sword and prepares to behead the teacher. Then the samurai warrior sees his own anger and the teacher's wisdom. So he sheathes his sword and bows to the teacher, and the teacher says, "Enter the gates of paradise."

When we fight any other human being, we enter the gates of hell. When we bow to another human being in reverent surrender, we enter the gates of paradise.

We have to say yes to life and all its risks. They really aren't risks; they just look that way. The riskiest, most dangerous thing we can do is try to control life to avoid risk, because we always fail and the only person we frustrate is ourselves, because we never control life, we just think we do. I've heard a lot of people say, "What's going to happen to the world if I give up controlling the world?" And the answer is, "The same thing that happened before you gave up controlling the world."

St. Catherine of Siena said, "All the way to heaven is heaven itself, for have I not said, 'I am the way.' "

This is a battle we wage with our bodies. How do we get up courage to leave safety behind? We do what we can with what we have. We change the things we can change. And our marriage partner is the very last thing we should ever change, because typically most of us have wrought the very carnage we condemn. And the minute we wake up to see the carnage we've wrought, we want to say, "Well, isn't this awful what this person is doing to me and, by God, I'm going to go and get a new one." And typically the answer is "We'll get a new one and wreak the same carnage on them as we did the old." So if we're going to learn to stop wreaking carnage on the marriage partner, a good place to start is with the present marriage partner, or sexual partner if you aren't married. You say, "But I want new ground!" Sure. But there's a bond there, and we'll talk about that next.

CHAPTER 7

Bonding and the Healing Power of Love

I want to talk to you about bonding. I think bonding is the most misunderstood topic in America. When Ben-Gurion was going to be made Premier of Israel, they found he hadn't troubled to get married, because in the Jewish tradition, when a man sleeps with a woman, they are married. The religious or civil ceremonies simply recognize a fact that has, in those cases, already happened. When a man has intercourse with a woman, he takes a lifetime responsibility for her. Furthermore, if that man dies, in old Jewish law that man's brother has the responsibility to care for the woman. That is a religious and, I guess, cultural tradition of the Jews.

I think what we do in this day and age in our culture is we think that our cultural and religious rules on bonding are just myths. We think religion as we see it practiced has little or no consequence or substance in people's lives. I think that the religious view of marriage and the legal view of marriage is not only valid, I believe it doesn't go far enough in recognizing a deep psychological principle that I see is unrecognized by most people today even among so many of the people who stoutly defend marriage on religious grounds.

The way I see it now is that in any relationship there is a bonding. In a sexual relationship there is a deep bonding. What the Jewish tradition Ben-Gurion operated under does is recognize that the first sexual intercourse between two people is the best place to draw the line between the little bonding that's in all relationships and the big bonding that's in a sexual relationship. The Jews have had thousands of years of experience as an intact culture, and I think their judgment is wiser than most people today understand.

In the Jewish tradition as I understand it, from reading the "Rabbi" detective novels like *Friday the Rabbi Slept Late* and other important Jewish sources, the center of religion is in the family rather than the church. So when Ben-Gurion and his wife say to each other they're married and are a family, that's the most important step for them. The public ceremony in the synagogue is a very secondary matter, partly involved with the proper appearances on the surface, rather than what's in the heart.

In the Christian view, the church has more importance in religion, and marriages are to be performed in the church. But even here, as the marriage ceremony indicates, what is created is not as much a marriage as an opportunity for a marriage to happen in the protected unit of two which is sheltered by religious and cultural belief.

Even for those who have no belief in church weddings, there is, for most, a desire to recognize the legal and cultural role of the wedding. So they get a license and get married by some public official.

But in any of these forms, the marriage doesn't really occur in the church or judge's chambers. As a young person, I always wondered why that ceremony could make things right that up to that minute were wrong. I wondered how that ceremony could be so important. I see now why I felt that way. The ceremony wasn't that important. What was important was the bonding that would occur in the marriage. So marriage really happens in the bonding that goes on between the two people. The marriage is simply an aid and a recognition of this blonding. But, in our society, not just for this generation but for some generations we have seen the ceremony as more important than it is and not seen the bonding for what it really is.

They say marriage is in trouble today. Marriage has always been in some trouble. Just look at some of the marriages in the Bible three thousand years ago. For generations marriage has been in lots of trouble. Today's divorce rate is astronomical but it doesn't tell the true story. The marriages I saw in Bricelyn, Minnesota, as I was growing up a generation ago in an idyllic small town were probably about as troubled as today, but they didn't break up because most couldn't. Social pressure was too strong, jobs for women were too few and money was so scarce people had enough trouble just living, say nothing of being able to afford living separately.

We think of the younger generation as having more trouble today with marriage, and the statistics seem to back it up at first. The number of people who are living together without marriage has doubled just since 1970. Among couples under forty-five, the increase has been fivefold.

But in the older generation, we are also having our troubles with marriage. Three out of four women over fifty are on their second marriage and five out of six men. A good part of that is due to the death of the first spouse, but a good part of it is due to previous divorces.

I don't think marriage can get in trouble. It's an institution that exists in a pretty stable form in most every society ever studied. What I think has always been in trouble in some percentage of our people of marriageable age. When a person has too much trouble with his ego, his self-centeredness, or too much emotional deprivation, or both, there's almost no way that person can make any relationship work well for very long. So, to me, today it isn't marriage that's in trouble but the people who are trying to make those marriages go. When we're crippled, how can we make good basketball players?

I don't mean this as a way of making us feel bad. But, as I've said, if we're going to solve a problem, it helps to know what the problem is. There's no need for me to defend marriage. It's strong enough so it doesn't need any defense. Rather than launch attacks on marriage, I think each of us had better search his own mind, heart and soul and look at his or her abilities to build and sustain a long-term, permanent relationship. And I think we need to see that bonding, as recognized by the Jewish law followed by Ben-Gurion, is going on in our lives to some degree whether we recognize it or not.

What is bonding? Bonding is just what it implies. When two pieces of material are bonded together, they become one. Between two people, sexual bonding is an emotional, psychological, physical and spiritual link so strong that the two become one at least for a moment in a small way. The more emotional and spiritual openness and the deeper the relationship goes into physical and sexual openness and surrender, the deeper the bond. Now, because people don't know about sexual bonding, especially at first, people are bonding sexually all over the place to one another and to one degree or another, not realizing they are. They tear apart, taking a little or a big piece out of each other, and go on to the next bonding. And then eventually they wonder why they hurt so much.

As I said, the common view is that bonding is something the churches and other religions of the world talk about as marriage and that it is a myth with no reality. There is little understanding of the psychological and physiological basis of bonding, which applies to anyone with or without reference to God. From the psychological standpoint, you can pretty safely generalize that the more people a person bonds with in sexual intercourse and then tears away from, the more emotionally disturbed they are—with prostitutes, paid or amateur, at the top of the scale.

There are drastic physiological consequences when the war of emotions upsets the whole body. We don't see that we have a heart. We think that our big head is so great. There is a sad story in Studs Terkel's book *Working* where he interviewed all kinds of people in different kinds of jobs, and he interviewed a prostitute. The prostitute had a boyfriend. When the prostitute would have sex with a customer, she would turn her feelings off, and then she would turn them back on when she was with her boyfriend. Pretty soon she found her feelings stayed off. She couldn't get them turned back on.

You see, the big head keeps telling us we're so smart. Who is it that's telling us we're so smart? The same big head that listens to itself telling us we're so smart. It's the big head, the huge, big head.

Bonding is a very complex process. There has been very little research done on it. Part of the problem is that we don't even have a concept in Western society for one of the vital elements of bonding—energy. Touch is a central part of sexual bonding. One of the big things communicated by touch is energy. The Eastern religions recognize this energy. The Hindus call it prana. Health is an abundance of prana, and sickness is a lack of prana. They see the lack of energy as the cause of the disease, and the physical symptoms as just a side effect.

We call that energy vigor or vitality, and we're well aware of the obvious changes in vigor or vitality in illness, and its disappearance is death.

There are some experiments that demonstrate the power of touch and perhaps of the transfer of this energy. At McGill University in the early sixties, a man named Grad took three hundred mice and wounded their backs with a cut of a standard length and depth. One hundred mice were allowed to heal naturally without any outside assistance, a second third were touched and held by medical students who did not purport to heal. The final third were held by a world-renowned healer, Oskar Estebany, who visited this country for a few weeks each year.

Careful measurements of the rate of healing demonstrated that by the end of two weeks the rate of healing in the mice held by Estebany had accelerated to a level where the outcome could have occurred by chance less than once in a thousand times.

The study was repeated on plants. Barley seeds were soaked in salt water to make them sick. The containers the sick seeds were in were not touched. Only the water they were irrigated with was touched. The first group of seeds was irrigated by water from the tap. The second group was irrigated with water from the tap put in flasks which the medical students handled and touched. The third group was irrigated by water from flasks held by Estebany.

After five days it was found that the barley seeds treated by Estebany sprouted earlier, the spouts grew taller and they contained more chlorophyll.

Another study was done on the enzyme trypsin, an enxyme essential to metabolism. One set of test tubes of trypsin were the controls, another set was exposed to high magnetic-field radiations and a third group was held by Estebany. After the first hour, the values of the sample held by Estebany dramatically exceeded the other two samples.

A nurse, Dolores Krieger, R.N., PH.D., of New York University, was intrigued by this work and wanted to see if she could apply this therapeutic touch to nursing. She says, "I realized that my basic assumption was that human beings are open systems, that they appear to be a nexus [connection or link] for all fields of which life partakes; that is, inorganic, organic, psychic and conceptual . . . and as such they are exquisitely sensitive to wave phenomena, i.e., energy. The healer [Estebany] I saw as an individual whose health gave him an access to an overabundance of prana. His health was an indication that he was in a highly efficient interaction with the significant field forces. His strong sense of commitment gave him a certain control over the projection of his vital energy for a well-being of another. The act of healing, therefore, would entail the channeling of this energy flow by the healer for the supplementation of that of the ill individual."

Krieger set up a couple of experiments. In the first one, Estebany did the touching and the hemoglobin of the patients touched was increased. Krieger came to believe that one didn't need to be a chosen person to do therapeutic touch. "Rather, it seemed to me that therapeutic touch was a natural human potential which could be actualized by those who had a fairly healthy body, strong intent to help or heal ill persons and who were educable."

Krieger had thirty-two nurses and sixty-four patients in an experimental-control, before-and-after research design. Lab technicians didn't know the study was in progress. Hemoglobin values of patients who were touched therapeutically improved, and the control group showed no change.

That research suggests what touch can do. If some nurses touching the hands and bodies of people can improve their hemoglobin, what can the massive touch of two loving people in sexual intercourse do to each other's bodies?

We see another sign of this in the bonding that goes on just after childbirth. I talked of that in Chapter Two. I mentioned that babies who were separated from their mothers at birth were later held on the side away from the mother's heart. Other studies show that lack of bonding in premature infants results in increased child abuse.

So a dangerous thing happens when a premature baby is rushed from the delivery room to an incubator to save its life without having the chance to be held and loved by its mother in the first few minutes of life. The bonding process can't be carried through. The lack of that bonding has grave consequences for the baby's physical and emotional health for the rest of its life.

What, then, happens when a man and a woman are together in sexual intercourse, yet don't let down the shields that guard their separateness? To me, there is a lack of bonding between them that has grave consequences for their sexual relationship, for their emotional relationship, and for the closeness between them, that will be more and more important as they face the difficulties of life together.

I see our immaturity in sex in our escapes. I see our maturity in sex in our bonding. The path to maturity is through immaturity. There's just no reason we should delay maturity forever.

Dan Casriel, the psychiatrist, in his book *A Scream Away from Happiness*, written in 1972, points out that we have a biological need for bonding in the same way we need air, food and water. This is a need that was met when we were in the womb and to some degree when we were babies. But then we went out into the great deserts of life, where no more were we touched or could we touch.

When we get an adequate amount of bonding it produces a neutral state that he calls well. When we go join our fellow human beings in life and embrace them, we get an abundance of love and pleasure. This changes our whole body in ways that can be measured, and we become weller than well, as my wife and Walther Lechler discuss in their book. "I Exist, I Need, I'm Entitled."

When we don't meet our biological needs for bonding, we experience hunger, just as we do when we don't eat. That hunger shows itself as pain. We tend to react to that pain in one of two ways: fear (the anticipation of pain) or anger at what we see as the cause of the pain, the others around us.

When we react with fear, we tend to show it through running away or withdrawing within ourselves like a coiled snake.

When we react with anger, we lash out against the world or we try to control it. My reaction to my lack of bonding was to lash out at the world in anger. The hostility and aggression of extreme Type A people like myself is an expression of anger coming out of the pain of our hunger and thirst for bonding with people and all the rest of life.

My deprivation—not getting enough bonding as a baby and since then—changes my whole physiology. So as I learn to come back into the human race and to go join each of my brothers and sisters—you—I start getting my needs met. I reduce my pain, so I automatically become less angry. This lets me bond more deeply and reduce pain more, and on and on. My body stops being so negative, so I get rid of pain by reducing my hunger and thirst for people. Someday I will be a neutral, where I stop damaging my body. And someday past that, I will be "veller than vell," as my German friend Walther says it. And my body will be changed from the negative system of constantly expecting pain to the positive one of constantly expecting love. When this happens, my whole physiology will be different. Instead of producing the hormones that are needed to fight or flee, I will be producing the hormones of a state of pleasure and relaxation. That's happening some already, but later it will be the predominant state.

As I mentioned at the beginning of the chapter, there is very little understanding in our society of bonding and the consequences of careless bonding. We don't understand the depth of the physical consequences of deeply loving and being naked to the other person.

We don't see the consequences of our bonding, so we don't see we have a responsibility for our bonding the rest of our lives.

A prominent movie star saw a Fellini movie that showed movingly the consequences of bonding. The star was very deeply moved and said, "I didn't realize before the harm I was doing when I carelessly touched a woman in a personal way." I'm sure all of us know what he means. It is any wonder, with all the careless bonding going on, that we recoil from trying again?

Bartley's book of Werner Erhard tells of an unusual recognition of bonding. Jack Rosenberg deserted his wife and children at about twenty-three and ran away with another woman. They both took new names and started a new life as Werner and Ellen Erhard. Later, Werner had a number of affairs, including one that taught him so much about loving. About six years ago, Erhard went back to make amends with his first wife and family. But what is unusual about his story is that his former wife is now working in his office staff. She has remarried and divorced. She realized she still loved Erhard. He couldn't remarry her but did evidently choose to have her in a position where he could give her daily emotional love and support as well as financial. If the woman Erhard had the deep loving affair with was on his staff from the *Parents' Magazine* days, then there is a good chance she, too, is still working close to him.

So, while Erhard and Ellen have a close and honest marriage, one and maybe two of what might have been bondings he made in his past are now in his daily environment in a good way with the bond and its consequences being recognized to as great a degree as possible while still avoiding playing any games.

The Eskomo culture doesn't have a word for war. That tells us about Eskimos. Our culture doesn't have a word for *confianza*. That tells us about our culture. *Confianza* is a Spanish word. Jerry and Marilyn Sexton of Marriage Encounter gave me the meaning of the word. "At a wedding, the families of the new bride and bridegroom, before their assembled friends and before God, freely choose to enter the relationship of 'confianza.' They pledge themselves to each other in a sacred bond. Once they are in this special relationship, they pledge to come to the other person or persons, no matter what. They can depend on the other. In fact, they are obligated to depend on the other in that relationship. In effect, they are saying: 'I will come to you for help in my needs, in my times of trouble, in my moments of joy, in all my life.'

"The bond formed is much stronger than any blood relationship. Because the bond is made by choice, and not by accident, it is a very solemn commitment.

"As an example, say I've entered into such a bond with you. Also suppose that I suddenly become financially distressed. If I go to another person to reveal this need, rather than to you, I would have broken the bond. I would have failed in my obligation to come to you. This is the bond of confianza. Confianza involves, then, more than mere trust. It involves a pledge of intimacy to each other that we freely choose to depend on each other for the fulfillment of our needs."

So here the Spanish have a word for something we can all see the need for; yet it is so uncommon in our culture we can't understand it really or talk about it without using three paragraphs.

When it takes three paragraphs to describe a word, then that says we don't have that idea much in our society. In the movie *The Godfather*, there is the scene where the undertaker comes to the Godfather. Here are two Sicilians. One has chosen to go the American way. When his daughter was raped by two punks, the undertaker went to the police. The two men were tried and released and laughed at the undertaker as they went by him in court as free men.

The undertaker then came to the Godfather for jus-

tice. The Godfather scolded him. He said, "Why did
you not come to me first?" I think the reason he didn't
come to the Godfather first is the desire that is in all
people for separateness. "I can do it myself." Going to
the police was nice and impersonal. Coming to the
Godfather in fulfillment of the bond of confianza that
existed among Sicilians was not nice and impersonal
and cool. It was very intimate and hot.

I think part of all our fascination with *The Godfather* was a feeling for the intimacy and passion in
their family life. I don't mean sex-passion; I mean
passion-passion, the intense life that most of us experience only in sex.

I was out cross-crountry skiing after doing the final
editing of this book. I saw a woman be with three
magnificent men—her husband, her ski instructor and
me—and she spent the whole time complaining, being
a victim. The ski instructor and I had a good time.
Her husband later got stuck with the victim. What
sadness to see a woman forty-nine years old living out
a fiction, a role she had learned from her mother! She
had the opportunity for passion: to romp in the snow,
laugh, holler at the fear of sliding downhill too fast
out of control and roll in the snow and laugh when she
finally fell. But she was so full of her pain, which was
coming out of her as fear and anger, that none of
those passionate things happened.

That evening, she talked about how strong her religion was. Yet, by stressing her religion instead of her
God, she gave an indication of the limit of her religion. She loves her husband and children. Yet she is
blind to the way her role as victim limits the flow of
love to her and from her. And she lacks a God that
has enough power to remove old, unconscious patterns.

As I saw this clearly the next morning, I shrunk
from telling the two of them what I had seen. Her
husband had asked me what having a living God
meant. So it wasn't that I didn't have an invitation. I

saw that I was like all the rest of you in being afraid of openness and intimacy and love. I saw that, to be true to myself, I had to broach the subject. The next morning, I called the husband and explained what I saw. He was happy to hear what I had to say and invited me to sit down with them and talk about it.

If I hadn't said something, then we each would have gone our separate ways, with me feeling uneasy about the information I had for them yet hadn't done anything about and them feeling some other feelings I didn't know. This way there is a golden thread between us the rest of our lives and a little confianza. It is bonding, confianza, golden threads, that holds us to society in a good way and holds society together. Marriages, families, communities, nations, the one world we can see plus all the rest of creation we can't see need all the bonding and confianza we can get. Also, the more confianza or bonding or golden threads, the richer and more passionate the moments in each day can be. And when we are passionate all day long, do you think that might increase the joy and passion we feel as we meet the loved one?

The big point here is that there is some confianza available to us, usually more than we will take. We won't take it, because it threatens our separateness. But you and I are one, and we also hunger for that. We need to find ways to put our separateness down anyway we can so we can join the brother and the sister that makes us whole. When we do that and meet each other openly and wholeheartedly, it does so much for us that whether there is or isn't a permanent sexual bonding for us down the road all of a sudden isn't the central issue any more. We are whole because we are bonded with the brother and the sister. The sexual thing just adds another dimension and helps in opening up our souls where that is the appropriate path for us.

It would be nice to be able to describe clearly just

what bonding is. We can see what it is in the infant. Dan Casriel, the New York psychiatrist, has a picture of a naked baby lying on his mother's stomach by the naked breast. The baby is looking into the mother's eyes with a look that says, "You're mine and I'm entitled to you." The mother's look back says the same thing. We know the immense physiological consequences of such a deep touching of each other, and the result of the physical, emotional, and spiritual contact.

We can also see the bonding that goes on when there is a real openness in sexual intercourse. But we can go from that kind of sexual bonding to the bonding I do as I go for a horseback ride. I greet my horses and bond with them. I walk up to my favorite horse and we play our little game of her not wanting to be caught and then waiting to be caught. I bond with her as I pet her and tie her up. I bond with her as I curry her. I bond with the saddle as I pick it up, remembering my dad's same basket-weave design, and admire all the silver on it and put it on the horse.

I bond with the horse as I get on, and my seat and legs squeeze the horse and my body hooks up to the roll of her body. I bond with the other riders as we move out, picking a way for everyone. I bond with the scenery, the rocks, trees, grass, fence posts, gates, hills, mountains, sky, all the sights I have seen so many times before.

It's winter, so we plunge through the drifts and deep snow. After a while we get off, tie the horses and scrape the deep snow away for a fire. We bond with the snow, the firewood we gather, the smell of lighter fluid I squirt on the twigs; I set a match to the wood and bond with the heat, and the feel of the cold thermos and hot tea, and feel the raisins and taste their sweetness.

All this is bonding, because it is the connection we make with things when we are awake and seeing and not asleep. You know how it is when you've gone through a few minutes of your life in a daze? You've turned off to everything? Well, that's being asleep when we're awake. We aren't experiencing what we're experiencing, so we aren't bonding with what we see and feel because we aren't aware. We're someplace else.

There are two Zen stories on this. Two Zen monks were walking through a small village on a muddy main street. They saw a young woman in a beautiful kimono on one side of the street who obviously was looking for a way to cross the muddy street. One monk went over to her, picked her up and carried her across the street. They walked on, and the other monk was silent until that evening. He finally said, "About that woman back there in the marketplace. We monks aren't supposed to have anything to do with women, let alone carry them across the street."

At this the other monk said, "Are you still carrying her? I put her down in the marketplace this afternoon."

This is us being asleep. We're still carrying all the women of the past, all the old memories and fictions and all the fears for the future. Our mind is so full of that junk, we can't even see what we're doing each moment, say nothing of bonding with it. It's always past or present with us, never the passion of now. Very few lives have too much passion. Most of us admire the passion of a Zorba the Greek, because most of us are like the college man in the story, with his mind filled with old fictions, questions, doubts, fears and resentments that he couldn't be like Zorba but yet why wasn't Zorba like him.

A new Zen master fresh out of school went to visit Hakim, an old Zen master. It was raining and the young Zen master left his sandals and umbrella at the door. He was very excited at the idea of meeting the great man. The first question Hakim asked the young man was, "On what side of your sandals is your umbrella sitting?" The young man had no answer and gave up his Zen mastership to go back to school to Hakim for three more years so he could learn to practice every-minute Zen.

We can't really see what life is offering us, we can't bond with life, unless we get an eye for life like Sherlock Holmes's, which saw everything. So this is how bonding works, as well as I can see.

I believe you can see from what I've said how the higher power, surrender and bonding all fit together. We need to surrender to the higher power all the things we can't change right now. (That's who's handling them anyway.) Then we can concentrate all our attention on every minute to see what life is offering us to bond with. The more we bond with life all day long, the better we can deepen the sexual bond in its time. The deeper the sexual bond, the more we can bond with life the next day. So that's how it fits together.

What does life look like when we look at it from this perspective?

Like I mentioned earlier, the people who bonded the most, often had the least sense of what all that indiscriminate bonding was doing to them. Some of my younger friends bonded and bonded and all of a sudden found it didn't work out very good. It didn't work out like their head had told them it would.

One of the saddest stories I had seen came up about six years ago when I was teaching at the college. The word was out that my classes were something kind of special. A guy stopped by from one of the eastern universities. He was hitchhiking across the country. He visited one of my classes, a really big guy in an old lumberjack shirt. He really liked what I was saying. "Wow, this is great." That was about noon, I guess.

About two-thirty I got this telephone call and here's this frightened little voice on the phone. It was this guy's old lady, his traveling companion. "Can I see you?" "Sure." "Well, how long are you going to be there?" I said, "Well, I don't know. Why?" "Well, I'm downtown and I don't have a car, so I'd have to walk up there." I said I'd wait; why not?

So the gal came up and walked in. She had an old sweater on and jeans and just a terrible-looking face. I went around on her side of the desk and sat by her, holding her hand. I said, "How are you doing?" She was just trembling like a leaf. "I'm not doing real good." I could smell sex on her. I said, "Have you just had intercourse?" "Yeah." "What's the deal?" "Well," she said, "that's the problem. I've had lots of anxiety and I've been able to use intercourse as a means of quieting down my anxiety. And it's stopped working. I just had intercourse a little bit ago, but right away my skin is crawling with anxiety. And now, because of all the sex and sex not working, my anxiety has really gotten worse."

"Well," I said, "tell me about your life." Her parents were in the foreign service. They were stationed in other countries and she was left behind in the care of servants. She said, "I haven't been able to make any peace with them about the bad feelings I have toward them for leaving me so much."

"Why don't you go home and make peace with them?" "Oh," she said, "I couldn't do that. They wouldn't stand still for it." "Well, why don't you try? What have you got to lose?"

So she went home and found she could make peace with them and started a new way of life for herself.

It was an interesting example to me how the big head of ours so often deceives us. For years she had a lovely rationalization all worked out for herself. And I'm sure that big guy was going around with the feeling, "Boy, when I have intercourse with a gal, it really calms her down. I'm really fantastic in bed and the gals that I lived with, it was so great for them."

That's not quite so. But we don't like, it seems to me, to look very carefully at the contradictory evidence that lies behind our own foolish ideas. We don't want to look at the havoc all our careless bonding leaves behind. When you bond two pieces of wood together and then break the bond, there isn't a clean break. Part of each piece of wood is torn away by the other. Same when a deep bond is broken, in my opinion. So we bond and break away a number of times and we can't figure out why we hurt so. I know that men I talk to are painfully aware of the women they bonded with and broke away from even if it was thirty or forty years ago.

It's just like the thinking of an alcoholic. Alcohol is so important to the alcoholic that, to him, all of us are drinkers; it's just that some of us are secret drinkers. He knows that everybody else in America is drinking. If they aren't drinking, they're cheating in some other way. He uses this twisted thinking to justify his own drinking and to help convince himself that what he's doing isn't so bad. So, to him, everybody else is drinking or, even worse, they're lying or stealing.

We maintain these same deceits in our own lives. Who are we hurting? It's just like when I was a businessman; I was crooked. Not out-and-out crooked, but I did business with two guys who were stealing people's money and I figured it was okay as long as I could get my money. I didn't want to look at the fact there were some people who did business in an honest, forthright way. Why would I want to look at something like that? So it's very easy with us to rationalize our deceits and justify them. But that's what's so dangerous: our distorted attitudes.

My friend Walther Lechler was teaching at the school I run on my own each January and July for my readers who come to Bozeman. He was speaking about the attitudes of smokers. Walther spent part of one of his days with us telling what a terrible thing smoking was, not so much from the consequences of smoking, but because of the justification of our addiction to ourselves. We tell ourselves it's not harmful to us when it's really hurting us. He said, "I don't care if you smoke if you'll admit that smoking is a terrible thing for you and that there's no reason for you to smoke. Because," he said, "what you're doing that's so bad isn't the smoking, it's the screwing up of your head so bad by justifying and rationalizing your smoking. You're saying, it isn't any problem to me or anything else that I'm smoking. That's the terrible thing. If I can get you to give up your twisted attitudes towards smoking, I don't care if you keep on smoking."

Can you say, "Yes, smoking is harmful to me and everybody else around me and it really hurts my family to see me killing myself with cigarettes and I'm a weak person not to be able to give up the addiction?" Say that and you can keep on smoking with a lot less harm to yourself.

Walther says that any time we have a part of us that is telling lies to ourselves and others, that's like a cancer that affects the whole rest of us. That's why the twelve-step programs talk about rigorous honesty. What rigorous means is not perfect honesty, because that's not possible for humans, but it means attempting to get rid of all areas of dishonesty in our lives. So we need to look at the consequences on ourselves of our careless bonding and we need to honestly recognize the consequences on others of our careless bonding, and this is typically not done. Once we know what we are doing and what the consequences of our actions are, then we can begin to act responsibly.

Imagine somebody driving a great big Sherman tank right down the middle of the Seattle main street with ten steel spikes sticking out in all directions and his windshield all muddy. Is he going to do some damage to other automobiles? And to telephone poles and pedestrians? He sure is. But because he chooses to be blind to it, he's not aware he's doing any damage. That's what I mean. The minute he opens his eyes and cleans off his windshield and looks out the window, he says, "Hey, I can't drive this tank down the main street here in anything except the absolute midnight time or I'm going to hurt somebody. I don't want to raise hell with a lot of people. I don't need to do good to people, but I do need to avoid raising hell with them." Careless sexual bonding is a big way we raise hell with ourselves and the other.

Earlier I mentioned the commune down in Summerton, Tennessee, formed by some hippies that were in the Haight-Ashbury district, out in San Francisco. They follow a spiritual teacher named Stephen, who was their teacher in San Francisco and led them to Tennessee to form a commune. I know Stephen and some of the people from the Farm. They found out how to make a commune go. Theirs is the longest-lived and the biggest commune by far, with over a thousand people there and six to ten other communes that they helped start under their direction in different places in the country. They have some basic rules for living there. Number one is that they acknowledge Stephen as their spiritual teacher. The rule they've got in the commune to handle relationships is that when you are sleeping together, you are engaged. When she's pregnant, you are married. Now, if you want to have a little marriage ceremony by Stephen some Sunday morning on the hill, you can do that, too, but the marriage happened when the gal got pregnant if they hadn't married on their own choice earlier. If you don't like the rules, then you leave.

The rules on the Farm aren't too different from the Jewish tradition. I could never have conceived of the necessity for such a set of rules when I was younger. But I'm completely convinced now of this bonding I see. It exists, and its existence has had to be recognized by any society where its members are going to stay in contact with one another, rather than drifting in and out of each other's lives.

Another student of mine was telling me a similar kind of story. She said that before she got married, she was willing to jump in the sack with most anybody, and did. She didn't think anything of it. But she's had god-awful sexual problems because of it. I don't see any recognition of the consequences of careless bonding in the psychological literature today. In fact, it seems to me that many of the psychological studies attempt to support careless bonding as a necessary and good way to cope with today's problems. The literature today by and large encourages people to do a bunch of things that, as near as this rat psychologist can see, produce destructive results for people. But I've got a suspicion I'm talking to people who have had some experiences that very possibly validate what I'm saying. But even there, whatever. Because I'm just telling you what I've found, anyway.

I've also come to see that there is at least a little bonding in any sexual encounter, because, like I say, there is some surrender in the sense of some nakedness to each other, psychically, emotionally, and physically. The larger the degree of awareness and surrender the more bonding. The better sex is, then, the more you are bonded to that person you have sex with. So the person who is looking for a fantastic number of great sexual experiences is looking for a contradiction. Because as great a sexual experience as you have, to that degree are you bonded to that person forevermore.

Now those are awful things to say to a group of lovely people. But that's what I see. I've seen overwhelming evidence to convince me of it. Now, like I say, I'm speaking in two guises here. I'm speaking in the guise of psychologist who is in the position to generalize about human behavior based on the evidence I have seen and my own intuitive judgment of

the meaning of that evidence. But since the evidence I
have seen doesn't consist of a bunch of carefully controlled studies, I'm not in a good position to argue
with you about my psychological generalizations. I'm
really not interested in debating about that. I'll discuss any of my conclusions with you, but I won't
attempt to defend them. I left the debating society
long ago.

I'm also speaking from another standpoint, which is
the more crucial one. That is, I'm speaking as a person who is conducting his spiritual quest. Now, in
conducting my spiritual quest, as I said earlier, all I
get is light on my own path; I don't get any light on
your path. So I don't know about your bonding or
about your sex. All I know is for me. That's the only
thing I'm interested in speaking on. So if you don't
agree with my spiritual quest, that's no problem. In
fact, it's impossible to agree with my spiritual quest.
And of course, in no way do I have any right to say
anything about your spiritual path, because I don't
know anything about your spiritual path. So this is
what I've seen as I've moved down my path.

I had an illustration of the bonding principle that
came to my mind that helps illustrate it in action.
Picture a man and woman on a desert island, and say
the conditions were such that they knew that there
was no way they would ever get off. In other words,
those two people are going to be on that desert island
until they die, both of them.

Okay. Under the pressure of their loneliness, would
they have intercourse, do you think? Probably eventually. Would they continue to have intercourse? Maybe
not. This is what I think would happen. I think they
would eventually have intercourse for a while and it
would either stop or continue. I think the only way it
would continue would be if there was a true emotional
bonding between them. The sexual bonding wouldn't
be enough, because it hurts more to have intercourse

without an emotional bonding than what you would get from the intercourse. You see my line of thinking there? I think they would have intercourse some, for awhile, and eventually, I think, they would come to say, "Hey, this isn't working" or "It is working." But if it wasn't working, I think they'd say, "This isn't working; we will get along much better as two people if we don't have intercourse."

There is a very touching story of a Mexican guy and a young girl who survived a plane crash up in Alaska. They were stranded in the cold for two or three months without hardly any food. It's a very famous story that was in the magazines and dramatized on television. This guy was sure he was going to get out of there. His religious faith kept him going. He had a very interesting way of handling the sex problem. What he said to the gal was, "I will call you sister so that I will not in any way sexually be with you." He used the incest taboo as a way of protecting them against careless bonding and the harm it could do to them and their chances of survival. This gal, as I recall, was a kind of cantankerous one, and she was raising all kinds of hell; she didn't like this and she didn't like that. But he had a tremendous belief, and she had a lot of guts. She had a lot of dumb ideas, too, but a lot of guts. The combination of all kinds of things pulled them through. So either the bonding is there or sex doesn't work on the long term.

Somebody said, "Are there stages in the marriage scene or play?" and I think the answer is yes. This is another thing that I have just recently come to see. I see so many goal-conscious people in search of this great sexual experience, the Everest, the equivalent for the mountain climber of climbing Everest for the first time. Not only do they want the Mount Everest sexual experience, they want it every day for breakfast. I think that's impossible. Yet when you listen to these people argue for their particular experiences they are also implying that each of them have experienced something no one else who ever lived has ever experienced. It's just like I said earlier about when an adolescent falls in love the first time. The experience is so big compared to anything they've ever experienced before that they are sure no one else has ever experienced the same thing. They each feel that they personally invented love and no one else in their own age group can understand their feeling, to say nothing of the old fogies of their parents' generation.

I think that, in the sexual relationships, there are stages. There is the initial excitement of romantic love; then, as the people succeed in surrendering to each other more and more, there are increased heights of sexual closeness, but those peaks, by and large, can't last. Because I don't think even the Zen masters succeed at doing something the ten thousandth time with the same feeling they did it the first time. When my family was on a camping trip and we came over the Wind River Mountain range and saw the Grand Tetons for the first time, Jackie cried, it was so beautiful. The tenth time she sees that beauty, she's not likely to cry.

There's also the nature of the human body and the human mind. It tends to grow quickly tired of anything. No matter how fantastic an experience we could let you have, about two hours later you'd say, "Well, when does the fun start again?"

What I see is that the great passion of romantic love does not have to last, because it has accomplished its purpose. Say that in a sexual relationship, the two people achieve a fantastic degree of surrender, even if just for a rather brief period of time. That degree of surrender, to me, produces the glue that is bonding. And when there is a sizable degree of surrender achieved between the two, that bond is made particularly strong.

That passion, in a sense, has not only pleased, but it has fulfilled its bonding purpose. Not that that intense passion can't come back into the relationship again, and not that it won't come back to a much greater degree. In that case, there's deeper bonding. But the deep passion produced by surrender has fulfilled its bonding purpose by leaving a lasting feeling towards the other person.

I saw this on an Archie Bunker show the other night. The man down at the meat market was giving Edith roasts and stuff at half price. The son-in-law said to Archie, "Doesn't it occur to you, Archie, that the grocer likes Ma and finds her attractive?" Archie says, "That's impossible." So then Edith goes down to the laundromat and the butcher is there. She says, "Isn't it funny that I ran into you; this is the time I regularly come here." And the butcher says, "I know." So he proceeds to talk to her, and Edith, of course, is a fantastically innocent woman. He tells Edith, "My wife died and I'm very lonely." Somewhere in the conversation, Edith says, "Well, gee, you could get another woman." He says, "Do you think I have a chance?" as he stares right at her. She says, "Well, sure you have a chance." He misunderstands her and thinks she means he has a chance with her. He likes to sing songs, so Edith invites him over, telling him how she likes to sing too. She says, "You come over tomorrow night and we'll sing songs, you and Archie and I."

So he comes over, but Archie has got to go down to the tavern that night, because there's something he needs to check on. "But," she says, "I told you Mr. So-and-so, the butcher, is coming in." And Archie says, "Don't hold me responsible for anything you say. You know I don't listen to you."

Archie goes down to the tavern, and Edith and the butcher are having a good time singing these songs.

Down at the tavern, one of the guys comes in and it turns out his wife has just left him and run away with the exterminator. The exterminator came in and knocked off the cockroaches, came back and knocked off the ants, and then came back and knocked off the wife.

All of a sudden, Archie starts thinking, "Here's the butcher at home with Edith." He heads for home. Meanwhile, the butcher starts getting romantic towards Edith, and it begins to dawn on her what kind of a situation she's in and she tells him, "Oh, no, I'm sorry." And he, then, is embarrassed that he's taken it wrong.

Just about this time, Archie walks in with a bouquet of flowers, and in a rare moment of madness he shows his true feelings for Edith, that he really cares about her.

I know that the mere mention of Archie Bunker makes many women so angry they go right through the ceiling. But that's just a play, girls. That isn't really happening.

Now, that little play about the Bunkers will never wipe out Romeo and Juliet. But that play is close to life and shows the deep bonding that has occurred between Edith and Archie despite all the surface things that seem to indicate otherwise, all of his and her thoughtfulnesses for each other's needs. And perhaps with Edith and Archie, theirs was more of a bonding than there is in a lot of places where people say, "Oh, we're just lovely together, we just love each other so much," but then, one day, one of the two comes home and the other hasn't even left a note, they're just gone. I would think that what Edith and Archie have is one hell of an improvement over what I've seen in a lot of other people, who pretend to have a lot more but really don't.

So an original deep passion leaves a contentment and a knowledge of what was there at one time and a knowledge of what there can be again at the right time.

Now, instead of bonding, a lot of people want to talk about commitment. And, to me, commitment isn't so bad, because we need it in marriage. The "for worse" part of "for better or for worse" in the marriage vows wasn't just put in there by accident. Commitment means two of us are going to work together the rest of our lives to each give up our separateness and go deeper in ourselves. But, for me, one of the big problems I see in marriage is the misunderstanding of the word commitment. To avoid marriage, people live together at first, and like I said earlier, they think that that's like marriage. Then they get married and find living together wasn't like marriage, because most people can live together without marriage a lot better than they can be married together. They can live together for two or three years, get married and in six months be divorced. The minute each person gets a ring in the other person's nose, they start jerking on it real hard and that hurts, doesn't it? A lot of the time, people use commitment to mean staying together with someone so they can be mean to them. I think there are some other reasons for being together. I think we need a commitment, but I'd like to see other reasons too. Deep bonding is another good basis for being together, and there are others.

It's like a lady said: "We've had a long sex relationship without marriage. Will this hurt when we get married, later?" From the things I've said to you you can see that I believe it will. It usually does. The fear that one or both of them had of marriage to the other is going to leave a mark.

To me, commitment is something we give from our side, rather than something we can insist on. Because if we have to insist on commitment from the other person, it's pretty much a sign it isn't there. To me, a better way of looking at commitment that takes the ring-in-the-nose out of it, is the question, Who is the person I most want to come home to tonight? And hopefully that was the basis for Jackie's and my commitment and continues to be after thirty years of marriage. I don't think we change that much. A lot of people want to say, "Well, that isn't the same person I made the commitment to; they're a lot different." I don't think they really are a lot different, or that we are either.

I think a good reason to be with a woman is that she's the person you most want in the world to come home to and to continue to work together with the rest of your life. Or, in the case of the man, that's the man that you most want in the world to come home to and work with the rest of your life. Well, the minute we say it like that, then why don't we act like it? If that is the woman I most want in the world to come home to, then why don't I act like it when I come home?

There's a lot of talk about how we should have a renewable contract for marriage. Well, we have had one throughout history. When we don't renew the contract, it's called divorce, desertion, even murder or execution of the spouse.

I think we can see the problem in the idea of commitment, in a way, if we look at a gold mine as an example. If you had a gold mine and you could go there and fill up buckets of gold anytime you wanted, would you have to make a commitment to the gold mine? "Gold mine, I promise you I won't forget you, I promise you I won't forget to lock the door, I promise you I will come back to you." No, no way do you have to make a commitment to a gold mine. So, if our partner is our gold mine, then why don't we act like it? If we don't think our partner is the gold mine, if we don't think our partner is the best person in the world to come home to, I think we've got an obligation to do something about it. To me, the first obligation we've got is to work on our half of the marriage as hard as we can for five or ten years. Then, if we become finally convinced that there's absolutely nothing more than we can do ourselves or together to improve things, we can consider splitting. We can sit down with the partner and say, "Hey, I'm sure there is somebody else who would really be the gold mine for me or the best person in the world to come home to, so let's you and I split." To me, it's a far greater kindness to the partner to admit to that if it has clearly been established through many years that the problems in the marriage can't be solved.

What kind of deal is it if you're living with this person and you don't think they're the best person in the world for you to come home to, you don't think they're a gold mine, they aren't doing anything for you?

I don't see much working together in lots of marriages that end in divorce. As near as I can see in about half the divorces, the two people who got married were good for each other, they just weren't able to learn the lessons they had to learn together, so each will have to go out and learn those lessons with someone new who isn't as well suited to them for life as the first partner was.

There's a terribly sad story in Maribel Morgan's second book. In her first book, she tells the woman to think of something nice that the husband has done for her and compliment him on it and show him how much she appreciates what he has done. In response to that first book, some woman wrote Morgan and told her this story: "I thought back over our 22 years of married life and I couldn't think of anything he'd ever done that I liked. But I finally remembered that, at the time when we were first married 22 years ago, he did something I liked and I told him the other night about it, how much I appreciated that and I thanked him for it. 'Twenty-two years ago you did something I liked and I really appreciated it.' " Now, ain't that beautiful? I bet that guy was just tickled pink. What a kick in the pants, you know?

There's a mystery in life that we can't ever define, but to me that lady wasn't doing a real kindness to that man, staying with him. I think that man is showing a fantastic fidelity to that woman, a fidelity that, I think, very few of us could manage. If there's a person I'd like to nominate for sainthood, it's a man or a woman who shows fidelity in that kind of situation. I don't know that that's my idea of what I'd like to do with my life, but I have a great respect for people who are willing to wait in loyalty and whatever devotion they can manage as they lay down their lives in a good spirit for the loved one.

One of the students in my college classes said, "Jess, gals are so strange, they just want that little old piece of paper. This gal that I'm with now, she just wants that little old piece of paper." I said, "Tom, if that's just a little old piece of paper, why don't you give that little old gal that little old piece of paper?" And he just blanched. He knew that wasn't just a little old piece of paper. That's a real big piece of paper.

A lady said, "Jess, my husband had an affair and told me about it and I forgave him for it and we're going on and I know he's not doing anything more, but I have so much trouble living with the fear." I had to point out to her that some of her feeling was fear, but some of it was anger and punishing and what have you.

There's a beautiful saying about forgiveness: If we have aught against any, it's a poison within us. This is something that's so crucial. A lot of us are carrying a load of resentments around. The load of resentments that we're carrying around is like carrying acid in our hand. That's real hard on your hand. The only time that load of resentment hurts the other person is when you are around the person you resent, so they can feel it in you. But that load of resentment hurts *you* twenty-four hours a day, because you're carrying it. When you ask the person to put that load of resentments down, it's like you're asking them to give up the ranch. "Oh, never. I'll never forgive that person and what they did to me." They hang on to their resentments like they were hanging on to a life rope. They don't see that the big benefit of forgiveness is to them, rather than to the person they are forgiving.

When you've experienced some surrender and some bonding in love, you can start to see the healing power of love. I mentioned earlier the idea of adding to Ashley Montagu's definition that love is for healing of the individuals.

I think that inside each of our bodies is a part of us that is as handicapped as any physical handicap any of us can have. At the second day of the Seattle seminar, we had a young man named Tim in a wheelchair with cerebral palsy. One of the young people with him was a lovely gal named Jay. I told the group: "We've got good old Tim sitting back there in that wheelchair and he doesn't really belong in the thing. He's just faking it. Some people think that Tim is physically handicapped. But he hasn't got any kind of handicap compared to the kind of emotional handicap that every person in here has got.

"His friend Jay sits back there looking so beautiful and she's already shown us she can do a lot of things very few gals her age can do. But, despite all that, I know from general experience that she's got some deformities, some handicaps, some twistedness inside."

If you and I could have these external costumes we wear that we call our bodies lifted away so the emotional side of ourselves could thereby be revealed more clearly for what it is, every one of us would be in a wheelchair at best. Our minds seem adequate. We can solve all kinds of crossword puzzles and we can answer a lot of phony tests in a college classroom. But our bodies and minds aren't what we're really working with.

It's that internal twisted and dwarfed and handicapped emotional self that's our problem. And in that, you and I haven't got an inch of an edge on Tim. It's in that deprived, twisted emotional self of ours where our healing is needed.

This is the dimension of love I don't see much talked about. As I mentioned, Montagu's definition of love was that it worked for our welfare, our development and our growth. But I have also seen love heal. By healing I don't mean welfare, I don't mean development, I don't mean growth. Welfare is like giving the body the food it needs. Development is like some capacity is expanded. Growth is like lengthening out and getting taller. Healing is something different than that. For example, my left arm was broken right at the joint when I was five years old. Part of the ball was broken off that fits into the elbow socket. It was never set properly, because they didn't have X ray in that little town. Consequently, I don't have the mobility in my left arm that I have in my right. I can't rotate it nearly as well. It doesn't have the flexibility. Okay? No matter what physical therapy I did to strengthen that arm, it would not be as good an arm as my right arm. Now, the kind of healing I'm talking about, a healing of my left arm, would be that that joint would be structurally changed so that it would allow the full rotation of my arm and would allow me to develop the same strength in it as in my right arm. As it is now, I could lift weights for ten years and my left arm would never be as strong as my right, because it is twisted and needs healing.

Okay, this is what love does to that twisted emotional part inside us. It literally removes the deformities, it removes the handicaps in some certain area of our emotional life so that when the block is removed, we can finally see that area gradually grow and develop in a way it never could with the block there. So we become healed in that area of our emotional life.

This is the answer to that childhood deprivation and the marks it left on us. The little boy or little girl inside us who is twisted and deformed and handicapped can be healed by love if we will allow it, if we will allow the love to enter our lives.

Going back to the chrysanthemum story, it's like the sun on the chrysanthemum bud. The only way for us to see the flower is to get sunshine on the bud. But you've all seen flower buds that, as they opened, there was a deformity in the bud. It's like love not only is the sun that opens our chrysanthemum bud for us to be the thing we were meant to be, but love then touches that spot that is deformed and smooths it out so the bud becomes a more perfect bud.

That, to me, is a dimension of love we haven't seen or haven't thought about so much. It is a dimension of love that is so crucial because it can remove those internal handicaps that we were all given to some degree in infancy. Because those handicaps were with us before we had words or could remember, we thought they were part of the human condition and thought we were doomed to live that way. But we are not doomed to live that way.

I have seen people healed by love. In some cases sex was a part of that love. In other cases there wasn't any sex in the love.

A good example is an old friend of mine who came off skid row at the age of forty-five. He was a piece of garbage in a metropolitan ash can. He was so weak he couldn't lift a twenty-pound bag of tomatoes. He couldn't make enough money each day to buy wine, say nothing of food to feed himself. He slept in the back seat of an abandoned car.

He was in Salt Lake City and he was trying to save up enough money to buy some warm clothes and a blanket so he could ride an empty refrigerated car over the mountains to California so he wouldn't freeze in the winter. But he used his little savings to go on a drunk, got thrown in jail and came out of there on Sunday morning. He went and laid in a park and decided all he could do was get a big jug of wine and get in that empty refrigerated car with some newspapers to cover him and hope he could get across the mountains without freezing to death.

Two guys walked up to him and said, "Hey, there's a way out." He could see that what they said was a true statement, because these were two guys he had seen on skidrow himself and said, "Boy, if I ever get as bad as they are, I'm going to do something about it." But he got as bad as they were and worse and didn't do anything about it. Now here these two guys were with white shirts on and shoes that matched.

So they gave him a cigarette and set him up between them on a park bench and they started talking to him. He could see that they had what he wanted and he was finally willing to surrender and say yes to life.

The "winitis" in his knees was so bad that he had to crawl on his hands and knees to a second-floor AA meeting that night. He was that far gone. He was just one step from the undertakers.

That was nearly twenty-eight years ago. He since remarried, has a wife and five children. And his body is very similar to a man as much as ten or twenty years younger than him. You can imagine what his brain was like from the attacks of alcohol, all the brain cells that were killed. You can imagine what his liver was like. You know what all the organs of his body were like after fifteen years of assault by all the malnutrition and privation you find on skidrow. It was a miracle he was able to live that long. Very few do, but he did.

His whole body has been substantially restored. In this case, it was partly the love of other men, who would sit on either side of him holding his hand while he cried. But he was willing to let that love come into his life because he was desperate enough to do so. That is the kind of thing love can do for us in addition to all the other things it can do. It can literally heal ravaged physical bodies. Once I realized the war was over for me, I could stop hunching up my shoulders to protect myself from my imaginary enemies. Gradually my shoulders have dropped two inches and my physiology has changed. My blood profiles are very different now than they used to be.

But even more crucially, love can get at the emotional side of us, that twisted and deformed side of us, and bring it back. To me, this is the dimension of love that is so powerful, because it shows me that love can help relieve us of both of our two terrible handicaps: Our self-centeredness and our deprivation are our two terrible handicaps to loving. Like the monkey deprived of love, we push away the love we need. If we can find a way to let down our walls a little bit, we can let love come into our lives and heal us so we don't keep pushing away so much of the love we so badly need, so it can heal us some more so next time we push away even less. And the warmth of the love makes us less concerned about the walls we build up to keep ourselves separate.

That is the vision I have recently come to see of the effect and the power that love can have in our lives. I used to think love was just something Elizabeth Barrett Browning wrote sonnets about and something high school kids had. Sure, adults had it, but it didn't seem to be worth much, because I looked at the marriages around me as a young person and I didn't see a lot of love there. I now see there was a lot more love there than I thought there was.

We don't see love in its true power, because we think the body and mind and feeling are separate and we've got the big head in charge of all three. I've seen all kinds of other people healed by love, because I've been around a lot of AA and other twelve-step-program people, who have had that same kind of healing, a physical healing and also a healing of the inside, the emotions and what have you.

People asked me to go further into the healing power of love. I've gone as far as I can. I don't really see that there's that much more to say. I know it's enjoyable to think about the healing we could enjoy from love. That's lovely to talk about and think about, but the only real point is to experience it for yourself. And you do that by getting deep into the messy business of giving yourself up to a personal love relationship. Most of us recoil from this. But this whole book has been focused on how to be a better lover. As you are a better lover of a person, of God, of a rock or a tree, there's more love in your life.

When Werner Erhard had his transformation on the freeway, twenty pounds dropped away, he stopped smoking and drinking twenty cups of coffee a day. He had been doing things like I've been talking about, so he was doing his work. And he was seeking. So a little more love was coming in his life each day. But then, one day, a sudden rush came into his life and gave him a big healing of the subconscious and unconscious fictions he had been ruled by up to that point. All of a sudden he was free, healed so he could finally be the creative, outgoing person he was meant to be.

I've recently watched my wife change from a tired forty-eight-year-old woman to a beautiful, laughing young woman who is far prettier than she ever was as a young woman. She was so pretty then, it took your breath away. But her eyes were a little haunted with the emotional load she was carrying. Now her eyes are clear, and she's so beautiful at times it almost hurts. And I also saw that the old romantic love that I thought just came and then went, can come back when the two partners are both really working freely at doing their own work.

This transformation Jackie has recently experienced was a healing, and that healing freed her creative powers that were there all along but were locked up by her inhibition.

As we go through life, we're meeting God's little people along the way. There's a funny thing that happens as we meet these people that life hands us. With each one of these people we either share life or we refuse to share life. With you, I have shared life in some small ways. To me, that's one of the most crucial reflections of this business of surrender.

As I say, a key here is to continually improve on our concept of a higher power. If I get my little Volkswagen stuck in the mud, I can go for any kind of tow truck I want, ranging from a little dinky Volkswagen tow truck all the way to a big Mack tow truck, the kind they haul semitrailers out of the snowbanks with.

I'm not going to settle for a Volkswagen tow truck. As long as I'm going to the trouble of getting a tow truck, I might as well get a good big one, just in case my little bug is stuck tighter than I think. So I'll go get a big semi tow truck to pull me out of the mud.

It's the same way with the higher power. I saw that I could believe in any kind of higher power. I could believe in a higher power that had a very limited power, one that couldn't even pull a tooth, and all it did was sort out the sheep from the goats and sit in judgment. But I thought, "Hey, why settle for a little Volkswagen tow truck? Let's get us a great big higher power. Let's have a higher power that has nothing but the best in mind for us."

I think there's a line someplace that says, "Who, when asked for bread, would give his son a stone?" So I'll have a higher power that has nothing but good in mind for me so that anytime anything, including a

loved one, is taken away from me, it's only because
there are better things in store and that there's something good that can come out of it. If it's just a cruel
circumstance like a traffic accident, it isn't the higher
power's work that takes a person, it's the work of the
person who's driving one of the cars. So the higher
power didn't take that person away in that traffic
accident, circumstances did.

The higher power that I have allows me to take any
circumstance in my life, transcend it and turn it into
something good. Consequently, there are no ways that
there can be any bad circumstances in my life that
can't be transcended and no events the higher power
would ever cause in my life that would be bad; nothing
but good. The higher power that I have is one that
speaks to me when I need help and instruction. Now,
sometimes I don't hear very well, but the message is
there nevertheless. It isn't necessarily always printed
out in typing on a sheet of paper in front of me, but I'll
get the message if I pay attention. More and more, it's
getting clearer to me that before, when I felt the
message got garbled, it was more because I garbled it
up instead of because it wasn't made clear to me. My
friend Bill Gove calls his inner voice of the higher
power Simon. I asked him why he called him Simon.
He said it was because that's his name.

So that's the kind of higher power I've got in my
life, and it's a lot neater deal than what I used to
have. Now, I don't say I don't have any problems. I've
got plenty of problems. Anybody who knows me will
testify to that.

In my system, I've got a higher power, like I say,
where everything is provided for me, and I've also
arranged with the higher power to provide for all of
you. And she said she would do that, so that everything all of you need is all provided for you, too. Now,
my higher power is also one who doesn't care if I
speak respectfully to him or not. If I want to say to

her, get your butt down here and get to work, why she'll come down and get to work just as much as if I say thee and thou. She's not fussy about language. You can tell that from my books.

If any of you idiots have any questions out there, I'd be glad to answer them in my usual perfunctory, sarcastic fashion.

"When you speak of playing God, what you say puts me in an uncomfortable position. . . ."

Well, good, that's my business, to put people in uncomfortable positions where the only way they can escape is by thinking.

"Well, I am in an uncomfortable position because you seem to do whatever you can do with whatever you've got to work with at the time."

Right, but that's not an uncomfortable position. That's just life. You just do the best you can. If it doesn't work out good, then you do different next time, like riding the bicycle.

"If you have a mate who has a lot of anger, you can't change anybody else until you change yourself; you start from that premise. If you give this person all the positive love you can and not tear down the part of him that is undesirable or negative, whatever you want to call it, do you think that can change a person too?"

Yeah, but you don't ever do it for that reason.

"No. No."

But if you don't ever do it for that reason, what's the point of the question?

"Well, you care about the person."

What do you care about them?

"Because there is a bonding and I don't want any more pain."

Even though they are a mean son of a bitch, there's a bonding?

"Right, and I don't want any more pain. It's selfish."

Okay. You've got another problem. You're judging the other person.

"That's right. I recognize that."

That's a bad business. We'd best only compliment the other person.

"Yeah, but I'm human."

Sure, but how come you have to act so much like a monkey?

"Right. But what the other person does hurts and bothers me. Okay, it's my fault."

Okay. That's your feeling. Don't confuse your feelings with your justifications of your feelings. It's different to say, "Hey, it really hurts me when he screams and yells at me," versus saying, "He's an angry person, and how can I get him out of this by acting nice?" The first is a feeling and the second is a thought and a justification. I can go with you on "God, that husband of mine makes me so damn mad I could kill him. He's so full of anger, I can't stand him." That's a feeling. Okay, express that feeling to me; that's fine. But when you turn it into a logical justification of yourself, it stops being just human and becomes diabolical.

"Right."

That's all.

"I believe you made the statement that your mate should be the person that you most would like to come home to every night. Then you said people who live in a situation where they come home to someone who isn't the one they most would like to come home to every night are saints. And then earlier you said there are no stores to cash in all the Brownie stamps we earn."

I was speaking of an ideal, something we're working towards, and in a way it's a paradox, because if you took me literally, over half of the husbands and wives in America wouldn't come home to each other tonight. A recent survey showed that half of all husbands and wives thought they could do a lot better than what they had.

But in all the talking I've done about relationships,

there is one exception to all the things I've said, and that is in the marriage situation—because of the bonding. I think there is a very special, special allegiance we owe to our partner as opposed to anybody else in the whole world. In other words, the Brownie stamps I was referring to were primarily from going out and doing good for other people than my husband or wife.

Now, we have to be careful about this attitude. "Oh, I'm just a martyr." That's one of the most poisonous attitudes. But there is a fidelity, an honest and devoted and deep kind of fidelity, that is a beautiful thing to see. There also is martyrdom, which is the much more common thing to see, and that's the rottenest thing in the world.

Now, this is a very difficult problem. Someone came up at one of the breaks and said, "Jess, you've given me a bunch of paradoxes." And I said, "That's my intention."

I have spoken on one side of the matter and I have spoken on the other side of the matter, and you're going to have to find where the truth is, which is somewhere in between.

The point is I don't want you to follow orders, but to think. And for God's sake, think for yourself, even if it's wrong. And it will be. Because everything we do, in a sense, is wrong, imperfect, on the way to being somewhat more perfect.

My friend Gerry defines an educational experience as putting you in a situation where you cannot escape except by thinking. Okay, that's what I've attempted to do, present you with a group of paradoxes and contradictions and different ideas. The result is you will think, some of you, most of you, hopefully all of you. Because of it you will do better. You will not be right or wrong. No one will ever know whether you or I are right or wrong. But we'll get better results. We'll do better and we'll get better results. That's what we're here for.

If any of you are here as an intellectual exercise of an assignment for a college professor, why, that's your problem. A year earlier, when I came to Seattle, a nun came to the first session I had, and at the end she got up and said, "I want my money back." She was asked why, and she said, "I can't take any notes on what this guy is saying. I've tried for an hour and a half to get some notes. I can't get any order, any structure out of what this guy is saying. There's no structure here." That's perfect. I don't want a structure. It's like Zen. Why will a Zen student be sent to think for a year or two about the koan: what is the sound of a single hand clapping? In a way, there is no real answer to that koan. The benefit of the koan is in thinking about it and stripping away this surface logic that can delude us so. In Zen they call it breaking the bubble of rationalism, this foolish idea that we've got everything figured out. As long as we figure we've got everything figured out, we're in a terrible mess. The minute we understand we haven't got everything figured out, we're in good shape. Someone says, "I'm confused." Beautiful; that's just perfect. That's my student. You see?

"You talk about self-centeredness. I'd like to know more about it and the difference between self-centeredness and selfishness."

Self-centeredness and selfishness as we commonly use it is that you are the stage producer for the whole world and you're sitting there watching the play and you've got the script written out on how everybody in your life should act, what they should say to you, and what they should do towards you. "Don't any of you do any different than this or you will hurt my feelings. You'll make me feel bad." Okay, that's self-centeredness and selfishness.

Now, there is what we call an enlightened selfishness which says, "I must see what my real needs are and meet them by finding other people who share my feelings and with whom I can take what I need to meet my needs. They meet their own needs as they meet my needs." That's an enlightened selfishness. You see the distinction? Now, it's a big topic, so think on it for ten years and you'll get a lot wiser on it, because that's right at the very heart of what we're talking about here.

"You said, don't bother with the people in your lives you can't handle. Throw them away, because you don't need them. So the people you actually want in your life are the people who will respond to your needs without your saying, 'Do you mind smiling at me today, because I need that.'"

Right. They don't belong in your life.

"Well, then, in your husband-and-wife relationship, now, your husband is not going to respond to every one of your needs, so you said, 'Tell him, don't leave him in doubt.'"

Right. But that's different, because that's the husband-and-wife relationship. Furthermore, if you need to get smiled at, go find somebody else to smile at you. Get five women friends to smile at you. Pay attention to your kids and they will smile at you. Start treating the butcher nice and the baker nice and everybody else nice. Soon there are people smiling at you all day long. Then, when the old man comes home a big crab, it doesn't bother you so much. Most people, however, honey, do not have hardly anybody else in their life. They are all attached to this one relationship, and that person has to do everything and be everything for them. If that person doesn't do all the things they want from them, they don't have any alternatives and they get angry and resentful and pout. But if I've got twenty-six people smiling during the day and somebody gives me a crabby face, is it a big problem?

"No."

That's what you're doing while you're practicing fidelity. You get in your life and clean the whole thing up. Get in some kind of growth group like all the twelve-step groups that are around, like Emotions Anonymous, or Al Anon for the relatives of alcoholics. Everybody's got emotional problems or is related to an alcoholic. Get five friends, be nice to the rest of the people in your life. Surrender your husband. Let him be. Surrender your marriage. Let it be. After you've done that for twenty years, then you are in a real position to decide whether you need a new husband or not.

But it's simple on that kind of basis, because when you spend your days during the next twenty years doing all those things just for you, you've had a big reward for the twenty years, which is twenty years of a life well lived. And you've created a big open space for your husband to change and grow in instead of having him locked up in the same old groove. In a typical relationship, we've got all our chips on that one relationship and if it doesn't work out, we've got nothing in our lives. No wonder we go up and down like a yo-yo. It's our own stupidity, yet we want to blame the other person for it. How can anybody provide everything we need? In fact, asking them to do so is one of the surest ways to ensure that they won't. How do you like being in a relationship where the person says, "My whole life is involved with you. Everything that comes into my life comes from you." That's not a relationship, that's a parasitic dependency. It's a sick thing, not a good thing.

If we're in that position in our husband-wife relationships, why are we going around blaming them? We're the ones that are really causing the problem. We're at least one half of the dependency and maybe more. Maybe they're dependent on us, but if they are that's their problem. That doesn't mean we are justified in staying sick and depending on them. Do what we can. Change the things we can change.

Like I say, the things you can change are get five

friends and go to a growth group and love everybody else that you can and surrender all the rest. Once you start doing that, life all of a sudden picks up and it's a pretty lovely life unless the other person's a real ox, and in most cases they're not. Then, of course, once we stop being so sick and so overwhelmingly needful of one person. it makes it so much easier for them to change some things too. It isn't so much that they change, it's just that we make it less hard for them to do what they would like to do anyway. Many of us are making it impossible for anyone to love us. Then we piss and moan because the person doesn't love us. That's not intelligent and it's not fair.

"How did you arrive at five friends? Why not three or four?"

Well, three is better than nothing. Three's a start. I arrived at five because that's what I had. And then I kind of lost one and gained a couple more, so it's kind of indeterminate right now. There's only two that I see as often as two or three times a week, and then it scales down from there.

But those five I can tell almost anything to. So between them there isn't anything I can't tell to at least one of them. Talking to Gerry about sex makes his head ache, so I can't talk sexual stuff to Gerry, but I can talk to someone else.

"You talked about our two walls and having sex through those holes in the partitions?"

Okay, how do you go about throwing away those partitions that I was talking about with the holes in them that you have sex through? Partly, that's where you get out of the god business, quit asking to be perfect. In other words, you get into bed not wanting to be perfect, but to just do what you can. So you don't need a shield to hide anything. "But," you say, "well, I'm inadequate." But inadequate compared to what? Compared, again, only to your godlike expectations of yourself. So get the partition down a little piece at a time. Saw one corner off the partition for a start, but go slowly. Don't make haste quickly and shock everybody. Really. We've got plenty of time. We don't need to hurry. There's just enough time when we pay attention. To really live life, we need to be aware so we can surrender where it is appropriate and bond with sunsets, fresh breezes on our face and the loved ones.

CHAPTER 8

Where Do We Go from Here?

Where do we go with all the sex energy we free up when we do all these things I've been talking about? I'm not sure. To some degree, it depends on the two people in the partnership and how they blend together. It also depends on the results you want. I'm not sure at all how this works out. If the result you seek is more wholeness, then the energy will bring you closer to yourself, your God and your partner.

What we've been talking about in the previous chapters amounts to a fundamental change in attitude, an ego collapse in depth. There's no way, for example, we can surrender to the partner in a sexual relationship without also surrendering more in all our other relationships. There's no way we can experience our wholeness with other people without giving up a big part of our sense of separateness and guardedness with our partner.

There are a number of consequences of this surrendering of our ego. Immediately, we experience so much more joy, happiness and peace in all our relationships with people, animals, trees, during the day. If there is the specific act of sexual intercourse with the partner in that day, intercourse is so much better for us, just as all our other intercourses with life were during the day.

As we live this way, there is a lot of new energy available to us. All the energy we were using to guard ourselves, hide ourselves and foolishly try to control the world is available for other purposes. All the energy that leaked out through our angers and resentments is more available. All the new energy we receive as we lovingly embrace the world is available to us too. And the walls that separated us from our partners are partway down and will be further down.

I've seen that people's first reaction to this new release and new freedom is "Wow, look at all the good sex we can have now." And they usually do take advantage of what's now there for the two of them that was never there before.

But I see that in the longer run there is usually a different resolution of the opportunity for all the new energy and closeness. Like everything else I've talked about, this is something each set of partners has to work out for themselves. I've observed many different responses to the availability of all this new vitality. One observation was particularly striking to me.

In June of 1978 there was a big conference in Los Angeles where many of the leaders of the human-potential movement were speaking. I was familiar with the writings of most of the participants, but I wanted to see their faces and bodies and hear their voices so I could get a more accurate feeling for how they were living. I watched two men both in their early seventies with two somewhat different ideas. Both men had faces and voices that radiated their vitality. One man had a younger wife and he was saying that orgasm was everything. As I was listening to him, I had the feeling there was something more than that for me. The other man had a very lovely, gray-haired wife. His idea was to live as if to live and to love were the same thing. I felt good about that result and felt that was the result I wanted in my life.

Where, then, does orgasm fit in that result? What part does sex play when to live and to love are the same? I see that orgasm can find its natural place in our lives with its frequency and its use depending completely on the two partners, their physiology, their needs and desires, their life philosophies and the daily ebb and flow of the woman's and man's bodies and lives. When a woman spends a day nearly overwhelmed by her children or her job, she may need orgasm desperately or it may be the thing she wants least. Same for the man. It may be that one or both just need to be physically close without the burden of any performance. When there's a true surrender to life on the part of both people, the whole range of sexual behavior is open to them, including just reading or watching television or playing cards quietly together. Or each can follow their own individual interests, knowing that they are still together.

There are many ways orgasm can fit in the surrendered life. I don't see any evidence yet that one way works a lot better than another to produce the life results I like. So I'll just mention some different approaches to orgasm that I've seen work well for people, and any that are new to you, you can try out and see if they belong in your life and if so, to what degree and at what times.

One important point is that for most of us the old life was a real roller coaster, with its constant ups and downs, highs and lows. When we first find some freedom, we think we would want a life with just highs and no lows. As we go along, we come to see that our lows are part and parcel of our highs; they're tied together. We see, too, that there are two kinds of highs. There is the manic high of "Whoopee, ain't life fantastic, wake up and come party with me." There is also the high of seeing that life is fantastic no matter what's happening, and quietly appreciating that without asking the whole world to wake up and join the celebration just because you or I feel good at this moment.

So I see that love, for me, is a quiet, sometimes exuberant, feeling that's more even and more steady than the old roller coaster. Things just smooth out, or mellow out, as my son says.

I see now that in those old highs of mine I wasn't really very happy, I was just noisy. I was as blind to the people around me as I was in my most depressed low. I have found I can't love people and life with my eyes blind to what is happening around me. I don't want to go back to that old, blind way of living.

"Until we draw our last breath." Those are words from one of the marriage vows. They say that two of us, in a full sense of what we are doing, or in as full a sense as mortals can have, agree our two souls shall be bound together and we shall go seeking. We will be together like Ben-Gurion and his wife until at least one of us has drawn their last breath.

That's a commitment, a tremendously strong commitment, and commitment is one of the two big things that holds a marriage together when times get really tough. But the important part of commitment and the reason most people don't understand commitment is, typically again, they don't make the commitment as an inner pact with themselves. I see it so interestingly in businessmen. A lot of businessmen will start businesses, especially in their earlier years, and then perhaps have a difficulty and their business is a failure. They will take it on themselves, because they gave their word, to discharge those debts by paying them back, rather than go through bankruptcy. In fact, it's much more common that the guy works in some way to pay off that dept than it is to go through bankruptcy, common as bankruptcy is today.

What is sad, to me, is that a man would see an obligation to some other businessman as being more important than an obligation made to a woman, typically in a sacred contract between himself and his God. I think what's partly involved is a feeling of commitment to the other businessman, but there's also a lot of ego. A lot of the reason for discharging that debt is: "What will people think?" But I think even more of what is involved in breaking our marriage commitment is that each of us, out of our ego and our deprivation, has this terrible fear of the oppositeness of that other sex.

I know I may seem to have stressed that too strongly. I know many of you who are single feel, "Hey, the single life is the best life for me. I don't want to get into that oppositeness." I think you might feel, "Boy, Jess really comes down hard on me." The answer is no. I'm not coming down hard on you. I'm not trying to tell you how to walk your spiritual path. I'm telling you that it has been my experience that the most productive thing most all of us can do is face that oppositeness and accept it. Whether we choose to relate sexually to that oppositeness is not the point. But if we don't accept that it's there, our freedom is limited.

A widespread idea today is that homosexuals are born homosexual. I don't believe that is always the case, because I have recently seen evidence of successful cures: homosexuals being relieved of their homosexuality. What it looks like is that what homosexuality frequently is, is a fear of women. I would guess lesbianism is a fear of men. It's very rarely that a homosexual would want to have his problem removed, because why would you want to have removed a fear of something that was so terribly fearful to you? But occasionally one will, and it has been demonstrated now. To me, it clarifies what I think is the most likely cause of homosexuality and that is some terrible problem, due to a number of reasons perhaps, but just a fear of women, or in the case of lesbians a fear of men.

The male homosexual and the lesbians are simply the very end of a spectrum. I think all of us have varying degrees of fear of the opposite sex. Each of us are coping with that fear in our own particular way as well as we can.

I see marriage as two souls who seek each other out and then make a pact to each give up their separateness and to spend their lives opening themselves to each other in a deeper and deeper way. So commitment is this soul of mine meeting this soul of the opposite sex and going deep into myself, stripping myself of my fear, taking my shield away, disclosing myself to that other person, surrendering to them and knowing that they have my best interests at heart. And knowing that, in a sense, they know what's better for me than even I do. So I'm doing it for me. And that's what marriage is; it's soul to soul. The deeper the marriage is, the deeper each of these two souls has opened themselves to each other.

A lady asked me, "Okay, I'm married but I just can't see that this deal between the sexes is that big!" I told her, "I don't think you've understood and discovered the depths that there are in marriages. I don't think any of us have, and I think when we start justifying the situation we're in as good, we literally put a block, an obstacle, in the path of our growth. I think we need to do the opposite, to take away those justifications and say, "Hey, I want to discover more about what this marriage can be and is for me."

I have seen that in my years as a married person I very frequently stopped working and going deeper as my soul very literally cried out, "Enough!, enough already! I don't want to reveal any more of myself to this other person. I don't want to surrender more. I don't want any more self-knowledge. I've had all the self-knowledge I can possibly stand in this relationship. I've seen too many troublesome things about myself already that I don't want to see. I don't want to go any further." I know that a number of times in our marriage relationship I've stopped that process. But I'll typically get brought up short one way or another and finally say, "Hey, I have got to go on." And then be rewarded, always, for that decision by tremendous things for me. Then, consequently, there is a tremendous improvement in our marriage, because one half of the relationship can't improve things that contribute to that relationship without making the relationship better. I see Jackie going through the same things from her side.

Now, in some cases, as I said, perhaps some of you are in a contract with a soul that's not ready and able to stand that pull even if you just continue to do your part in the deepest and quietest kind of way. I guess, in a situation like that, it would eventually come to the point that the other person would say, "Hey, I can't stand this any more," and leave. I would far rather have it that way than to make the judgment for the other person and say, "This other person can't stand this pull and we will split this relationship." I would rather fight with every fiber of my being to preserve that relationship. And only if the other person could not stand it and said, "I refuse to go on," would I want to be willing to think of giving up and saying, "Okay. If you feel that way, then that's the way it must be," rather than me deciding what's good for the other person.

As I said earlier, at least half of the people I see getting divorced made a good choice of a marriage partner. All their divorces tell me is, "Hey, I didn't want and couldn't handle going deeper into myself." What they're going to have to do is go deeper into themselves with somebody else unless they make a compact with the new person not to go deep within themselves. A lot of marriages are like that. Two people go to a certain depth within themselves and it's like they both mutually agree, "Hey, we don't want to go any deeper within ourselves; we'll both stop right here." To me, that's a contradiction. That was very common in the old days, when divorce was economically impossible.

In Bricelyn, Minnesota, two people had enough trouble feeding themselves as one unit, say nothing as two units. We didn't starve to death down there, but like my old man said, "If I could just get fifty dollars together, I could get through the winter."

So only if it's proven beyond the wildest shadow of a doubt that their two souls don't belong together would I see two people giving up their marriage contract.

The other thing I see we need for us to make a marriage go is rigorous honesty. I don't mean rigorous honesty about the cash register. I used to be cash-register honest, because I wouldn't steal money and I always kept my books right and didn't cheat on my income tax very much. So I was always cash-register honest. I didn't understand there was anything outside the material world. I thought, if I'm honest with property and don't steal things and don't lie to other people, I'm honest. That's just the poorest, merest beginnings of honesty. The crucial kind of honesty is in the non-material world, which is honesty to me about me. That's what counts, me honestly seeing and saying what my feelings, thoughts, attitudes and actions are.

If we see that our souls need each other and strive for rigorous honesty, the relationship can grow drastically stronger, and good things will happen throughout the whole relationship. There will be a good quality and feeling throughout each day.

One gal listened to a set of tapes on the two days of the Seattle seminar. She said, "Jess, I got from those tapes an understanding that the sexual area doesn't just start at the waist down and that foreplay starts in the morning at breakfast, not after the lights are out."

The sexual relationship is the whole relationship, all day long. When I'm talking with a woman at the grocery store, she and I are having a sexual relationship. A man can't be with a woman without it being a sexual relationship. No matter what activity I'm doing, my sexual instrument, from my tippy toes to the top of my old bald head, is in play. Every pore in my body is a sex organ.

You need to understand that sex starts in the morning, when you get up and sing your two songs. That's an assignment for you for the next week. Within the first half hour of when you get up, sing two songs. You've got to sing them out loud. I don't care if you've got to go in the shower to do it, you've got to sing them out loud. Just do it and see what a difference it makes. If it doesn't improve your life and make it better, let me know and I'll give you your misery back.

Once you understand all the new dimensions and richness you can add to your present relationship, that's how you can literally have an affair with that person you're living with right now. You don't need to go out and plow new ground and break a couple of hearts in the process. You can find a way to love more intensely the person you're presently living with. I know that's a thought that, to most people, simply blows their minds. "No way. Not that nag. Not that old so-and-so. I've tried. God knows how I've tried."

Yes, unfortunately, dear friends, God does know how you and I have tried and, frankly, I don't think he's very impressed. He's saying, "Hey, get back in there and get to work." In high school there's always the crybaby on the football team. He comes running off the field limping and crying. The coach slugs him and tells him, "Get back in there, you lazy dummy." So the guy gets back in there and really tries.

How intense can sex be? It can range all the way from sex being just a very, very deep, quiet joy that restores the soul, to where sex is such an intense thing that all the proverbial and classical things happen, like the world stops turning and time stops and two people are as one and all of those beautiful, lovely things. The one thing sex can't be any more, once you understand these things, is it can't be routine. Sex starts in the morning with the two songs and it goes all day long. Then the physical part of sex, in the evening, is simply not some big thing the whole day is pointed towards but one part of that whole day's process I mentioned to you earlier.

You see that this day is the whole of life. We have the spring of new life this morning. We have the summer of active life this afternoon. Tonight at dinner with the people we love we will have our fall, the resting time. At night we will have winter, the restorative time.

Here is this wonderful possibility where I see that we can open up a complete new dimension and depth between the two of us. But typically, when this knowledge comes to us, there's already some miles gone down the road and a lot of the women want to say, "Where's my youthful beauty and body that would be so nice to have again when here is this person who could love me?" And the man wants to say, "Where is my youth that I could use so now, when I was just like a rabbit or a monkey, I could copulate every ten minutes? That's all gone now and so I've had it."

Well, this is one of the pleasant surprises I've run into not too long back. To me, it's one of the best-kept secrets in the country. Men over forty (and you can put that lower if you want) were cautioned in the days of the old Chinese not to have ejaculations every time they had sex. I know with that statement men's manhood immediately is questioned. But that's really true.

Masters and Johnson have found this out too. They got into it with the guys who were premature ejaculators. You see, it's a funny thing about human sex. What would you think of a stud horse, where the minute he got on a mare, he covered her just like that and got off her? You'd be proud of that stud horse and say he was a good stud horse. Okay, when a man's got the problem and can't stay with the woman for two hours, he's got a problem. But it's a peculiarly human and peculiarly present-day condition that sex can perform a different function.

While Masters and Johnson were working on premature ejaculation, they developed this squeeze technique, which is to teach the guy who is a premature ejaculator to be able to not have an ejaculation until his wife has some degree of satisfaction. One of the outcomes of their work was a very funny surprise to Masters and Johnson, because they found some guys they were working on this with not only developed the ability to delay an ejaculation for quite a while, but they found they got a great deal of pleasure and didn't need to have an ejaculation. They got as much or more enjoyment out of sex by not having an ejaculation as by having one. Masters and Johnson say in their book *Human Sexual Inadequacy* that they can't explain why this happens but they have observed it clinically.

About seven hundred years ago, the Chinese Taoists had a highly developed view of sexuality. The Chinese were the most civilized of all our early cultures. They had civilizations thousands of years before Western Europe. In the Chinese school Pearl Buck went to, half of the education was focused on human relationships and the other half was focused on the subject matter. About seven hundred to one thousand years ago in the Taoist tradition, the idea was that the man did not have an ejaculation hardly ever. In fact, the ideal was that the man would have an ejaculation only once in a hundred times. There are some things that that opens up that are really good to look at. It opens up a complete new dimension in sex. Again, it's one of these problems where what we think we see in sex is not reality. It's like the story of the five blind men describing the elephant. One guy says he's got ahold of a rope, another guy's got ahold of a tree, another guy's got ahold of a waving thing. Well, one's got the trunk, one the leg, and one the tail. They all describe something different. They don't describe the reality of the elephant.

What I've come to see is that, by and large, we don't know what sex is, and we've only had the faintest kind of glimmer of it and there can be some very drastic surprises waiting for us in the world of sex. For example, we think guys are the highly sexed ones and they've got to have it. They can have intercourse with anyone that walks down the road, and women have a slower, less easily aroused sexual nature, although once aroused it can be very strong. But, the more I see of things, the more I think that men's and women's sexual natures may be way different from anything we've ever seen hinted at.

It's like the alcoholic drinking wine can't tell us anything about the delicate bouquet of a fine wine. We men have been so wrapped up in our escapes of work and hobbies and other interests and women have been so wrapped up in their escapes and each of us have been so much in our egos that I don't think it's ever happened that a man without an ego has gotten in bed with a woman without an ego. I think that only when that happens is there a chance to really experience sex as it can be.

And then I think an additional thing can happen and I've never really heard of this happening other than what I read of this old Chinese guy, Jolan Chang, in his book *The Tao of Love and Sex*. My friend Walther Lechler sent me the book from Germany. It was published in England.

Chang started to practice this old Taoist idea of making love without having an ejaculation when he was about thirty-five. What Chang found was just as the old Chinese Taoist ideas indicated. He found that the woman was prepared to have sex far more than he had ever previously conceived of if the woman was open to all these feelings, wanted them and wasn't afraid of them. We can't lift an idea out of another culture and use it intact, but we can borrow an idea and adapt it to fit us and our needs. In a typical sexual intercourse, where a man has sex with a woman and the man comes too soon, the woman is in the height of her desire, yet faced with a man who's spent for the next few hours, days or weeks. This keeps some women from really realizing their true sexual nature and keeps them from going on and on into two, three, four or five orgasms or six or ten over a period of an hour or two and a fantastic bout of lovemaking. All a woman would ever know was here was this guy who was gone with no hope for her, so she'd just have to get her satisfaction any way she could and pack it in until next time.

With the old Taoist system, the guy doesn't have an ejaculation. He uses an earlier version of the Masters and Johnson squeeze technique the Chinese developed over seven hundred years ago. The guy presses two fingers against the root of the penis behind the scrotum. The guy just kept erect and kept satisfying the woman and she would have orgasm after orgasm, deeper and deeper and more moving. When she stopped having orgasms and the time came to end, she would, but in the full knowledge she could wake up again sexually the minute she wanted to. If she wanted to lie there ten minutes and start the cycle all over again she would, whereas in the old system, it's impossible, it's not available to her. How can we conceive, say, of the advantages of airplane travel when we've never been on an airplane? How can we conceive of what airplane travel can give us when we don't know how fast an airplane can travel?

So here's this woman who all of a sudden has no external constraints on her being able to truly realize and awaken to her sexual nature exactly as it is for her. Now, I'm not saying that all women are one certain way sexually, but I'm saying that what we've seen of women sexually is not what they truly are, be-

cause there is no way they could find out and be as
sexual as each truly is, because of our very unworkable
idea that a man has an ejaculation every time.

Old Chang really opened my eyes to this in his
book, because I saw the truth of what he's talking
about. I understood it. I saw that we are like the blind
men feeling the elephant, and each is just describing
some small part of the world of sex but stoutly insisting
that what we see is truth, that the elephant truly is
an animal like a tree. Or he is truly an animal with
ropes hanging on him. We're not ready to open our
minds and say, "Hey, what we are describing is not
reality but is a function of our limited perception and
our own limited experience and our own peculiar orientation and our own habit."

I used to spend a lot of time firmly maintaining my
prejudices: by God, I'm right. And I'd fight to the
death to be right. I'd rather be right than be Presi-
dent. I'd rather be right than be happy. I found I had
to give up that idea of what's right and what's wrong
and seek as well as I could for what is. I needed to
understand the limits of my perception and understand how my own perception and my own past tended
to distort evidence to fit my preconceived notions.

So I threw all those old ideas out as well as I could.
I wanted to get rid of that garbage, because it nearly
killed me. It not only did not serve me, it nearly killed
me. Worst of all, it was killing my days. There was no
love and no happiness and no excitement in those
days. So why wouldn't I want to get rid of that stuff?
But it was amazing how hard it was, even under those
incentives, to get rid of it.

What I have come to see of women's sexual nature
is that many women—I don't know whether it's most
and I would doubt that it's all—but, to me, many
women have a very, very different sexual nature than
I had previously understood some years ago. When
the constraints and expectations of each partner are

eliminated, there will be times in the sexual relationship between a man and a woman when there isn't much sex and there are other times when there is a lot of sex in the relationship. It seems to ebb and flow like the tides. It isn't just at one time there was a lot of sex and then it all went away. When a woman's sex is free to expand and move as it wants to without any constraints, as I mentioned, there can be tremendous depths in that relationship. In fact a woman sexually —they're finding now—is at her very strongest in the late forties, fifties and even into the sixties. Then also, in the daily life of a woman, she might find times when she needs the opportunity, as Chang points out, to have not just one orgasm, not just a bunch of orgasms, but as many orgasms as she wants, maybe two or three hours of orgasms at a time. And then she needs the opportunity, the complete freedom to come back to the man, ten minutes, two hours, five hours later, and have more orgasms.

So the dentist in the audience wonders, how can I run my practice? Well, there's a way. With deep love there is always a way. I find that when people are happy they find a way to get their work done a lot faster than when they're miserable and they're using their work to stay away from home. When I'm using my work to stay away from home I can stretch it out forever. But also, the woman I mentioned might have intense sex for days and then be almost completely uninterested in sex as she gets deeply involved in some other activity.

The guy may want to scream, "How am I supposed to make plans for something as erratic as this?" The point is, we don't make plans. That's what surrender means. It means we have to have enough freedom built into our days so we can move with what is, rather than ask what is to fit our schedule. You say, "I can't do that." You'd be surprised at what you can do as you open up your life more and more. Sure, you maybe can't do it all today, but you can start.

I've got six beautiful horses in my yard with a new colt coming this spring and mountains to ride in across the road and a silver-mounted saddle and bridle. But when I started I had a hundred-and-sixty-dollar horse, a seventy-dollar saddle and a six-dollar-a-month pasture at the edge of town to ride in. You start where you are with what you can do right now.

Those are some things I've seen about women's sexual nature. What have I seen about men's sexual nature?

I think that, in the man's case, and Chang makes a beautiful point of this, that men's emphasis on ejaculation is partly from our ignorance, but it is more from the goal orientation of us Americans. There was nothing that used to make my nineteen-to-twenty-one-year-old college students more angry than to hear me talk against goals. You'd think they owned stock in Goals, Inc. You'd think I was rending the very fabric of America. It was as if I was spitting on the flag or in some way desecrating it when I talked against goals. We are so goal-conscious in this country! Unless you can tell me what our goals are, I'm not going to have anything to do with you. Solid goals, that's us.

You go down to the locker room and tell the boys, "I had this fantastic night of sex last night and I didn't have an ejaculation." They'll throw you right straight out of the locker room. "What are you? Some kind of sis, wearing a skirt?" But at home you've got a wife who's smiling a great big grin and she's eagerly waiting for you to come home.

I think she's more important than the guys down at the locker room. If they've got their hang-ups, let them have them.

Now, in this kind of sex I'm talking about, I'm not talking about the kind of a thing that is written up so much, which as near as I can see is a bunch of sexual athletics where there's a preconceived notion of "We're going to have six hours of sex at eight o'clock. We're going to go through ninety-three positions, starting with sexual position number fourteen." We've got a sexual-position list written beside the bed and the pen to check them off as we go through them. If this doesn't happen just right I'll be disappointed, in the kind of thing I'm talking about. If you're thinking about sexual position your mind is way too far off the subject, tiger, because in the kind of thing I'm talking about the two people are so much one that they are going to invent ninety-three different sexual positions in the next two hours that haven't ever been written down. And they're going to be unaware they invented them. They aren't going to have anything in their minds at the end but "Wow! I feel good" instead of "Look what I did." Which is a totally different concept, to me, from what I see described in so much of the sex books and articles.

Ten years ago, I had the title for this book. It took me ten years to figure out what to say after I said the title. But I've got it figured out now well enough so I'm satisfied that my understanding is far enough along to answer my major questions. During my search, I've accumulated an eight-foot library of sex books and it's amazing to me how little help most of them were to me. A lot of them were headed in a way I didn't want to go. There aren't but four or five that I got anything out of. Most of the stuff in this book, I had to learn by myself and from friends I trusted to tell the truth. We all learned it the hard way, and we had to pay for our mistakes in pain.

So what we're talking about is sex coming into its own and finding its natural place, but we can't even know what that is, because sex has been under so many constraints.

Like I said, the two biggest constraints it's been under is first the constraints of the egos of the two people involved, both as big as houses. The second

constraint is really a lack of understanding of sex due
to the physical restrictions of the guy who's had an
ejaculation, and that just draws a line at that point in
sex for the next two, three, four, five days, a week
even. How can a woman, then, let herself be free
when she's operating under that kind of constraint
where she maybe doesn't even have the first orgasm,
to say nothing of the fifth available to her? Even if
she has the first, she knows the next one is automatically two, three, five, seven days away. Those two
constraints are what have given us a view of sex
where all we see is like seeing a mountain through a
cloud, we just see a dim picture of the mountain here
and there. We don't ever see sex as it can be. We can't
experience that kind of sex without getting our ego
out of the way. If we get our ego out of the way, then
all day long is a whole different day for those two
people. Then the sex is so much different because
we're so much different.

It's very important here that I repeat myself again.
I'm not telling you about Chang's way so you can do it
and become like Chang. I'm offering it to you just to
give you another perspective on sex. You can look at
it and say, that's not for me. You can try it and find
that's not for you. You can really get into it and find
it's something that's for you at some times that are
really right for you like little honeymoon periods tucked
in the year when both are really free for a lot of sex
and wanting a lot of sex. Or you can try his way and
see that when you've literally gorged yourself on sex
that you want to use those energies together in some
other way, like concentrating them on some higher
ideal. I'd guess only one in twenty, maybe one in fifty,
would take Chang's ideas and use them just like him.
But all the other forty-nine could have received a
great benefit from their new perspectives and new
experiences.

Now let's look again at what I mean by ego and

what I mean by surrender: A woman came up to me when I was saying *Ain't I a Wonder* down in Columbus, Ohio, and said, "Jess, I want my husband to do what I want him to do, when I want him to do it, the way I want him to do it." She's being the stage producer for the world. Is there ego in that? Yes. Is there any surrender in that? No.

The same thing is going on at home. Her husband is saying, "I want the wife to do what I want her to do, when I want her to do it, the way I want her to do it!" That's what I mean by two big egos, two self-centered people who want the world to go their way. The opposite of that situation is what I mean by surrender. Somebody asked, "By surrender, do you mean I should just take me and hand myself to another person?" No. Surrender doesn't work that way. It means surrendering to the higher power and what life has to offer you, surrendering to what is, and not by putting expectations on the situation and saying, "This is the way it should be. This situation has got to be different than this. I want it my way." That's not surrender, that's ego. That's self-centeredness, that's me. When I see what way is open for me and take that, okay, that's good. I have surrendered, pretty well, to the people in my life. I have said the prayer of release: "I release all things that are not a part of my inner perfection and I pray that all things not a part of my inner perfection release me." That's surrender.

If I'm claiming I've surrendered while there are some people I have decided must stay in my life before I can be happy, that's ego. Surrender is saying that the people who come into my life are the ones who are absolutely perfect for me.

Now, when I'm speaking to an audience, I can't seem, so far, to avoid going man to man on some of the people, because there's something about some of the faces, the bodies, the positions they hold or other things that are attractive to me. And especially in the old days, my tendency was to pick out someone like that and go after them. That's not surrender. What I have learned now, and I don't do perfect at it but I do real good at it, especially compared to the way I used to, is I accept what comes to me. If you watch the people who come up to me when I'm teaching, you can see that I welcome them pretty well, but also I welcome them in different ways. Now, how do I know how to welcome each of the people who come up to me? I welcome them according to how I read their bodies and faces as to what they have for me.

Surrender, for me, means being willing to receive what each of you have for me and not wanting something you don't have for me. The big problem in marriage is a lack of surrender on both parts, because we know what we want that other person to do for us. It's hard for us to say, "My God, look what he's doing to me," or "My God, look what she's doing to me," when we notice that they smiled at us. "But that's not enough; she *should* smile at me after all I've done for her." Not that; instead: "My gosh, she smiled at me, hard a day as she had all day long wrestling with the kids. Or doing her work all day long and then coming home to cook a meal, she's still able to smile at me." Isn't that beautiful? You see what I mean? See the difference?

So when we remove the constraint of our ego and this idea of if we don't ejaculate every time, we aren't a man, sex can start to find its normal place and it can start to ebb and flow in our relationship and start to do new things for us that were never possible before.

Now, what might surrender plus being willing to consider forgoing ejaculation lead to in sexual intercourse? It leads to different things. One, it might mean we don't do anything but regular intercourse with ejaculation, but that can be deeper, it can be more often if that's appropriate, but it's always with a better heart. It may be less often. It may be that sometimes we were having intercourse more than we really wanted to because we were trying to please somebody else or a bunch of other games were going on. Intercourse can now occur just as often as it should occur for us. It falls, then, into its natural free place, so that it can come and go just like the moon; it waxes and wanes, comes and goes. That's where it belongs as part of a natural, free-flowing life. And it can be more spontaneous.

Now, we can, if we want, go to regular intercourse but where occasionally there's no ejaculation. In the ebb and flow of the sexual life of two people, there are times when they have an intense feeling for each other and in those times it would perhaps be appropriate to have intercourse without ejaculation. Their feeling is, We'll have intercourse and use the Masters and Johnson squeeze technique or the good old Chinese technique where two fingers are pressed hard against the root of the penis, on the perineum, the area between the back of the scrotum and the anus. So they use this system for a while and then they come to a period where it isn't appropriate, they're in a different part of the woman's cycle, where her desire lessens or is gone. Or one or both are occupied intensely with interests, so some or much of their energy is consumed other ways. So maybe they just have regular intercourse and then go back and forth between the two ways.

Or they could go the Chinese way, the way of the Taoist, where he says, Hey, I'll have an ejaculation in about one out of three or four times as the spirit moves me. The real accomplished master of that kind of sex has an ejaculation once ever hundred times.

For example, I'll read you from my friend Jolan Chang a description of one Sunday morning for him.

Remember that this is in the perspective of the Tao, the book that's like a Bible for the Chinese. One of the main points of the Tao is to do nothing. In the Taoist philosophy you do not try. You don't try to do anything. It's a philosophy which is not only strange to us, it's absolutely heretical to the American way, 100 per cent heretical. I talk about doing nothing and everybody says, "How is anything ever going to get done without me out there busting my butt?"

I remember one time, last summer, I was in New York tooling along in the back seat of a friend's car and I was really feeling calm. Jackie was on one side of me and a gal from France I liked was on the other side and here I was holding two lovely girls' hands and I was just sitting there real relaxed, enjoying the day.

The other two people, up front with Dan Casriel, brought up the subject of doing nothing. One gal said, "How can you do nothing?" So I said, "Well, I've been sitting back here doing nothing." She said, "What do you mean? I thought you were being pretty active." Every once in a while I had chipped in on the conversation to say something, even if I didn't talk very long or say very much. "But," I said, "no, I'm doing nothing."

What does do nothing mean? Well, I'm doing no thing. Obviously I've got to breathe or I can't live, so obviously doing no thing means you're just doing those natural things that come along. You're just flowing in complete harmony with the stream of life. You're not making a ripple, just like a trout going through the water; he does not disturb the water, so the trout is doing no thing. He just floats along there in the water.

So what you also have to understand is that Jolan Chang is talking about this kind of lovemaking from the orientation of the Tao, giving up the ego. If you want to know what the Tao is, take all your cherished beliefs and turn them around and look at the opposite of them; that's the Tao. The only thing is, it works a lot better, in my experience, than our so-called cherished beliefs. You see, what our cherished American beliefs are is simply a set of escapes, and we've all gone into collusion with one another, saying, "You've got your escapes and I've got mine, and we'll both agree that each other's escapes are good." Then we'll build a philosophy out of our escapes. It's got nothing to do with finding our being and being it and getting rid of our egos. Anytime any one of us does that, we are an affront to any one of the people who have their escapes and want to hang on to them.

Now, you obviously are getting sick of your escapes and don't want to hang on to them or you wouldn't still be with me.

When Chang was a young man, he scorned his old Chinese way of thinking and followed Van de Velde, who wrote the book *Ideal Marriage,* which is a great old textbook on sex which says you should have an ejaculation every time you have intercourse or there's something wrong with you.

Chang says, "So although I did have some misgivings towards Van de Velde's guidance at that point, I did not give up his advice for nearly another twelve years. All my experiences during those years were nearly the same, dissatisfied love partners no matter how hard I tried or how exhausted I became. My general health was very different from my athletic youth, and it was not one minute too soon that I rejected Van de Velde's advice and returned to the ancient wisdom.

"Now I am nearly 60, the age many men have stopped making love entirely. Yet unless I am traveling alone I usually make love several times a day. Often on a Sunday, I make love two or three times in the morning and then go cycling for nearly the whole day about 20 or 30 miles and then make love again before going to sleep.

"The result is that I am not in the least exhausted and my health could not be better or my mind more tranquil. And above all, the hopeless situation of lying beside an unsatisfied mate no longer exists. What is the reason for this change?

"The answer is I now practice what the Taoist physician Sun S'su-Mo prescribed 1300 years ago: 'Love one hundred times without emission.' "*

At this, one of the older guys in the audience said, "I've got to get a bicycle." I told him, "What you can do is mount that book on the handlebars."

For the woman in that system, it finally allows her to experience her sexual nature. I haven't run into many women who have had any experiences along this line, but I've run into a few, and their general feeling is, My God, I didn't know I was as sexual as I am. Or some of them even said, I thought I was pretty sexual before, but I'm far more sexual than I thought I was.

But, again, it isn't that there's any degree of sexuality that's desired. The point is that a person be free to find out what their own level is.

For the man, big as orgasm is, there can be an orgasm without orgasm that has some things no regular orgasm can have. One of those is the intense joy of intercourse without end. The aroused and temporarily satiated woman can now be aroused again and again until she reaches as deep an experience as she can possibly reach, because she doesn't ever have the fear that she has to shut herself off because the man can't participate past this point.

By avoiding physical orgasm the man can participate with the woman to a depth neither could reach before. This also eliminates the hours, days, or weeks limit on when intercourse can happen again. Both can let their own lovemaking feelings be free of any kind of limit, and they can be on a long honeymoon, where their love is first and everything else is second.

Some young men, or sexually strong not-so-young men, may feel they can do as Chang says even if they do ejaculate, because they can handle a high frequency of ejaculation. This may be true or it may not be.

*Jolan Chang, The Tao of Love and Sex (London: The Wildwood Press, 1977).

There may be a depletion for the man in ejaculation that isn't recognized in this country. Today, we are currently arguing that the more sex we have the better and that there's no problem in changing partners. Maybe the truth for us, what works for good in our lives, is very different from that.

One of the many paradoxes in sex is that you can have lots of sex in a destructive way and destroy yourself and you can have lots of sex in a good way and develop yourself.

But there's another way of sex that on the surface seems completely opposite. That's the way of little sex or no sex in the name of a higher ideal. It works well, according to some people's testimony. In a smaller way, it is in all sexual relationships when the sexual expression is at a low and most of the attention of the partners is concentrated on some higher ideal, outside themselves.

So we have talked about four ways you can go with sex. The first was regular intercourse, the second was regular intercourse but withholding ejaculation sometimes. The third case was the Taoist system, with ejaculation withheld more often than not. The fourth way is the way of some of the followers of some of the great Indian religionists, for example Baba Muktanand of India. Some of his followers—husbands and wives—will renounce sex and take on celibacy in their marriage. And in some of those cases it works beautifully in the lives of the people. A modification of this celibacy is that sexual energy should be directed upward, towards God as much as possible, so intercourse is still used between the two people, but very sparingly. Intercourse is used no more than necessary, or once a month or so.

As near as I can tell from the American followers of these Indian concepts, those people have a great joy and a great comfort in their lives. We see this in some other health systems, like the Polarity Health Institute, in Olga, Washington. There, they use sex as sparingly as possible and only between two legally married people, because they feel the sexual energy when used in ejaculation and intercourse is a downward energy and depletes energy. They feel that same energy can be turned upward towards the shared ideal that the two have, towards God, and that it can result in a far greater wholeness in the lives of the two people.

It's interesting that a Jolan Chang, who is way over on the other end of the sexual spectrum, is doing something totally opposite to what the Indian-oriented systems are talking about, yet his life shows all the signs of all the same fruitfulness in it. What I see about this is something that I've seen so often, the paradoxes that exist in our search for truth or in our spiritual quest.

I see people doing some things that seemingly, on the surface, are very, very dissimilar things and yet they seem to be getting the identical results. What it has shown me is, it is very dangerous for me to lay down a set of rules or absolutes for myself, because I need to keep my mind open to the paradoxes of the higher power.

The best way I've ever found to say it is, if I can understand God, then I am God. If I can completely understand how the higher power works, then I have really reduced the higher power to the very limited scope of this Norwegian mind. And when you get a higher power scaled down to the understanding of one Norwegian mind, you have got an exceptionally poor higher power.

So I don't understand how these two seemingly contradictory ways can produce the same result. I don't know if old Jolan Chang's way is the way for me. Maybe some modification of it has value for me. But I doubt that extreme would be something I would ever realize. Maybe; all things are possible. I've got seven years to go before I'm sixty to find out. But that seems like it's on one end of the world of sex, and Sharon and Jefferson Campbell's work on Polarity seems over on the other end, but yet, to me, they both seem to produce beautiful fruits for the people involved, and I can't understand that.

It wasn't but a few days after I'd written that when I did begin to understand part of it.

My friend Walther Lechler, from Germany, came to visit us to do his part of a book Jackie was working on called "I Exist, I Need, I'm Entitled." It tells of her very different journey to roughly the same general ideas. It is a beautiful, deeply moving book and dovetails with this one. I had worked out the ideas in the last chapter of this book at a seminar with a group of dentists and their wives in Kansas City on a previous Friday. Walther came in from Europe the next Monday noon. We visited awhile and I suggested he and Jackie and I go for a horseback ride, because Walther loves that so. It had been warm in the morning, but by now the wind was blowing cold snow. We dressed up in lots of warm wool clothes and went anyway.

We saddled the horses and I knew they would be frisky because of being cold and not being ridden for a while. I told Walther to hold his horse's head up if he tried to jump or rear. Sure enough, he did rear up a couple of times and Walther hung on, even though he was frightened. We found his bridle was twisted, and then everything was fine.

We went for our ride in the snow facing the biting wind until we got over the hill into the valley, where it was all quiet and like a fairy tale. Our St. Bernard, Hexel, was running ahead of us in the snow. The horses were having a good time, and three great friends were together.

We stopped and gathered wood for a fire and piled

on dry sticks. Pretty soon the fire was roaring hot, so our clothes were steaming as the moisture evaporated.

When we got up the next morning, I was listening to Jackie and Walther talk. He was mentioning embracing the whole world and talked about all the parts of our trip in the snow the day before as examples.

Then I saw what I had been missing in the stories of Chang and the Campbells and the seeming contradiction. While there may be a small contradiction at the deepest level, there isn't a contradiction at the level of embracing the world.

Jolan Chang is embracing the world as much on his twenty-mile bicycle ride as he is in bed with his lover. The same with Jefferson and Sharon Campbell of Polarity. They embrace the world and the people in it all day long as well as each other. Whether they have a sexual embrace at the end of the day is not that big a thing in the way they live.

I've been talking to you throughout the book about this idea of embracing the day. But in the face of all the sex in Jolan Chang's story, I missed the point and focused on all the physical sex. When I told his story to the dentists, they all did the same thing; they laughed at the story of all the sex he had on that Sunday, but there was a lot of excitement in their laughter.

Do you know what the mark of a sexually mature and sexually satisfied and completely nourished person is? It's when they hear a story of a life like Chang's, they simply smile quietly and are happy for him that he's getting out of life, in his way, what they're getting in their own way.

Our excited response to Chang's way, again, shows our starvation, not just our sexual starvation but our total starvation as we go through life all day long guarded against receiving what our life is trying to give us.

In our starvation and deprivation, we see sex as like the chocolate malted milks of life. We are starved for chocolate malted milks and all other food. We only have a little taste of chocolate malted milk once or twice a week. When we see someone like Chang having ten or twelve big malted milks at a sitting we envy him and want that for us. When we see Sharon and Jefferson not having a malted milk very often we feel sorry for them.

What we don't understand, in our self-chosen impoverishment, is that, for both Chang and the Jeffersons, their whole day is filled up with beautiful food. Their food during the day is so beautiful that they're not especially conscious of whether they're eating a baked potato or an orange or a malted milk. Like a person who's outdoors a lot and has a sharp appetite, all their food tastes so good they don't fuss about one thing compared to another.

It's the same way with life. When we live in our ego, we are constantly wanting what we don't have. When we live in surrender, we are constantly appreciating and being grateful for what we do have.

Ego is when we constantly think we know what's best for us.

Surrender is when we see that the great stream of life, the higher power, God as we understand him, knows what's best for us.

This is why sex can't be a big thing by itself. If it seems to be, then it tells of our deprivation and our starvation when we are constantly asking so much of one part of life. It's only when we see that life has many parts, many sources for us to draw nourishment from all day long, that sex can fit in its proper perspective. Then sex can show us the greatness for us that we have felt was in sex all along. But that greatness doesn't surprise us, because we've seen the same greatness in all the other parts of our life that day. We see that sex can be greater, just as everything can be greater. As I begin to fully experience that in my life, then I won't feel: Sex: if I didn't laugh, I'd cry. What I'll feel about sex then is, I'll just smile quietly and bless you with the blessing that your life be full of the same good things I'm experiencing in my life.

It's been a long way from where I was when I first had the idea for this book, ten years ago, to here. It seemed like a tough trip at times. I can see now that it's been a good trip, through paradise, a trip full of just what I needed but what I often couldn't appreciate. I'm grateful that now I can appreciate all the love I was given by all the people in my life who loved me as well as they could, but more crucially, as well as I would let them love me.

I thank all of you for loving me and teaching me what I needed to learn.

I love you,
Jess

CHAPTER 9

How My Students Felt About the Ideas in This Book

Since this book was said as a seminar in Minneapolis (June 1977) and Seattle (February 1978) and was listened to by people from a set of tapes, it was possible to get people's reactions to this book before it was finally a book. I sent out a letter to people who had come to the seminar or bought the tapes, asking for their comments. Here are the answers I received. I put them in here so you could see how other people felt as they encountered these ideas and applied them in their lives.

"I only attended the first day of the sex workshop. The second day I spent talking with my husband who couldn't come. I think that the exploration of my own sexuality brought me to the question, 'Am I okay, am I acceptable, normal?' It's a sad question because there is no answer.

"In the love I feel for Jack I have always expected more in amount of sex and he less. Yet in the development of our caring relationship it has been a slow learning process to realize how out of focus I can get on sex.

"In one experience after the workshop I really felt depressed and thought that if only we'd share sex I'd be better. We were both unable to share under demand. It was another lesson, the mystery of loving and the mystery of sex are to be discovered in continued sharing of life, its pains, its ups and its downs.

"Also, the emphasis on sharing feelings verbally

has been a boon to our developing love rather than greater and more captivating sexual experience. I love the ecstasy of sexual love but I'm learning that it is meant to be a fruit of love, not necessarily a beginning of it."

"It has been a long time since the workshop in Minneapolis and I don't have your tapes but I recall thinking, 'Yeah, that's how I feel.' Sexuality isn't just below the waist. And foreplay doesn't start when you turn out the lights, but in the morning when you get out of bed and throughout the day.

"I feel grateful, threatened, afraid, aware, more compassionate, not so much alone. I don't need a sex manual, I need to love myself enough to want to love another person and to allow myself to receive love.

"I've been increasingly aware that I'm not willing to appear out of control. My sex life is lived in my head. I've become aware of how I feel about my body, and when I dislike my own body and its functions (periods, etc.), it's a losing battle to let my husband get close—it comes back to me and my brain. I need to hear a lot about how I can put my body and my sexual life *into* my spiritual life. I've got them separate and I need to have myself whole.

"The (only?) changes since the seminar have been *awareness,* willingness to work on these ideas, honesty, more openness and sharing. Good Luck."

* * *

"I heard a great many things from you but there were two words which changed my attitude on sex— 'Reckless abandon.' I had never associated those two words with sex and it really impressed me. There had always been a holding back on my part, afraid to let myself go, afraid to share all of me, afraid of I don't know what. I'm no longer that way simply because of those two words. Please include them in the book in BIG LETTERS!

"Sex is no longer one-sided at our house. I've learned that it takes two to tango and it's much more meaningful when both partners are giving and receiving. Thanks, Jess."

*   *   *

"Sex is beauty-full and the only way to approach it is in a positive way, as an act of love, as a part of God's plan for our fullness and fulfillment."

*   *   *

"I'm a minister so I see a lot of this but you gave me a better understanding of the part sex plays in our lives and a better understanding of self.

"The sex urge is so strong and difficult to control, and that is a reminder that we need the other. We cannot make it alone, we need others, a community. It is possible to live without sex, but not without the other—God and others. Sex is a reminder of how much we need others."

*   *   *

"Mostly I'm grateful. I'm taking more control and responsibility for my life. I have obtained a measure of peacefulness. I notice this in my stomach. I've had a couple of gastro-intestinal ulcers and have had many months of pain and problems. I found that when I listen to the tapes and follow the ideas I have less problems and more good days. We have your other books but the tapes are more helpful to me.

"I've been more able to let my real feelings of anger out and not keep it inside me. I feel better getting angry than I did when I went off by myself and felt hurt. I see the tapes dealing more with the realities of life than with sex. I wish you could elaborate more on healing. I could use more explanation on healing and how it works."

* * *

"All my life I practiced active life philosophy and now at my age of fifty-one discover that I still can and have to learn much! Sex was always very important to me. No, I am not a liberated freebe, I am very happy with my one wife and four children.

"Your lectures were just too much for me to absorb so I'm relistening to the tapes. And it hits me again.

"The seminar information was just terrific. Sex became the past summer more important and also less important! I recognized my 'orchestra' and how to reorganize it. So I did have more sex and more pleasurable sex. And that with my own wife . . . as you say, 'groovy!' I still have more to understand and put into practice.

"I never thought that love and sex can be so much better with advanced age."

* * *

"You gave me a better understanding of our brothers and sisters. I could hug the Chairman of the Board when our mutual friend died suddenly—we were both sobbing, and it was the most natural thing in the world to do. Before your school in Bozeman and the tapes, I would have stood there wringing my hands, probably."

* * *

"I felt very comfortable with what you said. It seemed so logical. I wondered why I hadn't become aware of it somewhere along life's path before. It is such a beautiful explanation and one I can wholeheartedly relate to. I know now that these truly are my values and I am free of any of society's pressures to hand out the bonding part of a relationship freely and without the logical steps to build on.

"It gives me courage to stand up for myself and my values in every relationship. I am able to guide and teach my children that concept in their lives. I understand and can analyze what happened in the breakup of a sixteen-year marriage which really helped heal the hurt I had. Now I can go on to other relationships with openness and without guilt.

I have been able to handle employees with a better outlook and understanding. Some of the things that have happened to me since attending the seminar are:

> I have accepted my life as a divorced person though before divorce was truly against my principles not only for myself but for my children.
>
> I have been able to handle many relationships (with men as well as women) that otherwise I would have run away from, not handled at all.
>
> I have recently been appointed General Manager of a small corporation with about seven employees.

"I thank the Lord for allowing me to *fall* into that seminar. It changed my life then and will continue to allow me to grow and grow and change and change. Thanks and a bundle of love to you."

* * *

"I belong to a group of non-drinkers and have not had a drink since 1975. I'm confused and perplexed in this vital area of sex and loving within the confines of the traditional marriage commitment. (I married 25 years ago.) All I'm sure of for now is I'm a loving caring person and I feel right with my higher power much of the time.

"The parts of the tapes which flow for me include surrender in sexual loving with one's whole mind and body and spirit. Also, I appreciate the part about fantasy being a hurtful thing and that the sexual loving journey without a specific goal in the way. I know this must be a mutual surrender and I know there must be a significant payment (commitment?) on the part of both partners and I know how difficult this can be in situations that are less than perfect. But as you said there is some very real, very significant good which comes from any kind of tender, unselfish loving.

"We must earn our loved ones' trust and this may be more appropriate under the traditional accepted modes and conventions. Your information on touching has also been helpful."

*   *   *

"When I sat down at the seminar in Seattle and heard you announce the topic, I wondered what I was in for—especially with my 19-year-old son with me. However to cut through all thoughts I can truthfully say it was what I needed in my life. It has made a change in our family of four children of what it means to truly love and how you need to love celibately before sexually or it just 'ain't right.' Before I heard you in Seattle there were two of my four children whom I could not 'touch.' Now I can touch one of the two a lot and the other one is coming around. Somewhere in my life I was deprived and felt 'I didn't need it.' Unfortunately I didn't pass a lot on to my children and I could have. I am sure changing that now and I am happier and it is real neat. I have three boys and one girl and it has been harder for the boys to share the need for touching.

"I can also share and communicate better with my husband, in areas we are now 'working on' after 31 years of marriage. This even includes the sexual part of marriage. So you can see what at first I experienced when I heard you announce your topic (a possible bit of embarrassment) turned into one of the greatest life learning things I needed in my life. I consider it a privilege to share my thoughts and comments with you."

* * *

"The ideas expressed in your sex tapes are super powerful. Thank God they are on tape to be played again and again, because they require a whole *new* way of training about a basic subject—feeling, that has been engraved into our basic being-personality-character.

"Sex without a love of the heart is a shallow thing like a quick shower compared to a relaxing swim in a beautiful freshwater lake. To have a love; however, that is a restful pleasant love, I find I must be comfortable and love myself first. When I am ill at ease with myself it just does not come off. My love for myself shows just how fickle I am—for it comes and it goes and therefore my ability to love and have joyous meaningful sex also changes sometimes on a daily, hourly or minute basis. This makes life less than a serene experience.

"Therefore my work is cut out for me: to get straight and love me, the son of the Father, not me the Great Ego, and to accept him in a consistent loving fashion, with *all* his goodies and baddies. Thanks."

*   *   *

"I went to the seminar in June 1977 and received so much from it that it's hard to put it into words. By the end of the weekend, I realized that what started out to be rather explicit talk about sex turned out to be more of an involvement in the subject of love. I felt as though you were talking directly to me. I felt loved, lovable and loving. I felt so good about myself and those around me that I know I went out of my way to do loving things for others. For instance, I would cook something extra special for my family, not because I felt I had to, but because I really wanted to. This feeling stayed with me for quite a few weeks, but gradually I got back into my old way of feeling. It wore off.

"For well over a year now, I have been praying every day to want what I have, for the willingness to want what I have. I have seen some subtle changes in my attitude as time has gone on. About six weeks ago, our sixteen-year-old boy was involved in an accident. He was riding his bicycle home late at night and was struck by a one-ton truck. He wound up in the hospital for five days, the first night in intensive care because they were watching for internal bleeding. My son had been drinking and smoking pot that night. The people who struck him had been drinking, too. During the time my son was in the hospital, we started talking about getting some counseling. We are now involved in family and marriage counseling, which I feel very good about. I think I decided that what I have is worth putting some effort into to improve our relationships. I have already learned that I have been very lonely in my family situation for a long time, but I have not shared that with anyone in the family. Instead, I have used manipulating behavior that has turned my husband off. Instead of telling him I'm lonely and need a hug, I have gone to him demanding a hug or some other sign of affection. I'm seeing how hard it is to put into practice some of the things I've learned, but I intend to keep doing the best I can from here on. I'm very grateful."

* * *

"I was reminded by our seminar that my parents had taught me that it was right and good to love all people, regardless of sex, etc. Our ability to love is boundless unless we allow society to set our standards and limitations. Then we endanger our freedom and become spiritually lonely people, perhaps not even aware of the cause of our unhappiness. I was made aware that I could, if willing to take the risk, become the kind of person I had started out to be, which presented me with a unique chance to start life all over, with the goal of becoming a loving, sharing person.

"I did a great deal of thinking about my relationships with people I was in contact with on a daily basis and particularly my family and friends in A.A. I saw what I wanted out of those relationships and what, so far, I had gotten out of them. I reflected on my life so far to see if I could find out which of 'society's' standards I had used as my own, that I was not comfortable with—thereby placing limitations on my chances for freedom. These I turned around, by trial (and sometimes in error) until I found a more comfortable standard with which I could live. I have taken the ultimate risk of sharing my deepest feeling with three people, two of whom loved and accepted me for it. The third person, my husband, didn't understand what I was talking about so I guess that is his problem. I am still changing: trying new relationships, adding depths and meaning to those old ones I treasure and trying to work your books, seminars and tapes into my A.A. program. So far I have had good feelings and results *most* of the time but never without some pain. This indicates to me I am growing and today at least, I feel in the right way. I am beginning to be comfortable with others and above all less lonely. Thank you, Jess."

* * *

"The seminar was great. I enjoyed it all. I have had a strict Catholic school education and could not suggest a girl have many premarriage sex experiences. Maybe for her husband it would be ok.

"My husband and I have cuddled more and have had more sex which is also more meaningful. Love."

* * *

"My actual feelings at the seminar were so many. It amazed me that a crowd of mixed sexes took so well to the subject matter. You definitely hit home or we wouldn't have all sat there soaking it up as we did. I am amazed also that you were able to put it across so well. I am convinced that your relating to us your own personal life and happenings, along with your letting your emotions go along with what you were talking about and opening your heart to us like you did was the only way it could be accepted. It is so refreshing to hear (especially a man) admit he has faults, admit openly it is okay to cry and show emotion, that it makes the group to which you're speaking very humble.

"My only other definite feeling throughout the seminar was that I wanted to ask you a hundred questions, but before I could think them out enough or get them written down, I answered them myself. It was very frustrating and yet very eye-opening. It all boiled down to 'me.'

"I've read many books on the subject of I'm ok, you're ok, along with the one with that title. Until I attended your seminar, I didn't realize what it all meant or how to apply it to my life. I guess it is just too easy, and yet the hardest thing to do: living *your* own life, making *yourself* happy, and like you say meeting *your* own needs. I can't believe how easy it is to *let* all the problems we have borrowed from others for so long, stay with the people who are having them. It is a revelation to know finally that *you* are the cause of the largest per cent of *your* problems. Once you change your attitude it's amazing how the others around you change! When it's really you that has changed! It's weird but wonderful. Most of the problems I had with my 'miserable husband and kids' turned out to be how I reacted to them not what they were having problems with. Letting them have their problems and helping them when I can and leaving them to deal with them themselves, not only makes them grow but saves me a lot of headaches. I see now that me getting involved to the extent that I was getting involved with their problems, only made me interfering so that they weren't learning how to deal with life at all, besides I was becoming mentally ill from worrying about things I had no control over. It's so nice now to see the kids handling things, my husband getting angry, and me not taking it personally, and he gets over it so much faster and we don't spend weekends pouting any more. It's cool!

"So consequently, I am saying that I have changed my attitude on life in general, practicing finally the things I have always believed only with more positive direction. I am sitting back letting people that bugged me before, do their thing and letting others react or get angry because there is no reason for me to get angry over something someone else is having a problem with. I am much more compassionate, and find myself feeling sorry for a lot of people who spend their life being miserable. And yet, I leave it at that and don't dwell on it.

"I can see however, that meetings like Emotions Anonymous must be a great help to us, and yet we don't have one close by. The nearest is 100 miles. I do backslide, and thank you for your tapes, without them I would be lost. I play them very occasionally simply to remind me of what I'm doing, or not doing.

"I can only thank you so much for sharing your life and ideas with us; they have changed my life and made me see things that I couldn't see before.

"I am anxious to get your book when it comes out."

* * *

"You have helped me focus in on the 'gut' issues regarding sex. First we all start out with our unique sexual appetites. Secondly, we all start out sexually inadequate; if we depend only upon our physical sexual appetite for guidance in gratifying and satisfying this sex appetite, we will experience insatiable sexual hunger, we can become sex cripples, even diseased, and contagious.

"In order for us to learn and understand our unique sexual needs, we must discover we are not only physical beings but spiritual beings and it is the spiritual voice inside each of us that must put our sexual needs in proper prospective. Our spirit must be healthy in order for our whole physical side to be healthy.

"Sexually, we are all generally reflecting our human predicament. We all feel inadequate and are inadequate until we begin to listen to that higher voice of the spirit. To the extent our lives reflect the spirit's selfless, unconditional love and acceptance of ourselves (just as we are with all our inadequacies and imperfections) and of others; to that extent we will find harmony and peace, satisfaction and fulfillment of all our needs. Of course this will be a growing harmony and peace and a growing satisfaction and fulfillment because we are unfinished on the way to being finished creations as is all creation on earth and in heaven.

"As human beings we are one package. When we isolate our sexual appetite from the dependence upon the spirit of love (selfless unconditional love and acceptance of ourselves and others), to guide us, our lives reflect disorientation and sexual drives because an overpowering obsession that has ugly and horrendous consequences.

"Your tapes put sex back in the human package under control of the spirit, and have helped me face more and more and more honestly my sexual inadequacy—helping me to realize that sexual inadequacy can be reflected and is reflected in the most 'macho' sexual behavior as well as the most timid.

"This realization that sexual fulfillment is not based upon how active or inactive your sex life may be, has led me further to let loose of my conditioning to judge my sexual behavior on the basis of other people's appetites and/or their misunderstood 'macho' standards of measuring one's success or failure as a 'lover.'

"You help me to accept my inadequacy, to realize it's all right to be sexually inadequate, that I can get better. It's all right to have my own unique sexual appetite even though when placed next to someone else's apparent 'macho' appetite I come out below last place. If I accept myself and love me unconditonally as the spirit guides, I accept my sexual inadequacy and I accept the whole package which is unfinished and on the way to being finished. I may still feel intimidated from time to time by these inadequacies, but I recognize I needn't be. After all, each of us have their own

unique appetites which are not meant to be used as a
standard of and for satisfying other people's needs. We
satisfy one another to the degree we accept ourselves,
love ourselves unconditionally and to the extent we
selflessly love and accept each other unconditionally.
Miraculously, two unique beings with unique appetites
by living selflessly under the guidance of the spirit of
unconditional love and acceptance, can find all their
needs, sexually, and the others, abundantly satisfied
and fulfilled by one another.

"Sexual compatibility is more than physical. It takes
us a while to realize this. Each of us experience our
own pattern of growth in this realization. The sexual
act and relationship when abused reflects the consequences of this abuse and reflects in this abuse our
failure to let the spirit in each of us be the construc-
tive and creative force guiding and guarding our relationships. Only when we surrender and commit ourselves to trusting in the spirit (in our lives and in the
lives of others) to be our guide, our wisdom and
strength-sustaining life, will we be willing and able to
commit, to bond our lives with another, recognizing
the seal of this bonding is the sexual relationship. Sex
is an imperfect expression of love, mutual love, selfless love. It is not the only way of sealing our bonding
together of two lives in a relationship of love, selfless
love. It is given too great a burden to bear in society,
but because it is the procreation of the human race
that depends upon it, the burden can be lessened when
the spirit takes over in guiding and enlightening our
understanding.

"Since accepting my own sexual inadequacy, I am
more patient with not only myself but with my husband. I am still struggling against my conditioning of
the past, knocking down those corks that keep surfac-
ing. I have a better understanding of my husband's
needs, of his inadequacies. And my own needs and
inadequacies less and less intimidate me. I stop de-

manding from myself what I cannot give and I have stopped more and more, demanding from my husband what he is not able to give. By doing this both of us are growing, able to give ourselves and each other more and more satisfaction, because we trust the spirit in each of us.

"Sexual perversion is a spiritual concern and must be recognized as an inadequacy unchecked, unaccepted and unacceptable—unaccepted by the individual who suffers this perversion and unacceptable to society. Until we can embrace and love selflessly ourselves despite our inadequacy and its ugliness, and until we can embrace and love selflessly others despite their inadequacies, we will suffer the consequences of this rejection—horrendous consequences. We must share each other's burdens—our inadequacies.

"Sex is abused constantly and we are abused by sex as a result. It takes time to heal, and sexual healing is part and parcel of the whole package needing healing. We get out of sex the measure we have given in selfless love, and acceptance of ourselves and others. Our sexual activity is hot and heavy today, but its lack of pleasure and satisfaction leaves a hole in our lives that cannot be filled without learning first to selflessly, unconditionally love and accept ourselves and others . . . sharing our mutual predicament.

"Thank you, Jess. Volumes can be written describing the effects of your shared understanding, unconditional love and acceptance, in my life. Love."

NEW FROM FAWCETT CREST

THE GLOW *Brooks Stanwood*	24333	$2.75
THE GHOST WRITER *Philip Roth*	24322	$2.75
LADIES IN WAITING *Gwen Davis*	24331	$2.50
DAMNATION REEF *Jill Tattersall*	24325	$2.25
SATAN IN GORAY		
Isaac Bashevis Singer	24326	$2.50
THE CATER STREET HANGMAN		
Anne Perry	24327	$2.25
DARK PIPER *Andre Norton*	24328	$1.95
SWEENY'S HONOR *Brian Garfield*	24330	$1.95

Buy them at your local bookstore or use this handy coupon for ordering.

COLUMBIA BOOK SERVICE (a CBS Publications Co.)
32275 Mally Road, P.O. Box FB, Madison Heights, MI 48071

Please send me the books I have checked above. Orders for less than
5 books must include 75¢ for the first book and 25¢ for each additional book to cover postage and handling. Orders for 5 books or
more postage is FREE. Send check or money order only.

Cost $ _____   Name _____

Sales tax* _____   Address _____

Postage _____   City _____

Total $ _____   State _____ Zip _____

*The government requires us to collect sales tax in all states except
AK, DE, MT, NH and OR.*

A NEW DECADE OF
CREST BESTSELLERS

THE LAST ENCHANTMENT *Mary Stewart*	24207	$2.95
CENTENNIAL *James A. Michener*	23494	$2.95
THE COUP *John Updike*	24259	$2.95
METROPOLITAN LIFE *Fran Lebowitz*	24169	$2.25
THE RISE AND FALL OF THE THIRD REICH *William Shirer*	23442	$2.95
THURSDAY THE RABBI WALKED OUT *Harry Kemelman*	24070	$2.25
IN MY FATHER'S COURT *Isaac Bashevis Singer*	24074	$2.50
PRELUDE TO TERROR *Helen MacInnes*	24034	$2.50
A WALK ACROSS AMERICA *Peter Jenkins*	24277	$2.75
WANTED! THE SEARCH FOR NAZIS IN AMERICA *Howard Blum*	23409	$1.95
WANDERINGS *Chaim Potok*	24270	$3.95
DRESS GRAY *Lucian K. Truscott IV*	24158	$2.75
THE GLASS FLAME *Phyllis A. Whitney*	24130	$2.25
THE SPRING OF THE TIGER *Victoria Holt*	24297	$2.75
TYPE A BEHAVIOR & YOUR HEART *Friedman, M.D. & Rosenman, M.D.*	23870	$2.50

Buy them at your local bookstore or use this handy coupon for ordering.

COLUMBIA BOOK SERVICE (a CBS Publications Co.)
32275 Mally Road, P.O. Box FB, Madison Heights, MI 48071

Please send me the books I have checked above. Orders for less than 5 books must include 75¢ for the first book and 25¢ for each additional book to cover postage and handling. Orders for 5 books or more postage is FREE. Send check or money order only.

Cost $_____   Name _____

Sales tax*_____   Address _____

Postage_____   City _____

Total $_____   State _____ Zip _____

 * *The government requires us to collect sales tax in all states except AK, DE, MT, NH and OR.*

This offer expires 1 June 81

CLASSIC BESTSELLERS
from FAWCETT BOOKS

ALL QUIET ON THE WESTERN FRONT	23808	$2.25
by Erich Maria Remarque		
TO KILL A MOCKINGBIRD	08376	$1.95
by Harper Lee		
SHOW BOAT	23191	$1.95
by Edna Ferber		
THEM	23944	$2.50
by Joyce Carol Oates		
THE SLAVE	24188	$2.50
by Isaac Bashevis Singer		
THE FLOUNDER	24180	$2.95
by Gunter Grass		
THE CHOSEN	24200	$2.50
by Chaim Potok		
NORTHWEST PASSAGE	02719	$2.50
by Kenneth Roberts		
THE RABBIT RUN	24031	$2.25
by John Updike		
JALNA	24418	$1.95
by Mazo de la Roche		
SPORTS IN AMERICA	24063	$2.95
by James Michener		

Buy them at your local bookstore or use this handy coupon for ordering.

COLUMBIA BOOK SERVICE (a CBS Publications Co.)
32275 Mally Road, P.O. Box FB, Madison Heights, MI 48071

Please send me the books I have checked above. Orders for less than 5 books must include 75¢ for the first book and 25¢ for each additional book to cover postage and handling. Orders for 5 books or more postage is FREE. Send check or money order only.

Cost $ _____ Name _____

Sales tax* _____ Address _____

Postage _____ City _____

Total $ _____ State _____ Zip _____

* *The government requires us to collect sales tax in all states except AK, DE, MT, NH and OR.*

This offer expires 1 June 81